FRENCH AND FRANCOPHONE STUDIES

French Fiction into the Twenty-first Century

French Fiction into the Twenty-first Century

The Return to the Story

Simon Kemp

UNIVERSITY OF WALES PRESS
CARDIFF
2010

British Library Cataloguing-in-Publication Data
A catalogue record for this book is available from the British Library.

ISBN 978-0-7083-2273-4
e-ISBN 978-0-7083-2274-1

Typeset by Mark Heslington Ltd, Scarborough, North Yorkshire

Printed and bound in Great Britain by
CPI Antony Rowe, Chippenham and Eastbourne

For Elizabeth Fallaize, with gratitude

Contents

Series Editors' Preface

This series showcases the work of new and established scholars working within the fields of French and francophone studies. It publishes introductory texts aimed at a student readership, as well as research-orientated monographs at the cutting edge of their discipline area. The series aims to highlight shifting patterns of research in French and francophone studies, to re-evaluate traditional representations of French and francophone identities and to encourage the exchange of ideas and perspectives across a wide range of discipline areas. The emphasis throughout the series will be on the ways in which French and francophone communities across the world are evolving into the twenty-first century.

Hanna Diamond and Claire Gorrara

Introduction

At the end of the 1980s a term began to crop up in the French literary press to describe a newly perceptible trend in fiction: *le retour au récit*, or the return to the story. One of the earliest appearances comes in a special issue of *La Quinzaine littéraire* in May 1989 devoted to the question, 'Where is French literature heading?' In his editorial, Maurice Nadeau figures the current literary scene as a collection of 'returns' to literature's traditional concerns in the wake of a period of textual experiment and theoretical formalism: 'A return to history, a return to stories, a return to the subject (after the description of so many objects), a return to "creation", a return to the "work of literature", a return to characters, to plot, to story-telling. From now on we have every freedom.'[1] The periodical asks a number of authors to comment on the phenomenon, and finds them broadly agreeing on its existence, although sometimes with certain provisos. Renaud Camus, for instance, replies:

> *Everyone is more or less in agreement about a 'return to the story', but the story isn't an unambiguous meeting-point for those, on the one hand, who never left it, and for those, like me, who went a little way out to see, from the outside, what it was made of it, and what might be made of it yet.*[2]

The concept is quickly taken up by criticism discussing 'l'extrême contemporain', a topic which has only relatively recently been considered appropriate for academic study in France. Aron Kibédi-Varga writes in 1990: 'What is perhaps most deeply characteristic of the new postmodern literature is the renarrativization of the text, the effort to construct stories once again.'[3] In the same year, Jean-Claude Lebrun and Claude Prévost critique the term, noting, as Nadeau did before them, that such a return need not imply a retreat to a Balzacian model of storytelling, and expressing a preference for the expression *retour du récit* as better encapsulating a sense of 'reinvestment in a broadened tradition, which can encompass

Faulkner and Proust, Diderot and Sterne'.[4] In 1991, Jean-Michel Maulpoix's history of recent French literature comments under the heading, 'Le Retour du Récit':

> *Throughout this decade [the 1980s] we nevertheless see a return to grace of narrative and fiction in the novel. No longer perceived as artificial and gratuitous diversions (as the New Novelists attacked them for being), they are now seen as bringing to life an imaginary universe, within which it might be possible to question and newly comprehend the meaning of the world.[5]*

In the years since then, the concept has flourished in French criticism, crystallizing around the term *retour au récit* at the expense of alternative formulations. *Le retour au récit* features in the titles of articles or book chapters by Dominique Viart, Anne Cousseau and Dominique Combe.[6] It is the focus of discussion in a host of other texts, including criticism by Marie-Claire Bancquart and Pierre Cahné, Yves Baudelle, Bruno Blanckeman, Olivier Bessard-Banquy and Henri Godard.[7] Anglophone criticism too has picked up on the idea: it appears, for instance, as 'the return of storytelling' in Colin Davis and Elizabeth Fallaize's *French Fiction in the Mitterrand Years.*[8]

The return to the story is now a commonplace in the analysis of contemporary French literature, so much so that it approaches the status of a received idea, propagated from critical text to critical text, often without being interrogated as to its precise meaning or its possible hidden assumptions. My own investigation intends to explore French literary fiction of the late twentieth and early twenty-first century in order to evaluate the term. What exactly is this *récit* that we are returning to? Where are we returning from? How might we go about judging comparative degrees of 'story' in different texts? If there is indeed a return to the story, then what cultural or other forces might have caused it to happen? These are the questions I shall be attempting to answer through the close study of narrative form in the work of five notable and very different French authors of the last thirty years.

There is consensus among critics on what it is we are returning from. Pierre Brunel describes the 1980s and 1990s as:

> *the period in which we generally see an ebbing away of the avant-garde thrust of the three previous decades, and in particular of that extreme and extremist avant-garde of the 1970s. The Sollers of Nombres, H, or Lois becomes more*

relaxed and better behaved in Femmes *or* Portrait d'un joueur. *Robbe-Grillet becomes an autobiographer while continuing to work through fiction. A new generation of writers receives the legacy of the recent experiments in the novel, while at the same time seeking to differentiate themselves.*[9]

Viart expands on this account with a sketch of the state of affairs in the 1970s which brought on the return:

> *The experimental and textualist practices which dominate the literary scene at the end of the 1970s reached their limit. Even the idea of a 'novel' was discarded in favour of the more general notion of a 'text' … Books like these [including those by Philippe Sollers, Renaud Camus, Pierre Guyotat and Maurice Roche] verged on the unreadable and no longer found an audience. The ideology of the 'new' led writers to outdo one another, and in the end had no legitimacy other than its innovative aspect, independent even of what it might have to say. Any aesthetic that calls itself avant-garde posits a need for rupture with 'old forms'. Getting rid of this one-upmanship means finishing with such practices. This is the major event of the last two decades of the century.*[10]

The rise of the experimentalists to which Brunel and Viart refer dates back to Jérôme Lindon's assembly of the *école de Minuit* at his publishing house in the early 1950s: Samuel Beckett, Marguerite Duras and the *nouveaux romanciers*, Alain Robbe-Grillet, Nathalie Sarraute, Claude Simon, Michel Butor, Robert Pinget, Claude Ollier and Jean Ricardou. The influence of the latter group in particular, who accompanied their fiction with often highly polemical theoretical essays, was instrumental in shifting the cultural dominant away from the Catholic novelists and politically committed writers of the earlier generation towards a self-referential form of writing in which, to borrow Ricardou's famous formulation, the writing of adventures would be replaced by the adventure of writing.[11]

Experimentalism did not spring fully formed from nowhere, of course, and the *Minuit* writers had important precursors. Fiction that subverted and critiqued the practice of conventional realist narrative has a long history, flourishing particularly in the eighteenth century with Denis Diderot and Laurence Sterne, and returned most notably in the early twentieth century with André Gide's *Les Faux-monnayeurs* (1925), a novel about the possibilities of novelistic representation. Radical revolt against prevailing aesthetic norms was also seen earlier in the twentieth century in the Surrealists, and the marriage of aesthetic theory and theoretical fictions was prefigured in Maurice Blanchot. Modernism itself, the early twentieth-century literary trend exemplified by Marcel Proust, William Faulkner, James Joyce and Virginia Woolf, has already inaugurated the restless reinvention of the conventions of narrative and representation, the valorization of what is new and different and, if necessary, at the expense of the novel's traditional function of storytelling. In breaking with Modernist forms and preoccupations in search of more radical experiments, the *Minuit* writers are in fact re-enacting Modernism's own avant-garde principles, and they will not be the last group of writers to do so.

Robbe-Grillet's first essay announces the element of writing about writing which will be an important part of all the *nouveaux romanciers'* practice:

> *it seems that we are getting ever closer to an era in fiction in which the problems of writing will be lucidly envisaged by the novelist, and in which critical concerns, far from sterilizing creativity, will be able to give it impetus.*[12]

The sentiment is fully endorsed by his fiction, which, particularly in his most radical texts of the 1970s, shifts between different levels of fictionality, all of which are composed of pulp-fiction clichés with little reference to reality; in which the actions of the characters frequently act as metaphors for the processes of reading and writing. In *Projet pour une révolution à New York* (1970), for instance, the 'story' appears to be a collage of clichés from violent and pornographic American *noir*, in which scenes merge with posters and book covers, and one character's habit of reading random selections from an extensive collection of pulp detective stories seems to mirror the novel we are reading. At the same time, the narrator is periodically interrupted by a voice which might belong to a police interrogator, but could as easily be a literary critic, questioning the structure and coherence of the tale recounted. Michel Butor, who published four experimental novels between 1954 and 1960, broke even more radically with conventional narrative form for his subsequent works. These mixed-genre texts, often inspired by art, literature and travel, enable him, in his words, to move freely 'within a triangle, the points of which are the novel as it is usually understood, the poem as it is usually understood, and the essay as it is normally practised'.[13] Sarraute's novels may be less overtly metafictional, tending more to reinvention of the psychological novel with their attempt to evoke in language the pre-linguistic processes of the mind. Yet they too define themselves with reference to earlier literary practice, and set rupture and innovation as their prime values in creativity:

> *The suspicion, which is now destroying character and the whole old-fashioned apparatus that ensured its power, is one of these morbid reactions through which an organism defends itself and finds a new stability. It forces the novelist to fulfil his proper function, Philip Toynbee says, remembering Flaubert's instruction: 'his deepest obligation: discover the new', and prevents him from committing 'his most serious crime: repeating the discoveries of his predecessors'.[14]*

Also coming to prominence in this period was another collective of experimental writers of reflexive texts, Oulipo, the 'Ouvroir de Littérature Potentielle' founded by Raymond Queneau and François Le Lionnais in 1960, whose diverse international membership would include Jacques Roubaud, Italo Calvino and, of particular note for French cultural history, Georges Perec. Oulipo's founding principles were more playful and less doctrinaire than the *nouveaux romanciers*. Their manifesto begins with a joke,[15] and the Oulipians avoid the *nouveau roman*'s monolithic theory-building, with each Oulipo text starting from a fresh structural premise. They also avoid the *nouveau roman*'s epistemological pretensions, being more concerned in their own work with the possibilities of play afforded by language and mathematics than by fundamental questions of the representation of reality. Their central idea was that, since writing has always been subject to certain procedures and constraints, be they the linguistic ones of grammar and syntax or the generic ones of poetic, novelistic or dramatic form, the goal of the Oulipo writers would be not to free themselves of all constraint, but, 'systematically and scientifically' to discover new ones by which their texts could be inspired and organized.[16] This led, in Le Lionnais's words, to texts ordered according to 'alphabetical, consonant- or vowel-based, phonetic, graphic, prosodic, rhyming, rhythmic and numerical constraints, programmes and structures', and in later work, less formalist experiments with a basis more semantic than syntactic.[17] Perec's *W ou le souvenir d'enfance* (1975) doubly splits its story, consisting of two strands of narrative, a fantasy and a memoir of childhood, which alternate chapters and are themselves divided midway through the text by a central gap which sends each in a new direction. Jacques Roubaud's *La Belle Hortense* (1990) plays with the conventions of the detective story with a parodic shuffling of its roles and incorporated figures of an author, narrator and reader to squabble over the plot. But the more formal linguistic and numerical constraints persist in Oulipo's novels too, most famously in Perec's *La Disparition*, a novel about mysterious disappearances and an uncanny sense of absence, written entirely without recourse to the letter 'e', and in his masterpiece, *La Vie mode d'emploi*. This text is subjected to a number of mathematical procedures which determine how the novel moves from room to room in the apartment block it describes, and which items from a set of forty-two prescribed lists are to be worked into the story of each room.

In the 1970s, experimental writers proliferated and practice became increasingly radicalized. Aside from the continued work of Oulipo and the *nouveau roman*, further experimentalists appeared on the literary scene. Some were unaffiliated individuals, like Renaud Camus, whose *Églogues* series forms a kind of annotated intertextual collage. Others shared the experimentalists' privileging of rupture and innovation, without having literary concerns as their primary aim, such as those writers associated with *écriture féminine*. Hélène Cixous's 1975 essay, 'Le Rire de la Méduse', inspires the movement, calling for a new from of writing which will attempt to break free from patriarchal structures inherent in conventional discourse.[18] The poetic, cyclical and highly metaphorical style of the essay itself puts Cixous's ideas into practice, as does her extensive output of fiction, drama and philosophical or psychoanalytic writing. Other writers who came to be associated with *écriture féminine* include Chantal Chawaf, Luce Irigaray and Monique Wittig, and writers linked to the publishing house, Éditions des femmes, which was founded by Antoinette Fouque. While the practitioners of *écriture féminine* may have more explicitly political ends in mind than the other experimentalists we have seen, their reinvention of style and form, accompanied or infused by metadiscursive reflections, has strong parallels with other experimental writing of the period.

There is one collective, however, that marks the extreme of French literary experimentalism. It is the journal *Tel Quel*, produced

by Le Seuil publishers and headed by Philippe Sollers from 1960 to
1983. In its uncompromising radicalism, which made few concessions to ease of interpretation or reading pleasure, its high degree
of theorization of its own practice and of literature in general
(including a reformulated canon which has done much to restore
writers such as Sade, Lautréamont and Bataille to academic notice),
and its influence on writing and publishing in the wider literary
sphere, *Tel Quel* was the high-water mark of the experimental era,
albeit one that owed much of its *élan* to the possibilities opened up
by the Minuit writers in the previous decade. In 1990, seven years
after it folded, Jean-Pierre Salgas is able to write that the journal
'determines, and above all, overdetermines, to use a buzzword of
the time, the whole history of the French novel up to the present
day'.[19] Experimental writers who participated in *Tel Quel* include
Pierre Guyotat, whose often pornographic subject matter (his 1970
novel *Éden Éden Éden* was banned for a decade) was expressed in a
manner that took it to the limits of readability: discarding sentences
and punctuation for *Éden Éden Éden* and, in *Prostitution* (1975),
disrupting even the lexis of the text with neologisms and phonetic
spelling. Maurice Roche produced similarly transgressive work in
this period. His trilogy, *Compact* (1966), *Circus* (1972) and *CodeX*
(1974), fragments discourse, with sliced-up sentences interspersed
with symbols and ideograms in a manner that borders on the illegible. Sollers himself is as radical in his practice as he is in his
theories (and, incidentally, his politics, which included a flirtation
with Maoism during this period). His own view of French literature,
expounded in *L'Écriture et l'expérience des limites* (1968), argues
against continuity of development, positing literature as a succession of ruptures with established forms, and literary history as an
ideologically motivated occultation of dangerous or undesirable
writing. Sollers's creative writing in the 1970s was itself an exercise
in aesthetic rupture, which sought to both critique and revolu-
tionize conventional forms, as he makes clear in his description of
his 1968 text, *Nombres*: 'it is indeed a *novel*, in that the narrative
process is simultaneously X-rayed and taken beyond itself. It is a
novel that aims to render novelistic exploitation and its mystificatory
effects impossible.'[20] His most famous work, *Paradis*, was published
serially in the *Tel Quel* review between 1974 and 1981, when it
appeared as a single volume. It consists of over a hundred thousand
words in a single, unbroken, unpunctuated stream, sometimes

structured like sentences, sometimes like fragmented phrases or lists of words. Its primary voice drifts into other persons and discourses, often parodically reproduced, in a discussion which centres around the themes of religion and sexuality, but draws in an eclectic range of topics from art to economics. Sometimes it proceeds by narrative or logical argument, at other times by associative links of sound or sense. A brief excerpt from the opening lines gives the flavour:

> *voice flower light echo of enlightenment waterfall thrown into darkness stripped hemp thread it's lost from the start lower down I shook hands closed with sleep and the current swelled once again choke the river the city of willows silver silk out of paper of jute flax reed rice quill cotton in the froth 325 lumen de lumine in 900 changing the currency 1294 Persian expansion after it's straight on to our deltas my fantasy for the moment is to stop everything to cross the lines swimming morning breeze fire lakes mirrors ...*[21]

Like many of the other experimental texts we have touched on, *Paradis* also theorizes the processes of its own production and interpretation within the text, dismissing punctuation marks as clumsy 'prosthetic crutches next to my inward-spiralling salvos', or, in later instalments, satirizing hostile reader responses to earlier ones.

Tel Quel is emblematic as the point from which the *retour au récit* returned, not only for the uncompromising texts of Sollers and his colleagues, but also due to its connections with other movements of note. *Tel Quel* is linked to the *nouveau roman* by the favourable analyses it made of its texts and the interviews it accorded its practitioners, as well as by the presence of *nouveau romancier* Jean Ricardou on the review's editorial committee in its first decade. Through Julia Kristeva, who would join the review and also marry Sollers in the mid-1960s, *Tel Quel* has an association with the feminist movement that harboured *écriture féminine*, and with post-structuralism, the movement in critical theory with which Kristeva, and other *Tel Quel* contributors, were closely associated. Almost all of the major figures of post-structuralism were associated in some capacity with *Tel Quel*, being published in or by the review, like Kristeva, Roland Barthes, Jacques Derrida and Michel Foucault, or, like Jacques Lacan and Louis Althusser, a major influence on contributors and the subject of debate. The high-water mark of experimental fiction is also the apogee of theory as a cultural force in the humanities, and there are many connections between the two. Barthes, for instance, wrote some of his earliest critical essays on the *nouveau roman*; Sollers *écrivain* would be one of his last. Kristeva would later accompany her careers as psychoanalyst and theoretician with that of avant-garde novelist. When *Tel Quel* comes to an end in 1983, it is also the end of the era of post-structuralism: Lacan and Barthes have both died in the early years of the decade, and Althusser has been committed to a psychiatric institution after killing his wife; Foucault is in the grip of the AIDS virus that will kill him the following year. Some, like Kristeva and Derrida, will continue into the twenty-first century, but the influence of post-structuralism is waning, and the following generation of French intellectuals will neither sustain nor supplant it on the world stage. The theoretical fictions of *Tel Quel* and other avant-garde writers lose their academic champions and a major source of their inspiration at a stroke.

The high-water mark is the point at which the tide turns, and since the 1980s experimentalism in literature certainly seems to have been on the ebb. As Brunel noted, this retreat from the extremes is in part performed by the experimentalists themselves. Duras, Robbe-Grillet, Sarraute and Sollers all turn to autobiography in their later careers.[22] Their memoirs are not the most orthodox exemplars of the genre: none gives a continuous, chronological account of their life; all reflect on the processes of life-writing within the text. Robbe-Grillet's autobiography intertwines his own story with that of a fantasy character, Henri de Corinthe, while Sarraute divides her narrating voice into two, who squabble over details and interpretation as they delve together into her memories. Yet as well as inhabiting a traditional genre of literature and engaging unambiguously with a non-literary referent in the form of their own life, all of these texts are noticeably more conventional in form and accessible to readers than work produced earlier in these writers' careers. Other members of the avant-garde, including Pierre Guyotat, Danielle Sallenave and Renaud Camus, have turned in later years to writing which makes greater use of narrative and greater concessions to readability than their work of the 1970s.

If critics are largely in agreement as to where the *retour au récit* has returned from, they also have certain ideas in common about what it is we have returned to. First, as Fieke Schoots points out, the *récit* in question is to be understood in its general sense of narrative fiction unfolding through time, internally connected via chronology and causality into a coherent whole which develops towards a denouement: in other words, a story.[23] The more technical sense of the word, used by Gérard Genette in his 'Discours du récit' to distinguish the manner of telling from the underlying *histoire* being recounted, is not at all the intended meaning: the *retour au récit* should be understood as a turning *away* from the procedures of telling to refocus on the *histoire* itself.[24] Secondly, there is concern that a useful shorthand like *retour au récit* should not become an unhelpful caricature of the phenomenon it represents. As Bessard-Banquy notes, a return to the story does not imply a complete absence of storytelling among the experimentalists of the previous generation: 'story was never absent from novelistic works, even in the darkest days of 1970s experimental literature. At most the concern for narrative gave way before other priorities.'[25] Neither does it imply that the current generation has abandoned its predecessors' suspicions about plot, character and mimesis to retreat to an 'innocent' form of classic realism that takes for granted life's faithful reflection in narrative. Nadeau says few writers in the 1980s have not taken lessons from Beckett or Sarraute, preserving the *retour au récit* from being a return to the 'old recipes of the Balzacian novel'.[26] Viart denies that the return to the story implies a blank slate, claiming that the majority of novelists 'accept the critical scope of the reflections [the novel] has been subject to' in the experimental era and create their own novels 'in a *critical* dialogue with the cultural past'.[27]

The novel has certainly been flourishing in France in recent years, at least in terms of numbers. The 2007 *rentrée littéraire* saw 727 new novels published in France between August and October, up from 683 in 2006.[28] Compare this to the *rentrée* of 1978, where in the estimation of the *Quinzaine littéraire*, the tally was between 160 and 180 new novels.[29] Around a third are foreign novels in translation, a proportion that has been increasing steadily throughout this period. The ever-growing numbers of novels are being produced by a dwindling number of French publishing houses, as smaller firms are acquired by giant publishing conglomerates such as Hachette (owner of, among others, Stock, Fayard, Grasset, Larousse and Livre de Poche) and Editis (which owns Pocket, Bordas, Plon, 10/18, Le Robert and many more). Yves Baudelle sees in this a danger of the mass-marketing power of the conglomerates distorting readers' choices, citing Paul-Loup Sulitzer, the best-selling author of *Le Roi vert* (1983), whose use of ghost-writers was exposed in 1987, as 'the product of market research and a commercial strategy based on a huge marketing push'.[30] Baudelle also casts doubt, as have others,[31] on the independence of jury members for the major French literary prizes, the awarding of which can increase a novel's sales tenfold. The novel, it must be admitted, has a limited impact on the French public at large: a third of French people read less than one book per year, and in 2005, 82 per cent declared that the *rentrée littéraire* was of no interest to them.[32] Compared to other cultural forms the difference is stark: the average print run for a novel is 15,000 copies, while television spectators are routinely counted in the millions, and in the cinema, directors like Jean-Pierre Jeunet and François Ozon reach international audiences beyond the dreams of French novelists. The disparity threatens to place literature in thrall to the other media: cinematic adaptation or televisual exposure greatly increases a novel's sales and can bring an author to public attention. Bernard Pivot's now-defunct *Apostrophes* television show was courted by authors and publishers for its perceived public influence; Philippe Djian found international fame with the release of Jean-Jacques Beineix's 1986 film of his *37,2° le matin* (1985).

Literary critics' verdicts on the current state of the art in France vary enormously, and sometimes tell us more about the temperament of the commentator than the material discussed. Among the more pessimistic diagnoses is that of Tzvetan Todorov, who sees a literary culture bedevilled by the three vices of *nihilisme, nombrilisme* and *formalisme*: writers (all unnamed) who lack any constructive engagement with the ills of the individual and society, writers who indulge themselves in narcissistic explorations of the self, and writers who continue to produce metatextual texts which deal with nothing beyond the processes of their own creation.[33] Pierre Jourde's even more damning report is unafraid to name the guilty parties. He finds much of the current literary scene composed of confessional mediocrity (Annie Ernaux), unreadable rehashing of the worst excesses of *Tel Quel* (Mehdi Belhaj Kacem), cynical provocation (Virginie Despentes) and a market determined more by a writer's media profile than the quality of their work (Michel Houellebecq).[34] Critics too are condemned for abandoning the polemics of earlier generations and avoiding negative value judgements, leaving the discipline insipid and moribund. More optimistic voices are in the majority, however. Lebrun and Prévost note that the theorizing tendencies of the experimentalists' generation manifested themselves most frequently in the negative: declaring certain ways of writing out-moded, forbidding forms of representation on the grounds that they were fraudulent. The absence of such doctrines and the lack of schools or movements among writers today is, in their view, grounds for a greater diversity in cultural production than has been seen in France for some years.[35] Blanckeman even sees the displacement of literature by film and television as having positive effects, a marginal-ization that acts a stimulus to creativity.[36] Colin Nettelbeck shares this view, pointing to the range of non-literary cultural influences at the disposal of the modern novelist, and cites Daniel Pennac and Jean Echenoz as two writers who have taken advantage of the opportunity.

The lack of groups and manifestos makes it harder to generalize about contemporary literature than in the days of literary schools and ideological battlelines. Attempts have been made, however, to survey notable trends. The rise of life-writing has been widely noted, both as avowed autobiography and in the hybrid category of *autofic-tion*. Writers like Serge Doubrovsky and Christine Angot specialize in autobiographical work; others, like Pierre Michon and Jean Rouaud, write the lives of others in works that remain deeply personal. Minimalism is another noted current.[37] Pierre Brunel dubs the literary present 'the era of brevity', in which novels that can be read in a couple of hours, like those of Amélie Nothomb, are increasingly popular, and longer works are as likely to be a collec-tion of fragments as a sustained narrative.[38] The sober, unadorned style of Annie Ernaux or Emmanuèle Bernheim is a form of stylistic minimalism, as is the 'impassive' *pince-sans-rire* of Echenoz, Jean-Philippe Toussaint or Christian Gailly. These latter also exemplify what Olivier Bessard-Banquy calls the 'ludic novel', writing which, in his view, inherits Georges Perec's legacy of literary renewal and reconnection through postmodern play. Such play generally retains something of the metafiction dear to the avant-garde experimental-ists, although it is more likely to be a subtle undermining of the reader's expectations about the novel's style, subject matter or plot development than it is a doctrinaire rewriting of the codes of fiction.

Set against this playfulness, though, is the resurgence of novels that engage with historical and contemporary social issues. François Bon's celebrated *Daewoo* (2004) mixes journalistic investigation with fragments of drama and personal meditations in a study of the effects of factory closures on a local community. World events like the Heysel Stadium disaster or the attacks on the World Trade Center become fictions from Laurent Mauvignier and Frédéric Beigbeder. Scabrous satires on current French society make a publishing phenomenon out of Michel Houellebecq, while the continuing legacy of France's twentieth-century wars is disinterred by writers like Jorge Semprun and Jonathan Littell.

The documentary impulse in recent fiction is complemented by a strain of magic realism, which draws on myth, dreams and folk tales, but may still engage with current issues. J. M. G. Le Clézio, France's newest Nobel laureate, and Michel Tournier rewrite the myths of old Europe and other cultures, yet can use these same novels to discuss twentieth-century historical issues, like the colonization of North Africa or French collaboration in the Second World War, or matters of contemporary concern, like the immigrant experience in France. Similarly, the dream-like fictions of Marie NDiaye, Sylvie Germain and Marie Redonnet can demonstrate very modern and committed sensibilities when dealing with sexuality, abuse or exclusion.

As can be seen already in Le Clézio and Beigbeder, French literature has also undergone a process of globalization as it responds to cultural influences and current affairs from all parts of the increasingly interconnected world. The last thirty years has seen an immense influx of new culture and literature into France, from the francophone writers of post-colonial societies in Africa, the Caribbean and elsewhere, from the second- and third-generation immigrant communities in France like Nina Bouraoui and Azouz Begag and from the growing fraction of translated literature disseminated by French publishers. Writers like Tahar Ben Jelloun and Assia Djebar bring a fusion of western self-conscious fiction with Arab narrative traditions into the French literary establishment, and thereby alter the character of the French novel in general.

Much of this recent fiction would support the thesis that innovative use of narrative form continues to flourish, but in a less radical way than that practised by *Tel Quel* or the *nouveau roman*, and that the subject matter of the novel has returned to a more decisive role in determining the manner of its telling. We must be wary, however, of constructing our own literary trends by what we choose to classify as literary fiction, and what we choose to see as dominant tendencies within it. Certainly, popular and middle-brow French fiction has maintained a continuum of classic realist fiction throughout the twentieth century. Just as Françoise Sagan, not Alain Robbe-Grillet, is arguably *the* French writer of the 1950s, at least in terms of readership, and Henri Charrière, not Sollers, is the writer of the 1960s, so our period belongs in the public's mind not to the literary writers like Olivier Rolin and Serge Doubrovsky, but to Régine Deforges and Marc Lévy. Popular fiction and narrative innovation are not incompatible, of course: we might think of Daniel Pennac's reflexive crime fictions or Philippe Djian's *Doggy Bag* novels modelled on the narrative format of American television drama. Yet the notion of a return to the story would seem to have little relevance to mass-market fiction, which has, if anything, continued to increase its experimentalism as avant-garde ideas filter slowly into the mainstream and the divisions between 'high' and 'low' culture become ever more porous.

In literary fiction too, radical narrative experiment was not the whole story of the post-war decades, and its decline is not the whole story of more recent years. Realist novelists like Henri Troyat and Marguerite Yourcenar maintain what Julien Gracq calls a 'literature of continuity' before, during and after the period of experimentalism, trumping the innovators in terms of readership, critical acclaim and establishment honours as they do so.[39] Equally, writers such as Olivier Cadiot or Gérard Gavarry maintain a cutting edge of experiment in the twenty-first century in texts at the limits of narrative (and sometimes of intelligibility). The post-war realists may lack the uniqueness, the cultural impact and the legacy of influence of their more radical contemporaries, just as the twenty-first-century avant-garde lacks the readership, the cohesion of a literary movement and the support of committed publishers and fellow-travelling cultural theorists enjoyed by its forebears. Nevertheless, these writers are not to be discounted for the sake of a more sweeping generalization: the story of the *retour au récit* will not be an entirely neat one, and we must expect to be left with some loose ends.

Annie Ernaux, the focus of chapter one, is one of the best-known women writers in French today. She is perhaps the foremost exemplar of the widespread interest in life-writing in current French literature, combining the self-consciousness of Doubrovsky with the confessional intimacy of Hervé Guibert and the generalizing discourse of Camille Laurens in her autobiographical texts, and standing with Michon, Rouaud and the later Yourcenar in the

celebrated subgenre of the historical-study-cum-family-memoir.
Like Begag, she uses autobiography as a sociological document; like
Bernheim, her style is spare and sober while dealing with highly
emotive subject matter; as with Bon, the sense of precision and
objectivity she produces from this stylistic restraint is exploited for
political ends. The first chapter explores how Ernaux uses the division between the time of writing and the time she is writing about as
part of her rhetorical strategy in presenting her sociological and
autobiographical material. Of particular interest is Ernaux's
tendency to re-narrate the same events from a different temporal
perspective, as when she accompanies a retrospective account of
her mother's decline into Alzheimer's with the subsequent publication of her private journals of the time. The chapter argues that
Ernaux uses the time of narrating to explore different qualities of
time in lived and remembered experience, as well as to divide her
identity into a writing and an experiencing self.

Pascal Quignard, the subject of chapter two, occupies a very
different position in contemporary French fiction. While the
prolific author has produced a small number of classic realist narratives of love and loss, the majority of his work is considered difficult
or even obscure, blending narrative, poetry and the philosophical
essay into texts that defy easy categorization. He shares with
Tournier and Le Clézio the passion for foreign cultures and ancient
myths, and has a similar seriousness in his tone and themes. He is a
philosopher-novelist like Butor or Kristeva, but is of a very different
stripe from either, and his work can be by turns as limpid as Troyat's
and as disorienting as Sollers's. I analyse the way his work combines
narrative and non-narrative forms of writing, examining how
Quignard's philosophical and autobiographical preoccupations are
served by the hybrid nature of his writing, which skips between
genres to renew its attack on abstract issues of memory and desire.
The aesthetic of fragmentation which prevails in his work, both
within and between the genres of his writing, is considered in relation to his ideas on the limitations of order, reason and coherence.

Marie Darrieussecq, born in 1969, is effectively of a younger generation than the other four writers, who were all born in the 1940s. In
the space of a decade of writing, she has established herself as an
important voice in French fiction, attracting both acclaim and
controversy. She shares with NDiaye an interest in the uncanny, and
with Laurens the recurring theme of bereavement, parallels which

led to two separate literary spats over unfounded accusations of plagiarism. From vicious social satire that recalls Houellebecq in its shock tactics, if not its sexual politics, she has moved increasingly into the territory of *autofiction* and an interest in psychological representation reminiscent of Sarraute. My third chapter explores her use of narrative voice and its relationship to her view of how the mind works. The chapter explores the forms employed to represent thought, from modernist stream of consciousness to other techniques better suited to evoking non-linguistic thought, and examines how far the particular use of narrative voice is determined by a particular conception of consciousness.

The fourth chapter focuses on Jean Echenoz, a writer associated with the postmodern, and whose stylistic links to both Oulipo and the *nouveau roman* are often remarked upon. His straight-faced irony and playful virtuosity of style and form link him closely to other twenty-first-century Minuit-based writers like Toussaint, Gailly or Éric Chevillard, while a fond and subversive attitude to genre fiction connects him to the Oulipians Perec and Roubaud, the *nouveaux romanciers* Robbe-Grillet and Butor, and best-selling genre-twisters like Pennac and Sébastien Japrisot. The discussion examines how Echenoz plays with readers' expectations through the espousal and subversion of formulas of plot development, often borrowed from popular fiction. It reads Echenoz's techniques as a strategy of displacement, shifting the reader's attention from the conventional interest and pleasures of the narrative type his texts inhabit, to centre upon other, 'irrelevant' elements of the story in order to bring the functioning of narrative to the forefront of the work. While Echenoz's stories-about-stories retain the closest link with the concerns of the experimenters' generation, my chapter suggests that the absence of a theoretical framework, and the pleasure taken in the proliferation of narrative, make this writer more akin to his contemporaries than to his predecessors.

The fifth and final chapter is devoted to Patrick Modiano. Modiano has the longest writing career of the five, and has most consistently combined critical respect with wide readership, creating in his extensive but homogenous body of work his own subgenre of the 'Modiano novel'. His revisionist interest in French collaboration and anti-Semitism during the Occupation links him to a number of current writers, Semprun, Didier Daeninckx and Philippe Grimbert among them, who write about France's role in the Holocaust, and contributes to the cultural atmosphere that brought forgotten novelist Irène Némirovsky spectacularly to the forefront of French literature with the posthumous publication of her *Suite française* in 2004. My chapter on Modiano focuses on the ends of his narratives, which merge thematic openness with formal structures of closure. It examines the balance struck in the writer's work between readerly satisfaction and the unresolvability of the issues of memory and identity which drive the development of the plot. The case is taken as a further demonstration of narrative form dependent on a writer's subject matter, in this case his concept of the self, which draws a distinction with the primacy of form among the *nouveaux romanciers* and their immediate successors.

In the work of these five authors we have writing from both women and men, from a writer born in 1940 to a writer born in 1969. We have a best-selling writer sometimes viewed with condescension by literary critics, and we have a critically acclaimed writer whose works are sometimes shunned by readers as wilfully abstruse. We have a writer famed for witty parodies of genre fiction, and a writer known principally for his explorations of the Occupation and the Holocaust. We have a writer of autobiographical narratives of political and sociological intent, a writer of fantastic stories of ghosts and transformation, and a writer whose texts leave us uncertain as to whether they are stories at all. There are deliberate limitations imposed on this diversity: I have not, for instance, included popular fiction from contemporary authors, nor have I included francophone writing with a dual heritage of European and non-European narrative traditions, neither of which can convincingly be argued to exist primarily in the wake of mid-twentieth-century French experimentalism. Nevertheless, the subjects of this study represent significant and varied currents across a broad range of literary fiction of the last three decades. In analysing their use of narrative form, I will be drawing on a range of narrative theory, including the French 'narratological' tradition of Gérard Genette and Roland Barthes emerging out of 1960s structuralism, and the diaspora of competing theories which develops from it, such as the psychoanalytic approach of Peter Brooks or the deconstructive method of J. Hillis Miller. The study moves from topics like the time of narrating that can be handled unproblematically by classic narrative theory, which strips *récit* from *histoire* like form from content, to issues like digression and closure, where the structures of narrative are harder to separate from the meaning of the text. The development through the course of the five chapters will thus also enable us to see something of the strengths and weaknesses of narrative theory, and evaluate the current state of the discipline. While this thread, and others, connect the five case studies together into one argument, the chapters are also designed to stand comfortably alone, should readers wish to pick and choose among them the authors that interest them most.

Chapter One
Annie Ernaux and the Narrating of Time

Since her first publication in 1974, Annie Ernaux (b.1940) has garnered increasing success and critical controversy with each stage of her oeuvre. To date she has published sixteen texts, which divide into four distinct categories. There are the three semi-autobiographical novels with which she began her career, *Les Armoires vides* (1974), *Ce qu'ils disent ou rien* (1977) and *La Femme gelée* (1981), first-person narratives dealing with issues of class and gender as the characters become distanced from their working-class origins through education, and experience oppression in social and domestic spheres. There are then the seven non-fiction texts on which her reputation largely rests, all of which share the 'flat writing' which has become her signature style as they explore her own or her parents' lives in an attempt to reach broader truths of society or psychology which transcend the personal subject matter.[1] *La Place* (1983) and *Une femme* (1987) are posthumous reconstructions of the lives of her father and mother respectively, territory revisited in *La Honte* (1997), which explores the rules and discourses which governed her twelve-year-old self in an attempt to understand the effects of her father's act of violence against her mother. *L'Événement* (2000) tells of Ernaux's illegal abortion in 1964, recasting the fictional account from *Les Armoires vides* as avowed autobiography with explicitly political purpose. Two of her most controversial texts, *Passion simple* (1991) and *L'Occupation* (2002), explore the obsessive nature of love and jealousy during and in the aftermath of two love affairs. *Les Années* (2008), her most recent book, encompasses aspects of all the previous texts as it attempts to use Ernaux's own biography to tell the story of all those in her generation who share with her a social class, a sex, a milieu, a marital history or a political affiliation. The third category of texts is the diary, of which Ernaux has published four volumes. *Je ne suis pas sortie de ma nuit'* (1997) and *Se perdre* (2001) are extracts from her private diary, not originally intended for publication, which deal with her mother's decline and death in 1983–6 and an affair with a married man in 1988–90, the events of which coincide with the previously published *récits, Une femme* and *Passion simple. Journal du dehors* (1993) and *La Vie extérieure* (2000) are two volumes of a single project, a fragmentary diary of things seen and heard in public spaces or occasionally in the media from 1985 to 1989, intended for publication from its inception. Lastly, Ernaux has published two collaborative volumes. One is an email interview on her work conducted with Frédéric-Yves Jeannet over the course of a year, entitled *L'Écriture comme un couteau* (2003); the other, *L'Usage de la photo* (2005), is a series of parallel commentaries by Ernaux and her lover, Marc Marie, on photographs of their discarded clothing, in which they discuss their relationship and Ernaux's experience of treatment for breast cancer.

Ernaux is an immensely popular writer with the reading public, her books invariably reaching the best-seller lists. *Passion simple* remained there for eight months; *La Place* has sold half a million copies, and been translated into sixteen languages.[2] For some of these readers, Ernaux's auto-socio-biographies have a profound emotional importance. Lyn Thomas, in a reader-response analysis of more than three hundred readers' letters sent to Ernaux, notes the strong sense of identification many of the readers feel with the writer, thanking her for 'finding the words to express their experience' or using the texts as '"turning points" in their own life-histories'.[3]

Critical reception of Ernaux's work has been more mixed. Isabelle Charpentier notes that her most controversial work, *Passion simple*, divided critics along gender lines, with female critics saluting Ernaux's courage, and male critics attacking the text as banal or obscene, while revising downward the esteem granted to the writer since the Renaudot-winning *Une femme* in 1987.[4] Charpentier also comments on the ad hominem nature of the most vituperative attacks on Ernaux, something the writer herself claims she has reluctantly become accustomed to: 'a type of criticism – which cannot be called polemical, as it is so lacking in ideas and arguments which brings up the writer's body, her lifestyle, her social origins and the fact she is a woman to nullify her book'.[5]

The brevity of most of Ernaux's texts, their tendency to revisit earlier material and their frank discussion of both sexual activity and emotional vulnerability, have all been used against her by newspaper critics. She incurs the risk of literary marginalization by centring her work on her working-class origins and female identity, as well as through her dialogue with (but never adoption of) the discourses of romance and pornography. She also dispossesses critics of their prerogative by including her own critical commentary within the text, a commentary which often dictates how the text is to be interpreted ('These pages are in no way to be read as an objective report on the "long stay" in a nursing home, even less as a denunciation'), or denies the right of readers to judge her by literary criteria at all, as with her declarations in *Une femme* to remain 'beneath literature', and to be producing 'something between literature, sociology and history'.[6] Her unadorned style can also seem a challenge to aesthetic judgements. Warren Motte suggests that such minimalism is 'antagonistically in opposition' to conventional art, creating a kind of 'antiliterature'.[7]

For a long time Ernaux's fortunes with academic criticism were also marked by a split: this time between strong interest in anglophone criticism, particularly British and American feminist criticism, and indifference in French academia. Fabrice Thumerel comments in his introduction to the proceedings of a 2002 conference on Ernaux that francophone publications on her work have increased 'exponentially' in recent years, particularly with the increasing prominence of studies into autobiography.[8] In secondary education too, Ernaux has made an impression, with two of her texts reissued by Gallimard in a commented edition for lycée students.[9] The negative assessments of the literary press are largely absent from the work of academic critics (for whom value judgements on the text are often a less central concern), but not entirely so. Chloë Taylor Merleau takes Ernaux's generalizing to task for imposing her personal feelings as universal female truths; Siobhán McIlvanney accuses her of setting up a 'regressive developmental paradigm' through her self-definition as Other, fixing her identity through the social structures she decries.[10]

Narrative form in Ernaux is, according to the author, determined by the subject matter of the text rather than being an area of independent concern:

It's always what I have to say which determines the way to say it, which determines the writing, and the structure of the text as well ... I couldn't really claim that I'm trying to renew narrative form; rather I try to find the form that suits what I see vaguely before me – what I have to write – and this form is never given in advance.[11]

The sociological nature of her projects often requires a complicated structure. In the autobiographical *récits*, retrospective narration of events is interspersed with other recalled or researched voices from the past. At the same time, Ernaux's 'existentialist' conviction that her writing should not be an end in itself, but rather a means to effect change in society, tends towards extreme self-consciousness, whereby the narrative is constantly interrupted by the writer's own reflections on her text, questioning its meaning, purpose and possible reception, or broadening its scope from the personal to wider issues of class and gender.[12] In several cases, the levels of polyphony and commentary are such that classifying the texts as narratives at all becomes doubtful. The interruptions become fragmentation, temporal progression is replaced by synchronic meditations. Ernaux herself remarks on this: *Passion simple, La Honte* and *Journal du dehors* all contain denials that they are narratives, for different reasons which we will encounter later.

Ernaux situates her writing very much within a heritage of twentieth-century French literature, with numerous references to Proust, Beauvoir and Camus in her texts.[13] Her attitude to the post-war experimenters is ambivalent. Her early, unpublished work, *Du soleil à cinq heures*, written in 1962, bore the clear imprint of the literary zeitgeist: 'I had a solipsistic, antisocial, apolitical view of writing. You must understand that at the beginning of the sixties, the emphasis was on the formal side of things, the discovery of new techniques for the novel.'[14] Ernaux was 'strongly influenced' by the *nouveau roman* in particular here, and intended to situate her writing in its current.[15] Although she continues to read, and indeed lecture on, the *nouveau roman*, her references to it tend to mark out the distance she has since travelled, as experiences of illegal abortion, domestic oppression and class difference raised her political awareness and changed the direction of her writing.[16] She sees the lasting legacy of the era of experimentation on her writing as twofold. First, the *nouveau roman* has made it impossible for her to return to former conventions of representation: 'the conviction – widely shared, it has become a cliché – that we can't write after them as we would have done before, and that writing is a search, and a

search for a form, not reproduction. So not a reproduction of the
nouveau roman either ...'[17] Secondly, Ernaux still belongs to the
nouveau roman's era of suspicion, as far as the hidden assumptions
behind language are concerned:

I now accord language a function that the nouveau roman *gave it, that is,
getting rid of ideologies ... The research is on two fronts: it's writing as a
means of acting on the world, but writing is a human creation like everything
else ... it's an institution. So if we use the institution, we question it. Writing
can be sexist, writing is ideological.*[18]

While she may share in Alain Robbe-Grillet's 'travail de déconstruc-
tion' of ideology in language, she is also quick to declare of the
nouveau roman, 'those aren't the kind of novels I write at all!'[19]
Ernaux also discusses the limits of cultural influence on her work,
dismissing writers who make no impression on her (Gracq and
Duras are mentioned), as well as the *écriture féminine* movement,
which she sees as a distraction from the woman writer's engagement
with society. Ernaux finds the canonical literature of the twentieth
century far removed from the working-class life she recounts in *La
Place*, and her semi-autobiographical narrator in *Les Armoires vides*
notes the silence in the literature she studies at university about
experiences like her own of clandestine abortion.[20] Indeed, she
questions the pre-eminence of the novel in forming this literary
heritage:

*Must we always define ourselves in relation to the 'novel'? What people call
novels are no longer on my radar ... Literary prizes continue to consecrate the
novel with all their might – which is evidence less of its vitality than its insti-
tutionalized character – but something different is also happening, which is
at the same time a break from and a continuation of the major works of the
first half of the twentieth century by Proust, Céline, or the Surrealists ...
When people talk about books, the word 'novel' is used in an ever broader
sense. There are the hysterical defenders of 'fiction'. But in the end, the label,
the genre, is not important, as we know. There are just those books that deeply
affect us, that open up thoughts, dreams or desires within us.*[21]

It is interesting that Ernaux's point of reference here is the early
twentieth century, rather than the generation immediately
preceding her; both continuity and change are with regard to the

pre-war writers, the 1960s experimentalists implicitly sidelined. In questioning of the novel as literary benchmark, we might also note, she puts in doubt not only fiction but narrative too as the 'natural' mode of creative expression.

The exploration of Ernaux's time of narrating in this chapter sets out to prove two main contentions. First, I wish to show that Ernaux's revisiting of the same periods of her life in more than one text is not mere recycling; the comparisons set up through differing relationships between time of narrating and narrated time have important and original things to tell us about experience and its problematic rendering(s) in narrative. Secondly, I intend to show that a key element in Ernaux's literary effect comes from the division of her identity between past and present time, and that a surprising omission in the presentation of her former self is vital to her reconception of autobiography as a genre.

The 'time of narrating' is Genette's *temps de la narration* from 'Discours du récit'.[22] It refers to the point or period in time from which the narrative is expressed, relative to the 'narrated time' in which the events recounted occur. Genette notes that while recounting is an activity that takes time, in literature the time of narrating is more often a point than a period, an 'instantaneous act, without temporal dimension', that can be dated but not measured.[23] He discerns four possible relationships between time of narration and narrated time. The two which are of greatest interest to us here are *narration ultérieure*, in which the narrator recounts events retrospectively from a point later in time, which is, of course, the most common narrative instance, and *narration intercalée*, in which events are recounted from a series of different points in time, interspersed among the action, as in the epistolary novel.[24]

The time of narration in Ernaux is unusual first of all in that it is always a period, never a point. Almost all of her texts are dated with month and year of composition, sometimes with a span of dates: *La Place* is dated '*novembre 1982 – juin 1983*', for instance. Ernaux explains this as 'the desire to show the real time of writing the book, without the preparations, the abandoned drafts, from the definitive starting-in on the project to its completion'.[25] The time span of the text's composition has for her 'great significance'; she describes it as 'an exceptional time', or 'another life'.[26] The duration of the time of narrating is also clearly signalled within the several of the texts themselves. The diary texts mark out duration through their changing dates. In the *récits*, Ernaux often refers to the time of composition and its relationship to narrated time. In *Une femme*, for instance, Ernaux follows the account of her mother's funeral with the remark that it is now three weeks later as she writes about it, and two days into the writing process; later she notes that it is now two months since she began writing, and in the final pages she records that it is late February, and that the text has taken ten months to write.[27] *Les Années* records the twenty-year progress from the original idea for the book in the 1980s, through its formal development to its final production.

The duration of the time of narrating is also noticeable in the fiction with which Ernaux began her career. In *Les Armoires vides* the narrating instance sees Denise Lesur recounting her story while alone in her room, awaiting the miscarriage which an abortionist has triggered. The main narrative of her remembered childhood and adolescence is framed by a focus on the present situation in the opening and closing pages, and counterpointed by ironic comparisons of her life then and now at intervals through the story. We are made aware of the time of narrating as a span through several references to waiting, including in the opening line: 'Ever hour I do scissor kicks, bicycling, or push against the wall. To make things go faster.'[28] More importantly, however, the time of narrating has its own narrative development, moving from despair and anger at the beginning to a suggestion of reconciliation with the narrator's class origins at the end, and a renewed desire for life implied in her final decision to seek help. In all of Ernaux's work, and to an increasing extent through her career, the period of narrating is not only the perspective from which the narrated time is viewed, but a focus of attention in its own right. Ernaux uses it to comment on the events she is recounting and on the writing process which expresses them, exploring her own feelings towards her subject matter and considering readers' reactions after publication.

Ernaux narrates her life in the *récits* from after the events recounted, or at intervals from within their flow in the diary-texts, but never as a voice from outside time, always from a position that can be fixed relative to the timeline of the text's events, and which itself has its own inner duration. The time of narration is thrust to the forefront of the reader's attention, not only by the preponderance of narratorial comment in Ernaux's texts, but more particularly by the fact that a change in the temporal relations of narrative can often be the most significant difference between two texts whose subject matter is largely the same. Ernaux occasionally declares her revisitings as companion-texts, creating 'official' pairings with earlier publications, as is the case with *'Je ne suis pas sortie de ma nuit'* (paired with *Une femme*) and *Se perdre* (paired with *Passion simple*), where the private journal accompanies the earlier *récit* of the mother's death, or the love affair with S.[29] *L'Événement* holds a similar relationship to *Les Armoires vides*, being the explicitly autobiographical reworking of the abortion narrative rendered fictionally in the earlier novel. Such dyads are not entirely self-contained, however, since other texts often overlap them in certain details. For instance, Ernaux's voyage to Florence and a visit to her local *Secours catholique* trigger impersonal observations in *Journal du dehors*, but reappear in *Se perdre*, revealed as significant events in the final weeks of the love affair.[30] *Se perdre* itself contains perhaps a hundred references to previously recounted events and earlier publications, including a reference to the abortion very different from those seen previously.[31]

The majority of Ernaux's revisiting is in keeping with these less schematic overlaps, with autobiographical material resurfacing here and there across her oeuvre. The clearest example of this is the representation of Ernaux's childhood and adolescence, of which different aspects – such as her parents, *café-épicerie* life, her social milieu, education and religion, and her sexual development – form the major part of seven of her texts, and play a minor role in at least two others. *Les Armoires vides*, *Ce qu'ils disent ou rien*, and *La Femme gelée* offer fictionalized accounts of this upbringing, although *Ce qu'ils disent ou rien* makes certain changes to the autobiographical account, and each of the other two narratives continues beyond adolescence.[32] *La Place*, *Une Femme*, *La Honte* and *Les Années* all return to the same period, although only *La Honte* focuses on it exclusively. In each case, the perspective on the material is different, with the first two *récits* examining the father and mother respectively, the third exploring the ideologies which shaped Ernaux's understanding at the time, and the most recent inserting the period into the unfolding history of Ernaux's generation. If we include the passing references to this part of her life to be found in *'Je ne suis pas sortie de ma nuit'*, *Se perdre* and elsewhere, the repetitive nature of Ernaux's work becomes even more apparent.

When compared to the intermittently narrated texts, three characteristics of Ernaux's retrospective texts, particularly in her earlier work, are their coherence, their conclusive endings, and their definitive claims to truth. Circularity of narrative builds coherence: all three of the novels begin in the narrating present before a memory flashback introduces the main narrative. All three conclude when the narrated time has been traced back to the time of narrating, returning us to the opening. The process also gives us hermeneutic closure, since the extended flashback has served to explain to us the narrator's situation and state of mind as we met her. The first of the non-fiction *récits*, *La Place* and *Une femme*, have a more complex structure, with linked circularities in both time of narrating and narrated time. Both texts tell the story of Ernaux's father or mother beginning with their death, then going back in time to narrate their life, and ending with the death repeated. Both texts discuss the genesis of the writing project early in the text, then conclude with a backward glance to the start of the writing period. *Une femme* ends with Ernaux re-reading her opening pages, and in *La Place* she looks back over the time of writing, before ending with an anecdote on class barriers and social exclusion, pointedly dated only days before writing commenced.[33] Ernaux's metatextual comments on the form of these *récits* reinforce this sense of cohesion. She describes the purpose of *Une femme* as being to 'unite through writing' the elderly Alzheimer's patient of her mother's end with the powerful woman of her prime. At the end of the text, she claims to have successfully reconnected not only the phases of her mother's life, but also the temporal rupture she felt at the moment of her mother's death:

> *In the week that followed, I saw that Sunday again, when she was alive, the brown socks, the forsythia, her movements, her smile when I had said goodbye to her, then the Monday, when she was lying dead in her bed. I couldn't connect the two days.*
> *Now, everything is joined up.*[34]

There is a similar authority to the tone in which she declares her account of her father's death definitive, personal pain and the concern for truth forbidding any reworking: 'I cannot describe these moments because I have already done so in another book, which is to say that no other telling of it, with different words, a different order of sentences, will ever be possible.'[35]

The claim is rather paradoxical, however, given that the text in question, *La Place*, already recounts the scene twice, using different terms, as a consequence of its circular narrative. Even as she asserts the complete *lisibilité* of her writing, there are signs of the more uncertain and plural attitude her writing will develop in later works, and we have already moved away from the fully unified narratives of the novels.[36] Alison Fell notes of these two texts that Ernaux's aims of 'a degree of stability and integration in her representations of self and parental other' are approached with some doubts and hesitations, and the texts' fragmentation between various periods and discourses make a more complex representation than some of her comments might suggest.[37]

Later retrospective texts introduce dissonance into the representation of Ernaux's past, notably with the domestic violence of *La Honte*, which contradicts the harmonious view of her parents' marriage in previous texts. In their form, an increasing suspicion develops of narrative as a vehicle for truth. In *L'Événement* Ernaux baulks at the shape narrative imposes on her material:

> *I feel narrative's pull on me, imposing a meaning without my knowledge, and that meaning is the inevitable approach of misfortune. I force myself to resist the desire to race through the days and weeks, trying by all means – research, noting details, using the imperfect tense, analysing the facts – to preserve the interminable slowness of time that thickened without progressing, as in a dream.*[38]

La Honte and *Passion simple* go further in rejecting narrative. In discussing the choice of methodology for her attempt to 'reach my reality of the time' in *La Honte*, Ernaux states briskly: 'no narrative, of course, which would produce a reality instead of searching for one'.[39] In *Passion simple* she relates her avoidance of narrative to the temporal quality of the experience she is describing:

> *I am not giving the narrative of an affair, I am not telling a story (half of which escapes me) with a precise chronology – 'he came on November 11th' – or an approximate one – 'weeks passed'. There was no chronology for me, I only knew presence or absence. I am just accumulating the signs of a passion, constantly oscillating between 'always' and 'once', as if this inventory might permit me to reach the reality of this passion.*[40]

In fact, none of these later texts eschews narrative completely. *L'Événement* is given a high degree of narrativity, albeit grudgingly, in its representation of the pregnancy and abortion. *La Honte* opens with the story of the murder attempt and closes with that of Ernaux's awkward coach trip with her father shortly afterwards; the non-narrative 'ethnology of the self' which connects them acts rather like a textual commentary, dependent on the narrative it explicates. *Passion simple*, as Ernaux writes above, moves between narrated incidents in the *passé composé* and described states in the *imparfait*. Nevertheless, the texts do represent a further move away from the classic retrospective narrative of the early autofiction. The change is reminiscent of Nelson Goodman's distinction between the narrative of a biography and the 'exposition' of a character study, for which he argues that there is a limit to the amount of 'twisting' from their chronological sequence that the elements of a narrative can endure before they cease to be a narrative at all.[41] It is also worth noting that these texts place even more emphasis on the narrator's present, as Ernaux steps in to guide the reader through her unorthodox, a-chronological arrangement of the autobiographical material. *Les Années*, the most recent text, marks a return to conventional chronology, progressing from the 1940s to the present day. While it consists of fragments and static 'snapshots' of aspects of society at particular points (or literal snapshots in the descriptions of photographs which punctuate the text), it does allow the reader to piece together large-scale narratives of social change – the decline of the Left, the growth of consumer society, the fading memory of the war, or changing sexual mores – from the themes she revisits. The sheer scope of this book, covering sixty years of social, political and personal history, perhaps requires a more conventional narrative ordering than the brief sketches of the previous works.

Ernaux's most striking challenge to the unity and authority of her own earlier texts comes with the advent of the intermittently narrated texts in her oeuvre, appearing for the first time in 1993 and making up the majority of her publications since then. *Journal du dehors*, *'Je ne suis pas sortie de ma nuit'*, *La Vie extérieure*, *Se perdre* and *L'Usage de la photo* both complement and challenge the autobiographical picture offered in the retrospective texts, and also mark the coming to prominence of the time of narrating as an issue of debate within the texts themselves.

As early as *Ce qu'ils disent ou rien* in 1977, Ernaux expresses misgivings through her narrator about the effect of a retrospective viewpoint on the story it recounts:

> *Little did I know what I was heading for, like in serial romances, and even in* L'Étranger, *I remember, it said it was like four brief knocks on the door of misfortune, but I couldn't tell myself that because I didn't suspect anything, knowing now what happened next makes me see everything wrong.*[42]

This throwaway remark on the distortions of hindsight returns to become a repeated theme in her work of the 1990s and beyond. In *L'Écriture comme un couteau* she worries that the backward look over her writing career will impose a false teleology on the creative process:

> *These dangers and limits, then, are about the same as the ones you come across in any retrospective discourse about yourself. Wanting to throw some light, to link together what was obscure and unformed at the time I was writing, is to condemn myself to not taking account of the slippages and layerings of thoughts and desires that led to a text, to neglecting the action of life, of the present on the writing of that text ... What I'm afraid of, in talking about my way of writing, about my books, is, as I was telling you, rationalization after the fact, the path you see traced out after you've travelled it.*[43]

The problem receives a striking illustration in a surreal dream-narrative in *Se perdre*, which Ernaux takes as an allegory for retrospective narration:

> *And this troubling dream too: a girl in a bathing costume has disappeared (and is later found dead?). They reconstruct it with the girl, alive, who goes off walking. Because she's alive again they can find out what happened. But it's very hard, because we know how it turns out. (Precisely.) A dream that's the image of the novel, of writing: you know how it ends.*[44]

The analogy suggests writing is a replay of life's events, only now with an imposed predestination which was not present in the original, and which falsifies the copy. For Jonathan Culler, the phenomenon creates a 'double logic' in the causality of narrative, 'presenting its plot as a sequence of events which is prior to and independent of the given perspective on these events, and, at the same time, suggesting by its implicit claims to significance that these events are justified by their appropriateness to a thematic structure', a conflict which applies to factual narratives (Culler discusses Freud's case studies) as much as fiction.[45] In autobiographical writing, it is the perspective from a later time of narrating which creates this second, unacknowledged logic, selecting and arranging events to create meaningful coherence through prior knowledge of their outcome. As Sartre's Roquentin puts it, paraphrasing Kierkegaard, 'events happen in one direction and we recount them in the opposite one'.[46]

Ernaux's development into the use of an intermittent time of narrating and her growing awareness of its potential impact on the material narrated can be traced through the publication history of the five texts concerned. In *Journal du dehors*, the intermittence is almost a side effect, a consequence of the project's fragmentary nature as 'a collection of snapshots of everyday urban life',[47] and of its subsidiary status to her other, simultaneous writing projects over the years in question. Indeed, in the text itself Ernaux expresses some misgivings about the lack of a unifying retrospective narrative around the fragments:

I perceive two possible approaches to facts. You can recount them with precision, in their rawness, their snapshot character, outside of any narrative, or put them aside to (possibly) 'use' them, make them part of a whole (a novel, for instance). Fragments, like the ones I'm writing here, leave me unsatisfied; I need to be engaged in a long, constructed project (not one subject to the chance of days and meetings). Yet I also feel the need to transcribe the scenes on the commuter train, what people say and do, for themselves, without using them for anything.[48]

A year after the publication of *Une femme*, Ernaux shows herself still uneasy about the loss of coherence implied by intermittent narration. However, her scruples are overcome by the authenticity of this method of representation, retaining the unrefined nature of the fragment, which its enmeshing within the double logic of an overall retrospective narrative would contaminate.

A decade later, when Ernaux publishes her private diary for the first time in *'Je ne suis pas sortie de ma nuit'*, it is the immediacy of the fragmented narrative which strikes her as a contrast with the retrospective version of her mother's decline in *Une femme*. Being 'unaware of what was to follow' as she recorded what were to be her mother's final days took on 'a frightening aspect' on re-reading, which was itself a motivation for publication:[49]

For a long time I didn't think I would ever publish it. Perhaps I wanted to leave a single image, a single truth about my mother and my relationship with her, the truth I tried to approach in Une femme. *Now I think that the unity, the coherence that a work results in – no matter what your intentions to take into account the most contradictory data – should be endangered whenever possible.*[50]

The plurality which she earlier avoided in recounting her father's death is now seen as a virtue. Setting the diary account, written 'in the stupor and distress I felt at the time', alongside the reflective, interpretative account of the retrospective text, offers the reader a second way of knowing, an opportunity to feel the situation in its immediacy as well as understand it in its totality.[51] Even at the time of writing the diary, in 1986, she was aware of its peculiar temporal quality which a future *récit* would be unable to capture: 'I could probably wait before writing about my mother. Wait until I have escaped these days. But it is these days that are the truth, although I do not know what truth that is.'[52]

The capacity for intermittent narrative to encompass 'the most contradictory data' is clearly in evidence in *'Je ne suis pas sortie de ma nuit'*. One example is Ernaux's changing attitude to the spectacle of physical decline. Early in the text, in an entry for 14 April 1983, she writes of one of her mother's fellow residents:

Opposite us, an emaciated woman, a spectre from Buchenwald, is sitting very upright, with terrible eyes. She lifts up her gown, you can see the incontinence pad over her vagina. The same scenes on TV fill us with horror. Not here. This is not horror. These are women.[53]

She is far from such equanimity, however, when observing her own mother in a similar state three years on:

Thinner and thinner. Every visit there is a detail that overwhelms me, focuses the horror. Today it was the big brown socks they put on them, coming up to the knee, and, being too loose, always falling down.

My odd gesture: lifting up her gown to see her bare thighs. They are horribly thin.[54]

The initial denial of 'horreur' and its later assertion – indeed, the word becomes the constant refrain of the text's last pages – is striking, not because it shows a development in the narrator's character as the trauma drags on exhaustingly and becomes ever more personal, but precisely because this development is *not* shown to us. We see a moment of self-composure, and another moment of mental disarray. The path traversed between them may be inferred by the reader, but it is not developed in a narrative. There is no single narrative instance, no unifying narrator's perspective, to link the two instants together. With each narrator focused on their individual present, unaware of the future and forgetful of the past, we are left with a series of discrete, disparate 'nows' with no guarantee of coherence between them.

A similar effect can be seen in *Se perdre*, the publication of which was motivated by a perception of 'a different "truth"' from that in *Passion simple* to be found in her diary. Contradictions arise in the text from Ernaux's changing attitude to her lover. On four occasions in the text, for instance, between April and July 1989, she refers to S.'s habit of cadging her cigarette packets:

> *A bit of a gigolo: he drinks a half-bottle of my Chivas, asks for the open packet of Marlboro. I'm both mother and whore. I've always liked all kinds of roles.*

> *I brought him back some Marlboro cigarettes, a duty-free box. He pulls out a packet at once (did he not have cigarettes on him? he's used to helping himself to mine) and he won't forget to take the box when he leaves.*

> *I like it when he comes without any cigarettes – on purpose? – and asks if he can take the packet. I say, 'take the other one too'. 'Really?' He takes both without another twinge of conscience. The perfect gigolo.*

> *Sobering up, in a sudden burst. Seeing him as a playboy – or a gorby-boy – brutal (although not too brutal) and sensualist (and why not). Telling myself I lost a year and a half for a man who asks me when he leaves if he can take the open packet of Marlboro on the table.*[55]

Here the contradictory attitudes, towards an admittedly trivial character trait, do not even imply the coherent development which lay behind the '*Je ne suis pas sortie de ma nuit*' examples. They are simply the result of Ernaux's fluctuating moods and the ups and downs of the relationship. The intermittent narrator becomes a series of different narrators, interpreting this repeated event afresh each time, expressing, as Ernaux puts it, 'a raw, instant, contradictory truth, which finds expression more freely because it does not form part of the coherence of a literary work'.[56]

For Ernaux, the publication of the private diary is made possible only by the pre-existing *récit*, 'as if the latter *authorized* me to do it, as if life had to become "form", concerted literary form, with a coefficient of generality, for me to offer it subsequently in its immediacy, its unformed character'.[57] The 'concerted' and generalized nature of the retrospective versions of these events is immediately apparent in comparison to their companion diaries. In the sections of *Une femme* devoted to the mother's decline we see events in series which are recounted in parallel: 'My fear each time, at the moment of seeing her'; 'Several times, the brutal desire to take her away with me ...'[58] We see the linking together of individual moments into a coherent progression: 'In the space of a few weeks, the desire to keep up appearances has left her. She has slumped, walking half bent, her head hanging. She has lost her glasses.'[59] We see, too, the ordering capacity of a perspective that knows what is to come, marking the last time that the mother seems truly herself, or moving out of the iterative mode to single out a particular meeting which will prove to be the final one.[60] In *Passion simple* it is at one point the diary itself which is transformed by the retrospective narration, as Ernaux's habitual entries are condensed into a single, typical example:

> I would often write on a page the date and time and 'he'll come' with other phrases, fears, that he wouldn't come, that his desire would wane. In the evening I would return to the page, 'he came', making disordered notes of the details of our time together.[61]

The retrospective ordering of this account is 'endangered' by the publication of the raw material it transformed. Quoting Rousseau, Ernaux claims a desire to 'offer all the evidence', and to demystify the closed text by opening a new perspective on its material.[62]

The private journal as literature has been much criticized: René Girard notes objections to its banality and indecency of content; Maurice Blanchot takes issue with its dependency on the calendar, which, in his view, excludes the essential creative process of retrospective ordering of material, and grounds the material itself hopelessly 'in the everyday and the perspective that the everyday delimits'.[63] Philippe Lejeune, in a less polemical look at the form, agrees diaries are unsuitable for publication: 'book form is not made for diaries. Publishing a diary is like trying to fit a sponge in a matchbox.'[64] In addition to its repetitiveness, the diary's uncomposed, uncorrected nature, and the allusiveness of a discourse intended to communicate only with its own author make it a poor candidate for literature. Lejeune characterizes diary discourse as 'non-narrative', qualifying the judgement with the explanation: 'every sequence recounts, of course, but it is not constructed like a narrative with a beginning, a middle and an end – no phenomenon of sequence as Barthes, Brémond or others have analysed it: *it is written in ignorance of its ending.*'[65] Ernaux seems to a large extent in agreement with these characterizations, writing in *L'Écriture comme un couteau*:

> *[In the diary] time imposes the structure, and life in its immediacy is the subject matter. It is thus more limited, less free, I don't have the sense of 'constructing' a reality, just of leaving a trace of existence, of* setting something down, *to no particular purpose, with no publication time-lag, pure being-there.*[66]

These very characteristics which may exclude private diaries from the category of literature, however, are those which make Ernaux's diaries valuable companion pieces to her *récits*. The generalizing view of the *récits*, downplaying the personal in order to affirm commonality, is set against texts personal to the point of being cryptic, as with the many allusions to unknown people and events via initials and dates in *Se perdre*. The fragmented narrators with their banal detail and repetitions – *Se perdre* quotes the same line from Édith Piaf three times on different occasions – give us life in its disorder, rather than the condensed, reflective essence of the retrospective version.[67] Paul Ricoeur is critical of Genette's narratology for ignoring the experience of time arising from the order, speed or frequency Genette catalogues in its representation.[68] If narrative refigures time from clock-time to time as humanly experienced – *Zeiterlebnis* in Günther Müller's term – then the different narrative instances Ernaux employs demonstrate the plurality of this experience, from cool recollection to the heat of the moment.[69] Lejeune's comment on the ignorance of the ending suggests why these episodes in particular from Ernaux's autobiographical oeuvre should be chosen for the complement of the diary. As we have seen, they are both oriented towards an uncertain future event, a death or abandonment whose approach fills each text with foreboding, but whose arrival cannot be predicted. More than other episodes in her autobiography, then, these are falsified by a perspective devoid of uncertainty, as we find in the *récits*.[70] Moreover, the 'non-narrative' aspect of diary discourse (if we accept Lejeune's rather extreme characterization) is perhaps a reason in itself for the revisiting. We have seen already Ernaux's mistrust of narrative as a vehicle through which to represent experience; the diary's shapelessness, disjointedness and a-causality may be virtues in themselves to a writer striving to render reality with as little distortion as possible.

L'Usage de la photo takes further the notion of revisiting material, and perhaps stands as a rebuke to any critics who suspected her habit of recycling might be due to a paucity of material or a desire for an easy publication. The co-written text internalizes the principle through its parallel sets of commentaries on the same photographs by Ernaux and her partner, Marc Marie, giving rise to a double perspective on the periods and events in their relationship evoked by the photos. The project combines retrospective and intermittent modes of narration. While the discussion of the photographs, and the accounts of their relationship and Ernaux's concurrent treatment for breast cancer, are largely retrospective, the division of the text around fourteen chronologically ordered photos mimics the diary form, and for both writers the text is often as focused on the present of writing as much as the past of the photograph. The project's rule that neither writer should see the other's work brings an element of *inconscience* similar to that of the diary, with similar repetitions and contradictions as a consequence. At some points, Marie's account will unknowingly repeat what we have just read in Ernaux's: the image of a boot reminds them both of cartoon anglers with an old boot on the end of their line; scattered pens are compared by both to the *jeu de Mikado*.[71] The contradictions betray involuntary insights: Marie lists with confidence the tunes of their 'top nine' of the period of the photographs, but the list has only six tracks in common with Ernaux's version elsewhere in the book.[72] The dual narratives can be enlightening about the protagonists and their relationship, as when Ernaux recounts her unspoken suspicions during a brief absence of Marie's that he had left to telephone his ex-partner. Marie's subsequent version not only provides us with the missing account of his activities, but reveals that he is aware of, and secretly pleased by, her worries.[73]

These dual, more or less simultaneous times of narration are seen by Ernaux as having a similar function to the other pairings of different perspectives in her oeuvre. In being double, they offer the 'other truth' of a plural epistemology, the accounts undermining each other, and thereby undermining the notion of a definitive version of events. Ernaux admits to some trepidation about this, expressing a desire in the writing of the text to 'make the words and sentences unshakeable, the paragraphs impossible to shift', and confessing her fear of what she will find in Marie's alternative viewpoint: 'I'm scared of discovering what he is writing. I'm scared of discovering his alterity, this dissimilarity if points of view that is covered over by desire and shared daily life, which his writing will suddenly unveil.'[74] In being a series of interspersed images and texts, they avoid the totalizing effect of a single, coherent narrative, of which Ernaux is so mistrustful: 'the writing under the photos, in multiple fragments – which will themselves be broken up by M.'s, still unknown to me at the moment – offers me, among other things, the opportunity for *minimal narrativization* of this reality'.[75] The reader is destabilized by these fragmented accounts, doubled in perspective by their dual narrators, and doubled again by the 'double regard' of the writers' past and present views of the scene in the photograph – at one point, Ernaux's 2004 commentary on a photograph is interrupted by an extract from her 2003 diary from the day it was taken.[76] Such complex temporal play, to borrow Genette's phrase, serves to make time itself more prominent than ever as a theme, perhaps even, as Ernaux intimates in the closing pages, the subject of the book.[77]

In none of these revisitings does the second account invalidate or replace the first. They are correctives only in that they challenge the authority of the other text, demonstrating that the truth of events is not the property of any one perspective. Lejeune suggests Ernaux's paired texts employ 'a system of "triangulation" to evoke something which is finally unsayable', a truth existing somewhere between the imperfect and contradictory versions.[78] Not all of the significant differences between Ernaux's revisitings are necessarily dependent on the time of narrating. There are, for instance, changes of tone, as with the lighter and darker representations of her father in *La Place* and *La Honte*, or changes of discourse, as between the colloquial tirade of *Ce qu'ils disent ou rien* and the cool *écriture plate* of her subsequent depictions of adolescence.[79] Yet a change in narrative instance, particularly between retrospective and intermittent narration, is her most prominent form of revisiting, and also her most thought-provoking as the 'life illuminated' of the *récit* is followed by the 'being there' of her journal, giving us a sense of mingled familiarity and alienation from our shifted temporal perspective.

One major effect of different narrative instances is to alter the relationship between the narrator and protagonist in Ernaux's various texts. All Ernaux's texts feature a narrating self speaking in the present tense as she recounts events, and a narrated self (the protagonist) whose actions are partly or wholly the focus of the text, generally told in the *passé composé*. In the retrospective texts, the gap separating these figures may be decades long, and their characters clearly differentiated; in the intermittent texts, they may be mere hours or minutes apart, so that their identities become indistinguishable. For Tiphaine Samoyault, diary-writing time is not yet a true 'time of writing', and is in fact closer in quality to the narrated time than to the time of writing of the retrospective texts, so entwined are writing and experiencing selves in the private journals.[80]

There are also *rapprochements* between narrator and protagonist in the retrospective texts. They are often to be found in the endings: in the novels, the account switches to the present tense in the final pages as the protagonist's life comes up to date with the time of narrating. Similarly at the ends of the non-fiction texts, the figures generally come to coincide as the narrator drops the use of past tenses in her narration: 'I wasn't thinking about the end of my book. Now I know it is approaching ... Soon there will be nothing left to write.'[81] In *Passion simple* a footnote marks the point of change, expressing an awareness of and uneasiness about the division of identity it implies:

> *I move from the imperfect, what was – but until when? – to the present – but since when? – for want of a better solution. For I can't pinpoint the exact transformation of my passion for A., day after day, just dwell on images, pick*

*out the signs of a reality whose date of first appearance – as in general history
– can't be defined with certainty.*[82]

But, where the two figures do not coincide in time, Ernaux's texts
emphasize not the connection between narrator and protagonist,
but their dissimilarity. In *Les Années*, Ernaux rejects the Proustian
'palimpsest feeling' of merged levels of time while half-awake as a
means to recapture the past; rather, she works 'by an effort of critical consciousness' to expand upon a particular memory by
recovering typical words, customs and actions associated with that
moment in time.[83] Where the protagonist is many years younger,
the adult narrator designates the gap between their identities in a
variety of ways. Hindsight emphasizes the retrospective viewpoint
and exposes the protagonist's relative naivety: 'the signs of what
really awaited me, I ignored them all', writes the married narrator
of *La Femme gelée* ominously of her courting student self.[84] The alien-
ness of the child's mind is a source of fascination to the adult writer.
The narrator of *Les Armoires vides* says of her childhood self, 'when
you're ten, things are enormous, you're all at sea, you don't see
anything, the lack of experience'.[85] Ernaux writes similarly of her
own childhood, noting in *La Honte* that the social shame and awareness of class distinctions she ascribes to her former self might be a
connection between them, but the understanding she has of these
feelings now is far removed qualitatively from the instinctive, non-
verbalized sense of difference at the time.[86] The view which emerges
overall is perhaps surprisingly pessimistic for a writer who has
devoted her career to autobiography:

*The woman I am in 1995 is incapable of putting herself back in the girl of
1952 who knew of nothing beyond her little town, her family, her private
school, had only a limited vocabulary at her disposition. And before her, the
immensity of the time to be lived. There is no true memory of the self.*[87]

This emphasis on the division between writer and protagonist is
not only to be found in the memoirs of Ernaux's youth, where we
might expect some focus on difference. It is also present in texts
dealing with the narrator's recent past. In *L'Usage de la photo* she
notes the change from the 'I have cancer' of the protagonist to the
somewhat uncertain 'I had cancer' as she writes.[88] Similarly in
L'Occupation, the obsessive jealousy which is the subject of the book

is an attribute of the protagonist, not the narrator, as the latter makes clear: 'Writing has been a way of saving what has already ceased to be my reality, that is, a feeling that gripped me from head to foot in the street, but has become the "occupation", a limited time that is now over.'[89] *Passion simple* goes further in positing a qualitative difference between the time of narrating and the time of experiencing:

> *While I can remember precisely everything that is associated with my relationship with A., the October riots in Algeria, the heat and the overcast sky of Bastille Day 1989, even the most trivial details, like buying a mixer in June, the day before one of our dates, it's impossible for me to link the writing of a precise page to a rainstorm or one of the world events of the last five months, the fall of the Berlin Wall and the execution of Ceauçescu. The time of writing has nothing to do with the time of passion.*[90]

Yet despite all this focus on difference, there is one major difference between narrator and protagonist, perhaps even the most important one, which goes unexplored and unacknowledged in the text. The difference is simply this: at the time of narrating, Ernaux is a writer, but in the narrated time of her protagonist she is not. Consistently through her oeuvre, the acts of writing and publishing, along with Ernaux's status as an author of best-selling, controversial autobiographies and the effect of this status on those around her, are marginalized or passed over in silence wherever the protagonist is concerned. The narrator, of course, is largely defined by her status as writer: the majority of her comments concern questions of representation and narrative, re-readings of her text or anticipations of its publication. The protagonist is hardly ever seen in these terms. Her literary activities are an aspect of her life that the retrospective *récits* prefer to ignore.[91] Only in the private diaries – where the narrator and protagonist blur together, and where the text is so divorced in Ernaux's mind from writing-for-publication that she can write in *Se perdre* that she is not writing – does the writer-protagonist make an appearance.[92] Thus, in *'Je ne suis pas sortie de ma nuit'* we follow the writing progress of the first, later abandoned version of *Une femme*, and that of *La Honte* in *Se perdre*. Elsewhere in *Se perdre*, Ernaux recounts literary dinners and receptions, reads publishers' proofs, watches a stage adaptation of an earlier text, embarks on a book tour of Scandinavia, and struggles with embryonic writing projects. None of this appears in the corresponding *récits*, not even when it is of direct relevance to the text in question. *Une femme* recounts the mother's final months without mentioning that the original version of the text was written during this period, and that the guilt and distress the writing caused her would lead Ernaux to destroy the manuscript on the mother's death.[93] The narrator of *Passion simple* notes the difference between her current 'time of writing' and former 'time of passion', but omits to recount the anxieties occasioned by her inability to write as the time of passion overwhelmed her life to the exclusion of all other pursuits.[94]

Even where we do not have the private journals to highlight the *récits'* omissions, the silences in the representation of the protagonists are noticeable. In her relationship to others as daughter or lover, the protagonist's status as a famous autobiographer is apparently immaterial. During her mother's lifetime, for instance, Ernaux publishes four texts depicting the mother in stark, often unflattering terms, while exposing intimate details of her own life and sexual history. In *Les Armoires vides*, Denise Lesur recounts the joy and hatred she feels at the thought of her parents' humiliation should her pregnancy become public knowledge: 'they've got what they deserved, they pissed me off enough about being like they were'.[95] Of the reaction of Ernaux's own mother to the publication of this transparently autobiographical text there is not a word anywhere in the *récit*: neither *Une femme* nor *L'Événement* mention the effect of this self-exposure on their relationship. Elsewhere in these early texts Ernaux's narrator expresses contempt for her mother's uneducated, working-class ways, recounts her urinating copiously in a cemetery or, in both of Ernaux's first two novels, describes her with her skirt habitually 'stuck between her buttocks', tugged free with an 'ugly gesture'.[96] Despite the fact that this mother–daughter relationship is arguably the most important recurring theme of her oeuvre, it is not until she is directly questioned by Frédéric-Yves Jeannet in *L'Écriture comme un couteau* that Ernaux will discuss the effect on the mother of her daughter's chosen subject matter:

[Les Armoires vides] *was read by the critics as a novel, as an autobiographical novel by the readers. Not as a novel by my family, obviously. Particularly my mother, who lived with me at the time. With great intelligence, but also submission to the violence I was inflicting on her – she must have suffered terribly because of that book – she played the game, pretended it was all made up ... She had wanted me to write, she had never imagined it would be that, a book that had nothing to do with what she liked, love – 'romance' as she would say – and everything to do with the real, with our life, the shop, with her.*[97]

Wherever Ernaux's literary life impacts on her personal one, the autobiographies shy away.[98] In interview, Ernaux suggests that the writing of *La Femme gelée* was in part responsible for the ending of her marriage to Philippe (to whom the book is sardonically dedicated); this role of her writing is unmentioned in her oeuvre.[99] The affair with W. recounted in *L'Occupation* occurs nine years after the publication of *Passion simple*, of which W. must surely have been aware, but the book's effect on her subsequent relationships is unexplored. When W. refuses to describe or give the name of his new lover, Ernaux interprets this as 'a fear that I will get at her in a violent or underhand way, that I might make a scene'.[100] The reader cannot help but wonder if his real fear may be a well-founded concern for her privacy, given Ernaux's previous literary record. Any suggestion that her writing may affect the people in her life (rather than vice versa) is unwelcome: Ernaux frostily shuts down Bernard Pivot on *Bouillon de Culture* when he asks whether S. has read *Passion simple*.[101] And as Chloë Taylor Merleau points out, Ernaux must also be affected in her own life by the perceptions her work creates:

The memory [of her father's attack in La Honte *], if not confessed, would not have become a lens through which the public as well as Ernaux's intimates know her, and through which, consequently, she is increasingly required to see herself and to present herself, and according to which she will tend to structure her future behaviour. Similar to de Man's observation that autobiography produces life rather than life producing autobiographies, Ernaux's autobiographical discourse thus serves to produce an identity and pattern of behaviour for her rather than working as the position from which she can describe who she is and what she has done.*[102]

Les Années is a curious case in this regard, as, uniquely, it discusses its own development and production as part of Ernaux's life story, yet in other respects it is the most striking example of the suppression of the author's writerly self in pursuit of everywoman status. Unlike all her other works, *Les Années* lacks a narrator's commentary in the present, indeed, the narrator never refers to herself in the first person at all. In what is perhaps another Proustian allusion, the creative decisions taken in the development of the novel – the choice of the imperfect tense, and the alternating *elle* and *nous/on* with which personal and collective history are recounted – are enfolded within narrative time, attributed to Ernaux's former self at intervals from the 1980s onwards as the project gestates. However, more than any other text, *Les Années* occludes Ernaux's career as a published writer, to the extent that it presents *Les Années* as if it were the sole writing project of her life: in the late 1990s she clears her life 'to make space for her writing project', as if it were her first. Discussion of the development of *Les Années* is preceded by mentions of her writing ambitions as a student, and her abortive first novel in the 1960s, but in the intervening time there is absolute silence on her writing career. Her teaching experience is featured prominently – principally as a means of including comment on the younger generation – but of her life as a published author there is no mention. She even states of herself in the early 1990s, at the height of her fame following the publication of *Passion simple*: 'Besides her work obligations, lessons and marking, her time is given over to managing her personal tastes and desires, reading, film, telephone, correspondence and love affairs.'[103] Bernard Pivot appears in *Les Années* as a face on the television, not as a personal acquaintance. The people and events of her earlier works are all present, from the 'incident' of *La Honte* to the affairs of *Passion simple* and *L'Occupation*, but no word of their reworking into literature. Even as she acknowledges the important role remembering the past has played in her life, it is as memory exercises during bouts of insomnia that the topic is broached, without any reference to the subsequent fate of these recovered memories.[104]

Ernaux herself seems undecided on the question of her writing and experiencing selves. An aside in *L'Usage de la photo* implies there is no distinction between them: 'I wonder if not separating life and writing, as I don't, isn't a matter of spontaneously transforming experience into description.'[105] More frequently, though, her comments resist the idea that her experience is mediated through a writerly nature. 'I am not a writer; I write, then I live', she declares in *Se perdre*, and repeats the sentiment in the opening section of *L'Écriture comme un couteau:* 'I never think of myself as a writer, just as

someone who writes, who *has* to write.'[106] Here, once again, she
suggests a qualitative difference in herself as she writes from when
she is not writing: '[During the year-long email 'interview'] I could
take the time to tame this space, to bring up from the void what I
think, search for, and feel as I write – or attempt to write – but which
is absent when I am not writing.'[107]

More telling, perhaps, is the writer's reaction at moments where
writing might seem to contaminate the experience which gives rise
to it. In *L'Usage de la photo* this contamination seems to devalue the
photographs taken after the writing project has begun:

> *We carry on taking pictures ... But it seems to me that we are no longer
> looking at the spectacle we discover in the same way, that there is no longer
> this pain that pushes us to fix the scene. Taking the photo is no longer the*
> final *act. It is a part of our writing project. A form of innocence has been
> lost.*[108]

Elsewhere in the same text, Marc Marie's joking accusation that she
only had cancer in order to write about it elicits the confession that
he is right, in a sense, before a longer passage explains why he is
wrong, that she does not wait for life to provide her with subjects for
writing.[109] In *Se perdre*, the idea that the sexual experiences she
writes about might have been experienced with writing in mind is
firmly rejected: 'I don't make love like a writer, telling myself "I can
use that", or distancing myself. I make love each time as if it were –
and why wouldn't it be – the last time, as a simple living person.'[110]
There is perceptible discomfort in these few asides at the intermin-
gling of her source material and its representation, even if only
hypothetical.

The reason for this separation via the time of narrating into
writing and experiencing selves in all but the private diaries is that
Ernaux's particular conception of the autobiographical project
depends on it. Ernaux describes her writing repeatedly in terms of
an objective analytical study of its subject matter. She borrows the
terms of academic disciplines to label it: sociology, history or
ethnology. In the outward-looking texts she attempts to suppress the
personal, struggling to escape 'the trap of the individual' in *La Place*,
labelling *Les Années* 'a sort of impersonal autobiography', and prefacing *Journal du dehors* with the disclaimer: 'I avoided as far as I
could putting myself in the picture and expressing the emotion that

is at the origin of each text.'[111] In the texts focused on her own emotional and sexual experiences she continues to emphasize the general over the personal. In *L'Occupation*, 'it's no longer *my* desire, *my* jealousy, in these pages, it's desire, it's jealousy'.[112] *Passion simple* is not 'a book about him, or even about me'; rather it is concerned with the obsessive desire the relationship causes; it is public and outward-looking in its intentions rather than inward and private: 'I wonder if I'm not writing to know whether other people have done or felt the same things, and if not, so that they should find it normal to feel these things.'[113] In every case the protagonist is, as Ernaux puts it, 'the object of analysis' conducted by the narrator.[114] In *L'Écriture comme un couteau* she makes explicit this claim to objectivity even towards the most subjective material:

> *In all these texts [the non-fiction récits and the* Journal du dehors *project] there is the same objectivizing, the same distancing, whether it's a matter of the mental facts for which I am, or have been, the subject, or socio-historical facts. And, right from* Les Armoires vides, *my first book, I haven't distinguished between the private and the social ... When I write, everything is matter before me, exteriority, whether it be my feelings, my body, my thoughts, or the behaviour of people on the train. In* L'Événement, *the tube in my vagina, the waters and blood, everything that is considered private, is there, explicitly, but with reference to the law of the time, the discourses, the social world in general.*[115]

For such an autobiographical project to persuade us of its validity, two things are required. First, it is necessary that the narrator be separate from the protagonist, in order that the one can interpret the other and, secondly, it is necessary that the protagonist should be the object of the narrator's analysis, not her collaborator in it.

In dealing with personal matters, Ernaux's narratorial stance is closer to that of a biographer than an autobiographer. Her examinations of her recent or distant past mimic the processes of objective research; the narrator lists and interprets the facts of the protagonist's experiences as so much psychological or sociological evidence. In different texts, Ernaux's protagonist is explored as a woman in an unequal society, as a product of her class milieu, or as a human being in thrall to obsessions and desires. *Les Années* takes this tendency to its logical conclusion by banishing the first person from the text. Ernaux describes the changing beliefs, habits and attitudes she shared with others of her generation through a constantly shifting *on* or *nous*, which stands in turn for each of the groups in which she has a stake – as a woman, a French citizen, a lover, wife, parent and divorcee, an intellectual, a socialist and a middle-class consumer.[116] In the commentaries on personal photographs which appear at intervals as markers of passing time, the third person and a largely external perspective maintain the impression of objectivity, even as the photographs come up to date with the writer's present self in the final pages. In each of her roles the protagonist has a representative function, which, as we have seen, works to invite the reader's identification with the experience in question. The additional label of 'writer' would force the protagonist to inhabit her role less purely, damaging the figure's universality and impeding our identification. More importantly, writerly contamination of the experience as the protagonist is perceiving it would damage its validity as 'evidence'. If Ernaux wishes the experiences she recounts to be authentic, they must be seen to be lived for themselves, not in the second degree with an eye for their literary potential; if she wishes the experiences recounted to be meaningful in a wider sense than the personal, they must focus on what is representative of broader human experience where the protagonist is concerned, leaving the individualizing traits of the literary persona to the narrator.

Systematic adherence to these aims might result in rather a sterile, depersonalized oeuvre, so it is to our benefit as readers that Ernaux's ideal of objectivity is never quite obtained, as she freely admits in her texts. Cross-infection between the writer-narrator and experiencer-protagonist exists, as we have seen, with the writing self occasionally escaping the confines of the time of narrating. Elsewhere, the generalizing, objective intentions of the narrator are described as a struggle, bringing only limited success. She acknowledges of the *Journal du dehors* project: 'I put much more of myself into these texts than I intended.'[117] In recounting her father's life in *La Place*, Ernaux's intended focus on 'the signs of a condition shared with others' merges involuntarily with more personal recollections.[118] When she comes to write on her mother, this composite approach is planned from the start, with the *récit* situating itself 'at the meeting-point of the familial and the social, of myth and history', but tension remains from an urge to represent the mother via 'purely affective images'.[119] And as we have seen, the objective, generalized nature of the *récits* comes to seem to their author as a distorted or partial view,

which requires the immediate and personal perspective of the
private diaries, with their undifferentiated writer-experiencer
recounting time as it passes, to provide balance to the picture.
Even the rigorously impersonal *Les Années* is deceptively so: its shifting
group-associations not only universalize Ernaux's experience, but
also fix her individuality in the point of overlap where the various
groups meet. The majority of Ernaux's work may use the different
levels of narrating and narrated time to divide the self into investigating subject and analysed object, but Ernaux's scrupulous demand
for honesty requires that even this process, motivated as it is by a
desire for authenticity, be nuanced to avoid the possibility of falsely
representing the self.

André Gide's multifaceted representation of the self, compris-
ing published journals and correspondence, essays and semi-
autobiographical fiction as well as autobiography proper, led
Lejeune to coin the term *espace autobiographique* for such a network
of autobiographical perspectives. The work of few subsequent
writers has fitted the term as closely as that of Ernaux. Within this
web of novels and *récits*, private and public diaries, Ernaux shows us
her own and her parents' lives from many different viewpoints. This
variety, as we have seen, is in large part determined by the choice of
temporal relations in the recounting of the text, demonstrating how
the same experience can be transformed by a changed relationship
between the time of narrating and narrated time. As this implies,
narrative form is immensely important to Ernaux. It is important
enough for her to republish the same autobiographical material
cast in a new form, and it is important enough to be the chief
subject of the narrator's present-tense discourse, her meditations on
writing and representation sometimes rivalling the *récit* proper for
space allotted in the text. Yet this preoccupation has far from a
purely aesthetic motivation. Ernaux claims to be no more interested
in the pursuit of originality in her work for its own sake than in the
assertion of uniqueness in her personal experience.[120] Her texts are
not forms in search of content, as the works of the *nouveaux
romanciers* or Oulipians may sometimes appear, but rather, in
Ernaux's eyes at least, necessary modes of telling determined by the
particularity – or plurality – of the experiences to be recounted. She
may not be waiting for life to give her subjects to write about, but

she is, as she goes on to say in *L'Usage de la photo*, waiting for it to bring her '*unknown ways of organizing* writing', enabling her to write 'texts for which the very form is given by the reality of my life'.[121] This sense of the predominance of the text's subject matter, determining the form and engendering its innovations, is in keeping with Ernaux's suspicion of the literary. She states her aims in terms of communicating shared experience with her readership or using her writing to engage with social injustice, refusing readers' judgement on purely aesthetic grounds. As we have seen, the time of narrating is again key to her project here. Ernaux the outspoken, committed, taboo-breaking writer divides her textual identity via the text's own temporal duality, thereby bolstering her narrator's appearance of dispassionate, reflective objectivity and her protagonist's everywoman credentials.

Finally, there is a sense, though, in which Ernaux's narrative form is more than just a by-product of her choice of topic. As well as the critically dissected themes of gender, class, family and desire, there is another theme running through her oeuvre, and that is *time*. 'What is the present?' asks *Se perdre* repeatedly; *Passion simple* sums up the period of Ernaux's life it recounts as one in which she measured time differently, corporeally; *L'Usage de la photo* concludes with the suggestion that the entire text may be considered an exploration of her fascination with time.[122] Narrative is time represented in language. Ernaux's narrators describe the differing qualities of time in her life and writing; the autobiographical revisitings in her oeuvre strive to make such differences manifest in the reading experience, and the theme of time comes ever more to the fore as her career progresses. It would be a misrepresentation to reach the glib, deconstructionist conclusion that Ernaux's narrative texts are, essentially, texts about narrative. However, to the extent that she comes to focus on time as a theme and explores its representation directly through the structures in her writing, Ernaux's project is, in part at least, one of writing time, and that is a project as fundamental as any conceived by the *nouveaux romanciers*.

Chapter Two
Pascal Quignard and the Fringes of Narrative

Few writers have combined such renown with such eclecticism, such a wide readership for certain texts with such obscurity in others, as has Pascal Quignard (b.1948). He has been at the heart of French literary publishing with twenty-five years working for Gallimard, from professional reader to *secrétaire général des Éditions*, and has been awarded French literature's most prestigious honour, the Goncourt Prize (for *Les Ombres errantes*, 2002). He writes substantial novels of modern French life in a broadly traditional, realist manner (*Le Salon du Wurtemberg*, 1986; *Les Escaliers de Chambord*, 1989), as well as sober, reflective historical novels like *Tous les matins du monde* (1991, adapted into a hugely successful film by Alain Corneau, winner of seven Césars, and probably the work with which Quignard is most associated). He is immensely prolific, having to date produced eleven novels and twenty-eight volumes of non-fiction or semi-fiction, including essays, biographies, literary criticism and other forms more difficult to classify, plus two translations, six pamphlets of poetry, and nine *contes*. In the *rentrée littéraire* of Autumn 1990 Quignard published eleven books simultaneously.[1] He is the 'bass voice of great French literature', combining critical acclaim, academic interest and book sales in six-figure numbers.[2] Yet this is also a writer whose works can sell sixty-eight copies in ten years, whose most characteristic work, the *Petits Traités* (1990), languished unpublished for a decade due to repeated refusals, and whose Goncourt winner was dubbed 'resolutely uninterpretable' or an 'unidentified literary object' by baffled critics, going on to become one of the lowest-selling prizewinners in the history of the award.[3] He has published novels which seem more like essays, like *Le Lecteur* (1976), a disquisition on reading whose only characters are the narrator, the addressed reader of the book, and another, vanished *lecteur* who might be either or neither of them, or like

Carus (1979), a novel about a circle of friends, the 'action' of which largely consists of their intellectual dinner-party discussions on abstruse topics. He has published essays which seem more like stories or poems, like the *Petits Traités*, which mix anecdote with argument, or the *Dernier Royaume* sequence (from 2002), which take the *Traités* a stage further in their lack of cohesion, their clash of discourses and their gnomic poeticism. By turns accessible and wilfully obscure, Quignard crosses literary genres in a way that can still, in our postmodern era, trouble the reader who expects analysis and argument from an essay, and story and character from a novel. He poses a particular challenge to narrative theory: if much of his work is semi-fictional, it is also semi-narrative. Stories are accompanied by reflective essays on a related theme, like *La Leçon de musique* (1987) or *Le Nom sur le bout de la langue* (1993), and narrative and non-narrative discourses may be jumbled together in a collection of fragments, as in *Les Tablettes de buis d'Apronenia Avitia* (1984). Even where the nature of the discourse is not itself in question, there is often a sense of the borderline in Quignard's use of narrative. An aesthetic of disjunction is perceptible in many of his fictions, which employ various means to break connections and disrupt the narrative line. Lastly, Quignard's writing puts into question one narrative in particular which is important to our purposes here: that of the *retour au récit* and the story of twentieth-century French literary history which the phrase implies.

Investigating narrative form in Quignard will oblige us to hybridize narrative theory to some extent with modern genre theory, in order to explore Quignard's trajectories into and out of narrative discourse, and to examine the effect of the other discourses on the narratives they complement or interrupt. We can begin with Genette's basic definition of narrative as 'the representation of an event or a series of events, either real or fictional, through the medium of language and most particularly of written language', which is uncontroversial as far as literature is concerned, even if it does unreasonably sideline oral and visual narrative.[4] Subsequent theorists have questioned whether a single event is enough to constitute a narrative, requiring instead at least two, or suggested that a causal connection as well as a temporal progression must be implied in narrative's series.[5] All prose fiction – not just those texts which cross genre boundaries as Quignard's do – contains discourses other than narrative discourse, however. Mieke Bal classifies fictional discourses as narrative, descriptive or argumentative, the last of these being a catch-all term for direct personal expression by the author or narrator, be it analytical, informative or lyrical.[6] This tripartite division will prove useful, although we must bear in mind that fictions are not to be separated out in practice into narration, description and argumentation, either quantitatively by assigning particular roles to particular phrases, or even qualitatively by determining degrees of each within a single utterance. When Balzac writes, in *Le Père Goriot*, 'Eugène was starting to feel very ill at ease', how far does this describe a state, and how far does it narrate an event? When, in the same novel, he writes of 'one of those insubstantial houses with thin columns and parsimonious porticos that are what Paris considers *pretty*, a real banker's house' does this loaded representation itself constitute a description or an argument?[7] The discourses are inextricable in 'narrative' fiction, and may be equally so where narrative or descriptive elements appear within the 'argumentative' discourse of an essay, as will prove to be the case with Quignard.

The differing *addressivity* of these discourses is an essential consideration in examining their relationship in Quignard's texts. For Mikhail Bakhtin, addressivity is the particular communicative quality that makes language into an utterance. It is the implicit purpose behind the words, the implicit model coded within them of the person to whom they are directed, and the implicit expectation of a certain kind of response from this addressee. As Bakhtin puts it:

> *addressivity, the quality of turning to someone, is a constitutive feature of the utterance; without it the utterance does not and cannot exist. The various typical forms this addressivity assumes and the various concepts of the addressee are constitutive, definitive features of various speech genres … The choice of all language means is made by the speaker under varying degrees of influence from the addressee and his anticipated response.[8]*

We can see that there is a difference in communicative quality between the narrative/descriptive discourses that create the diegesis, and the discourses of a poem or essay. Narration and description serve to evoke a world and the actions taking place within it; they communicate an indirect invitation to their addressee to enter the diegesis they construct. Argumentation, on the other hand, interpellates its addressee directly. It highlights the writer as a thinking subject, and expects from its addressee, not acquiescence in a consensual fiction, but a direct response to the address. We have moved from a communicative relationship in which the writer facilitates from behind the scenes the addressee's imaginative reconstruction of a fictional situation, to one in which the writer steps onstage to engage the audience in dialogue. Literary forms like the *roman à thèse* which attempt to meld narrative and argumentation raise questions as to the purpose of the text. Is it an exposition of ideas, with fictional window-dressing? Is it a story hamstrung by the ideas it seeks to incorporate into its narrative? And with Quignard comes the further suspicion that the text is to be read neither as an essay nor a fiction, but primarily as a prose-poem. For the reader whose responses are conditioned by certain expectations of literary and non-literary genres – conditioning which few readers can escape entirely – Quignard's utterances can be particularly hard to tune into.

Let us open our investigation with a text which represents, if not the typical Quignardian form – for what would that be? – then at least a mid-point between his most novelistic (such as *Les Escaliers de Chambord*), his most essayistic (such as *Le Sexe et l'effroi*, 1994), and his most poetic (such as *Sur le défaut de terre*, 1979). This middle ground is the *Petits Traités*, and among these, 'Jesus stooping to write' is a representative example.[9] This *traité* consists of three fragments of narrative – the episode from John's gospel in which Jesus writes in the dust, a moment from Cao Xueqin's *The Dream of the Red Chamber* when Ch'un Ling traces a Chinese character on the ground with her hairpin, and a comic fragment from the early Roman author, Cneius Naevius, which lists actions performed by a dancing girl to entrance the men around her, while simultaneously writing to an absent other. The twelve-page *traité* is itself in five fragments, separated by asterisks. The first three contain the narratives with Quignard's commentaries, in which he develops the idea of writing as a withdrawal from human commerce. He draws attention to the witnesses present in each narrative who do not see or do not understand what is written, and whose direct, oral communication with the writer is either bettered or supplanted by the writer's secret

words. In each, the narrative is given through paraphrase and referenced quotation, and clearly demarcated from the accompanying
analysis. Some idiosyncrasies set the text apart from conventional
essay discourse: its fragmentation (countered here by cross-
referencing between the fragments, although this is not always the
case in the *traités*), its liking for obscure similes ('Language becomes
like the statues of gods'), and its curious combination of sweeping
assertion and faltering uncertainty. In a few lines Quignard can
move between a grandiose generalization – 'this abnormal, suspect,
brutal, contentious – to the extent that it should be interpreted as
evil, or interpreted as divine – "fission of the oral" that is every practice of writing' – and equivocations which seem to struggle for
words at the limits of the writer's language: 'it is the body of god
himself which, now rising, now stooping, enigmatically mimes or
dances a kind of division, or admonition, or hesitation between
these two worlds'.[10] When we reach the final two fragments, the
singular nature of Quignard's writing is in evidence. The penultimate fragment draws together the three narratives with a focus on
their shared characteristics of silence and withdrawal, yet it does so
largely through a discourse of description rather than argumentation. Quignard makes his point by redrawing the three scenes in
miniature with emphasis on their stillness. The final fragment,
where we might expect a conclusion, gives us instead narrative, with
a snatch of Cneius Naevius's life story that figures him unexpectedly
as a 'hunter', the relevance of which is not immediately apparent:

> *Cneius Naevius took part in the first Punic War. It is reported that he was*
> *wounded above the knee and on the hip. His arm did not shake. He still had*
> *the virtue of his origins, not that of the warrior, who is only human, but that*
> *of the hunter, who is every animal that pursues and devours.*[11]

Then, in the final lines, comes poetry, with a cryptic reflection on
the dancing girl's double play of writing and seduction of those
around her, drawing obliquely on the theme of hunting from a few
lines earlier: 'Monstrous simultaneity. Incredible and mysterious
intrusion for those whose hunting pack was of wolves, seeing,
amazed, the first letter at the end of a prostitute's finger.'[12]

Our interpretation depends partly on our understanding of the
traité's wider context in Quignard. The *traités* themselves form what
might almost be called a loose argument of associative thought. The

preceding *traité*, 'Tongue', meditates on spoken and written language, while also employing the metaphor of hunting to describe the process of reading; the following *traité*, 'Treaty on the red-breast', is nothing but a brief fable of the robin acquiring its colouring from the blood of the crucified Christ; this in turn leads to the next *traité*, 'The slit throat', which returns to the dichotomy of speech and writing through the idea of writing as a silenced voice. Both images and argument serve to connect the *traités* together, and what was an impenetrable allusion in one may be clarified and expanded upon elsewhere. Quignard has described his *traités* as a narrative of his thoughts in the sequence of their chronological succession in the way a restaurant bill is a 'narrative' of the meal consumed.[13] Thematic cohesion is true, not only of the *traités*, but of Quignard's writing in general, which returns obsessively to a small number of the same themes, regardless of the mode in which he is writing: voices and silence, reading and writing, the hermit and the hunter are principal among them. Two intepretative keys in particular are offered by a contextualized reading. The first is language. Quignard's fascination with philology – he describes himself, tongue-in-cheek, as a 'misologist' – leads him into extensive etymological meditations on certain words, unearthing former meanings and developing connotations, which then enrich his usage of the word elsewhere. 'Sidéré' (amazed), in the last line of 'Jesus stooping to write', is one such term, given a chapter of discussion in the later work, *Vie secrète*. The second key is autobiography. Confessional asides and fragments of personal memory abound in Quignard's writing, and are a common device at the close of his *traités*. Through these a picture of Quignard's life gradually emerges, which often suggests a personal, private dimension to topics presented in the text as neutral or universal, rooting the abstract in the personal, the essay in the life story. In our *traité*, the idea of writing as silent withdrawal from society echoes personal comments elsewhere. On different occasions, Quignard refers to himself as a hermit or a deserter; his own autobiographical sketch ends with an unexplained account of his renunciation of all public roles in the early 1990s.[14] The depiction of hermit-like characters in his fiction, and the choice of reclusive writers for many of his biographical subjects, begin to seem like so many partial self-portraits.[15] To take a more widespread example, the insistent return of the themes of intrauterine life, the primal scene, and the acquisition of a mother

tongue, expressed as universal human concerns, gains a new resonance with an awareness of Quignard's childhood trauma, never
confessed fully, in which he took his nanny, the German-speaking
Cäcilia Müller, to be his mother (absent through illness), only to
lose a language and a parent on her departure from the family.[16]
While these keys may allow us access deeper into the language of
the text and the life of its writer, they often bring as much mystery as
enlightenment. Linguistic definitions are more poetic than precise,
leading to uncertainty and proliferation in the meaning of a term.[17]
The autobiographical basis of certain themes is given only in teasing
hints scattered through his work; interviewers' direct questions are
rebuffed on the grounds that 'he who has no secret has no soul'.[18]

If Quignard's wider oeuvre surrounds the *Petits Traités* thematically as if by a collection of reflective fragments, how does it relate
formally to the *traités'* amalgam of poetic, essayistic and narrative
discourse? If we focus for the moment on narrative, we see a
number of distinct strategies by which the speech genres come
together. *Albucius* (1990) enfolds forty-six stories – supposedly
retellings of the Roman writer's own fictions – within a largely non-
narrative discussion of his life and work in its historical context.
Conversely, *Carus* enfolds argumentation within narrative: the
narrator's journal-like account of his and his friends' lives is the
framework within which the polyphonic 'essays' of their philosophical discussions are set, a technique which allows for debate without
conclusion, since the author's own view is not to be determined
behind the sometimes heated disagreements.[19] Elsewhere, we see
narrativity gradually drain away as argumentation comes to domi-
nate. This is the case with *Vie secrète*, in which the early chapters are
largely given over to accounts of episodes in the young Quignard's
first, brief sexual relationship, with a woman he calls Némie Satler.
The end of the relationship is narrated when we are not even a
quarter of the way through the volume, and from there the medita-
tion on the nature of love and desire, a subtext from the start, takes
precedence; when narrative returns it is in short, unrelated fragments determined by associations of his thought. Juxtaposition of
discourses is Quignard's most common procedure. His *contes*, which
are perhaps his most purely narrative creations, with their minimal
physical or psychological description, their lack of internal
commentary, and their rhythmic, three-part structure, are often
followed by a personal reflection on their themes.[20] The two most

interesting texts in this regard are *Le Nom sur le bout de la langue* and *La leçon de musique*. Each of these short texts is in three parts: one part is a pure narrative, the *conte* of the forgotten name in the former and a Chinese fable about an apprentice musician in the latter. *Le Nom sur le bout de la langue* prefaces its *conte* with a largely narrative autobiographical piece describing the genesis of the book, then follows it with a *petit traité* offering reflections from psycho-analysis, Classical mythology and his own childhood reminiscences on the topic of a forgotten word 'on the tip of your tongue'. *La Leçon de musique* places its fable last, preceded by two semi-narrative pieces: in seventeenth-century France, Marin Marais is dismissed from the choir on the breaking of his voice (a story Quignard will expand upon in *Tous les matins du monde*), and in Classical Greece, the young Aristotle comes to Plato's academy. Both of these use their narratives as the basis for reflections on music and the broken voice, the former figuring musical instruments as a replacement for the lost voice, the latter exploring etymological connections between the Greek terms for tragedy, the broken voice and the 'song' of the goat. Shared themes with the argumentation guide the reader in interpreting the stories, but do not exhaust their meaning: in the essay section of *Le Nom sur le bout de la langue*, Quignard refers to the preceding *conte* as 'mon secret', its deepest signification related to an episode from his adolescence which he will not disclose.

Lastly, *Le Lecteur* and the *Dernier Royaume* sequence, at opposite ends of Quignard's career as a writer, are perhaps the closest he comes to merging narrative and non-narrative discourse, albeit in different ways. *Le Lecteur*, subtitled 'récit', contains snatches of past-tense narrative as the narrator reminisces about himself and the vanished 'lecteur', but its primary 'narrative' is really an essay with emphasis on the chronology of its unfolding argument. The narrator's musings on reading and the loss of selfhood develop through changing moods from chapter to chapter and a shifting relationship with the text's implied reader from hostile suspicion to symbiosis, portraying the narrator-essayist's expressed thoughts and the reader's supposed reactions to them as the events of a temporal sequence. *Dernier Royaume* replaces this blend with a more coarsely chopped combination. In the five volumes published so far, prose poems, narratives fictional and autobiographical, and argumenta-tion from the rational to the oracular jostle together in myriad fragments. The books' chapters, which number close to a hundred per volume, may present a single short paragraph on a blank page, or group together a dozen brief texts in various discourses under a common thematic heading. There are sometimes connections, sometimes ruptures between the chapters themselves; the abstract, ill-defined topic of each volumes is a thread which emerges then vanishes again from fragment to fragment, each further approach to it as likely to diffuse and expand it as it is to render it clearer. This *macédoine* approach to literary composition, without progression or conclusion, preserves the specificity of discourses while bringing out their common themes as our attention flickers between them.

The *Dernier Royaume* sequence is the place where the effect of contrasting addressivities in Quignard's narrative and non-narrative discourses is most keenly felt, but it is to be found to some degree all across his oeuvre. The writer himself exploits the contrast to manipulate the reader's expectations of the text, as he explains in interview: 'Whenever the argumentation seems to lose footing in something soft, I make up a story ... In stories at least, you abandon the idea of knowing exactly what is being expressed in what is said.'[21] The mingling of discourses might therefore seem to offer Quignard a convenient slipperiness in his mode of expression. As Michel Deguy puts it: 'Can we refute a poem?'[22] The sometimes undecidable nature of these shifting discourses allows his essay-like pieces to shrug off the typical responsibilities of the form. Quignard warns his readers on one occasion, 'truth does not enlighten me, and the appetite to say or to think are perhaps never entirely subject to it', and on another: 'do not forget that I say nothing which is certain'.[23] Critics are sometimes unimpressed by such tactics. Bruno Blanckeman, who gave Quignard's writing the label 'undecidable', attacks the novel *Le Salon du Wurtemberg* for falling between two stools of narrative and argument: 'The story loses its way between fiction which does not take and thought which is mistaken. No revelation accompanies this latter. The narrator experiments jointly with the vacuity of consciousness and the vacuity of writing.'[24]

Indeed, Quignard's chosen mode can be the cover for erudition which is occasionally slapdash, or perhaps even dishonest.[25] But there are sound reasons within his subject matter for Quignard's multi-discourse treatment. Essay and narrative combine in Quignard's treatment of thinkers and writers from antiquity or early-modern France, the better to situate the thought within the living thinker. The uncertain boundaries between historical data and invented fiction may disconcert the reader, as when Quignard recounts in explicit detail one of Porcius Latron's supposed sexual encounters, or describes to us what Lu Guimeng's family library smelled like during the Tang dynasty.[26] However, the presence of these unlikely assertions within his biographical texts at least alerts the reader to their hybrid nature, and what such a method may lose in trustworthiness, it perhaps regains in its evocative reimagining of lost people and eras. The same holds true for Quignard's historical novels, which may embroider a life on very little historical fact, as in *Tous les matins du monde*, or place an invented character within a particular historical context to conjure up a voice, the like of which history has failed to preserve, as in *Les Tablettes de buis d'Apronenia Avitia*. Equally, the intrusion of poetic discourse into the essay is appropriate for a text which claims there is an underlying emotional basis to rational argument (*La Raison*), or criticizes traditional philosophy for its neglect of its own basis in language (*Rhétorique spéculative*). Both the poetry and the narratives in *Vie secrète* and the *Dernier Royaume* volumes justify themselves by the ineffable nature of the subjects they tackle, such as the nature of desire, or of our pre-linguistic past: allegorical narratives and suggestive metaphors are brought in to evoke to the reader what Quignard is unable to explain.

Quignard's slippages between different discourses with different addressivities are more than a pragmatic selection of suitable tools for particular jobs, however. There is at work in his writing a broader aesthetic of fragmentation, of which the genre-mixing is a part, but which can also be seen within his usage of single discourses, including narrative. In the opening lines of *Terrasse à Rome* (2000), we are informed that the protagonist, Meaume, has been an apprentice engraver 'with Heemkers in Bruges'.[27] Three pages later, in the second chapter, the narrator refers to 'his master, who was famous (it was Jean Heemkers)'.[28] Another three pages on and another chapter, in the middle of a scene which has already mentioned him twice by name, and for which his apprenticeship has no relevance, the protagonist is referred to as 'Meaume, the apprentice of Jean Heemkers'. This repetition gives a sense of narratorial amnesia between chapters. It seems to be not quite the same voice, or not quite the same mind, which would remind us of such things with no indication that we have been told them before. *L'Occupation américaine* (1994) has the same effect, this time within a single continuous episode, in which we read on one page, 'Marie-José was wearing a yellow and white striped dress buttoned to the neck', and three pages on: 'She had tied her black hair in a little bun on her neck … held in place by a yellow velvet ribbon. Her dress was striped yellow.'[29] Elsewhere, an unlikely echo between unrelated incidents produces a similar effect. In *Les Tablettes de buis d'Apronenia Avitia*, for instance, the 'historical' narrative of the first part recounts a character's death: 'In 397, Aurelius Ambrosius died in Milan. It was said that death interrupted him as he was writing the word *mortem*.' Eleven pages later, we read of another character: 'Aurelius Prudentius Clemens died writing the word *dolorosus*', again without comment on the coincidence.[30] The effect can be seen in discourses other than narrative. In the essay, *Le Sexe et l'effroi*, Quignard introduces a discussion of the Romans' sense of the terms *pietas, castitas* and *obsequium*. The analysis of the first term opens with the line, 'Roman *pietas* has an entirely different meaning from "piety", which derives from it'; the essay's next section begins: 'Roman *castitas* has an entirely different meaning from "chastity", which derives from it.'[31] The repetitions are close enough to ensure a troubling sense of *déjà vu* when the echo appears, but far enough apart that the source may not be immediately traceable. The lack of acknowledgement makes them a strongly disjunctive force in the text, paradoxically for what might seem a connective strategy. They are a reset where we expect a progression, a memory blank where we expect the narrating present to refer back to its narrating past.

Evidence for a wider aesthetic of fragmentation in Quignard's writing is not hard to find. The diary form in *Carus* and *Apronenia Avitia* is one example. We have noted the inherent repetitiveness of the diary in the previous chapter: it is an aspect that novels in diary form, like *La Nausée*, understandably seek to minimize. Not so Quignard, who uses extensive repetition in both novels to hypnotic effect. The routine life of *Carus's* narrator results in recurring phrases: 'I was passing by the rue du Bac' is a common opening to his entries. He notes the variety of flowers in the hallway on visiting A.'s apartment, and notes what they eat at dinner parties, as if for an *aide-mémoire*.[32] There is a similarly non-literary quality to the frag-mented narrative of Apronenia Avitia's boxwood tablets, which

Quignard's 'editorial' introduction describes as 'this sort of diary, calendar, memo-board, daily notes'.[33] Even more than the *journal intime*, which at least implies a measure of retrospection on and 'narrativization' of the day's events, the terms Quignard uses for Avitia's diary denote immediacy and disconnectedness, a lack of storytelling intention. So it proves in the text of the boxwood tablets themselves. Snatches of narrative recounting a notable event of her day alternate with records of profound or witty remarks she has heard, memories, miscellaneous thoughts and descriptions, lists of her likes and dislikes, and reminders of matters trivial and financial. What renders this unorthodox novel particularly rich and rewarding, and sets it apart from similarly fragmented texts like the *Dernier Royaume* volumes, is the chronological element to the tablets which encourages the reader to reconstruct narrative from the fragments we are given. Thus, a recorded 'remark by Q. Alcimius' implies an encounter between him and Avitia that day, a descriptive list shows what she has seen and provides clues to her day's activities, just as the lists of errands give us her activities in the days to come. We are aided in this reconstruction by the fake historical narrative, 'Life of Apronenia Avitia', which precedes the tablets in the volume. When we come to the tablets, we are already aware of the broad lines of Avitia's personal life, her affair and break-up with her lover, Alcimius, her husband's decline and death, as well as the historical events which affect her, famine and the siege and sack of Rome as Alaric's Goths invade. Quignard's faux-scholarly commentary in the first part of the novel on Avitia's responses to these private and public events helps to set up a coherent frame-narrative into which the flashes of everyday life can be set, and through which they can be interpreted. The single-entry tablets, '*Things to do:* Calends interest payments' and '*Bags of gold:* Twenty-four bags of gold' may be identical each time they recur in the text, but, with Quignard's introduction guiding us, we are able to read the increasing frequency of their appearances as the story of straightened financial circumstances in Avitia's widowhood. It is a bold move to fillet his narrative in this way, but, aided by the historical fraud which claims Avitia's tablets to be real archaeological artefacts, Quignard produces the impression of eavesdropping on the real private concerns of someone from another era. That the fragmentary form is central to Quignard's intentions is made clear by his uncharitable remarks about Marguerite Yourcenar's celebrated representation of

a Roman writing the self within a more conventional realist narrative: 'I have no interest in "making the great dead live again", I don't
care about bringing back the Romans, ressuscitating Hadrian to
have him hold forth in an idiotic nineteenth-century manner.'[34]
Unlike Yourcenar's emperor, Quignard's matron relies on disordered discourse to create the impression of the cluttered immediacy
of life as it is being lived.

On the large scale of the narrative's general structure and the
small scale of the syntax of its sentences, we find the strategy of fragmentation across Quignard's oeuvre. Even in the structure of his
most classically realist novels the aesthetic is discernible. In *Le Salon
du Wurtemberg*, the sense behind the achronological ordering of the
narrator's memories eludes even the narrator himself: 'The curious
way I note these memories. The order that links them continues to
escape me, and yet it imposes itself on me as obvious.'[35] The story of
Les Escaliers de Chambord is a series of abandonments, as the protagonist's haunting memory of his first love prevents him from following
through on the potential love stories life offers him, just as, while
climbing the double-helix staircases of the title, 'you were constantly
abandoned by the person you were looking at'.[36] *Villa Amalia* (2006)
switches unexpectedly from impersonal to first-person narration,
and slices its narrative into a succession of brief, disjointed scenes
set apart from each other on the page. All of Quignard's contemporary novels mimic in their narrative form the shapelessness of
modern western existence, as relationships form and dissolve, and
the protagonists drift onwards with uncertain goals, their rootless
lives disconnected once again with each move to a new dwelling-
place.

Chapter divisions, the inevitable element of fragmentation in the
most traditional of novels, draw attention to themselves in
Quignard. They may be an arbitrary slicing of the text, as when, in
Le Salon du Wurtemberg, the fourth chapter opens with a single paragraph continuation of the scene which closed the previous chapter,
before jumping forward several years with its second paragraph.[37] In
Carus, the chapter divisions are entirely divorced from the narrative,
following instead the dates of the diary to mark changes of season,
regardless of what is happening in the story. *Terrasse à Rome* changes
to a different mode of narrative (and occasionally to a non-narrative
speech genre) with each chapter break, a procedure underlined by
the amnesia as each new discourse takes over the text.[38] The

changes are not simply a matter of style: the whole epistemological basis of the narrative may shift. In one chapter our perspective may be focalized through Meaume's own thoughts and perceptions, as in chapter thirty-four:

> *The engraver smells a sharp odour.*
> *He raises his eyes to the face of the young man who is slitting his throat. He looks at him. He is overwhelmed by his features. He contemplates him. He does not cry out. Curiously, he thinks of an engraving on wood by Jan Heemkers, who was his master in Bruges.*[39]

In another, the narrative may have no more authority than the cautious hypotheses of a historical researcher:

> *It happened that in 1667 Meaume died in Utrecht at the house of Gerard van Honthorst and an engraving, signed on the left and dated December 1666, would provide the proof if it were needed. The engraver must have left Rome at the end of 1664. Or in autumn 1666. This point is uncertain.*[40]

The large number of chapters – forty-seven in a novel of only 128 pages, each different in form – puts the disjunctive nature of the story to the fore. The positioning of the breaks is likewise used for emphasis. The scene between the injured Meaume and his son, following the son's attack on his father, is split between two chapters. The first gives us Meaume's perspective on the scene; in the continuation, we see him only from the exterior, and make of his tears and silences what we can.[41] Whatever the mode of Quignard's writing, he employs its conventions to undermine cohesion. Historical narratives like *Albucius* use their paucity of material as a reason to switch between the historian's and the novelist's perspective, sometimes drawing our attention to the shift from fact to invention ('J'invente', the narrator will declare abruptly on occasion, just as Marguerite Duras's narrator does in *Le Ravissement de Lol V. Stein*), sometimes leaving us uncertainly in-between. *Albucius*, too, turns its historical sources into competing narrative strands, offering us repeated narrations of the same events according to the differing versions of ancient historians: the novel's final chapter, for instance, offers us three competing accounts of Albucius's final hours.

Albucius also offers us examples of Quignard's aesthetic of narrative fragmentation on a smaller scale, between or within the sentences themselves. Consider the following extract from Quignard's account of Albucius's childhood, for instance:

> *In 58 BCE the amphitheatre welcomed five crocodiles and a hippopotamus. It was there that Albucius saw them for the first time. He was eleven, and that is probably why he never stopped talking about them. And three years later he saw his first rhinoceros: brought back by Caesar himself. In January 58 BCE, Caesar has the books prepared that he plans to take with him to Gaul. Cicero in mourning clothes is chased through the streets of Rome by gangs of thugs paid by Clodius. They yell and punch. They intend to avenge the men who served Catilina, whom Cicero had put to death. Cicero is wounded by stones and covered by bucketfuls of human excrement poured over him. The people join Clodius's gangs and shout that he has infringed the right to liberty. Cicero leaves Rome. The Helvetii leave Switzerland en masse with a plan to set up along the Bay of Biscay. Cicero washes in a great grey stone basin. He hopes he will leave behind a putrid smell, Caesar destroys the bridge across the Rhône.*[42]

From a brief reference to Albucius himself, about whom, for this period of his life especially, information is understandably scarce, the narrator makes an associative shift via the linking figure of Julius Caesar to the historical background. Here, two narratives of early 58 BCE are recounted: Cicero's flight from Rome under threat of exile from Publius Clodius Pulcher, and Caesar's defeat of the Helvetii during his conquest of Gaul. These narratives are simply juxtaposed with Albucius's; we are given no guidance as to their bearing, if any, on the life of the protagonist. For contextualizing narratives, the accounts of Caesar and Cicero are themselves remarkably lacking in context. Quignard tells us Caesar is taking books to Gaul, without having mentioned that this is the year of the conquest; he shows us Cicero pursued by Clodius's thugs, without explaining who Clodius is, or what the Catiline conspiracy was about. It is not simply that Quignard assumes knowledge of Roman history in his reader: sporadic details sketch in the essentials for informed and uninformed readers, while offering to both a presentation *in medias res* which disorientates through its impression of a missing preamble. There is further disorientation in manner Quignard alternates the two narratives. Connections within a single narrative may not be apparent – it may not be obvious, for instance, how Caesar's books, Swiss migration and the destruction of the bridge over the Rhône form a coherent story – and are further obscured by false connections between them, as when the verb 'quitter' is used in consecutive sentences on Cicero and the Helvetii, or the rhinoceros and mourning clothes echo more distant parts of the text. What is most jarring, however, is the juxtaposition of great and small events, intimate (and perhaps fictional) details with the movements of history. As Caesar destroys the bridge over the Rhône to halt the advance of the Helvetii, Cicero washes in a grey stone basin, an action which itself introduces some chronological malaise into the account, since what might seem a literal response to his being pelted with excrement is separated from this event by his flight from Rome: we must read either it as analepsis or as metaphor. As well as the familiar Quignardian clash of different narrative perspectives (we know of Cicero's feelings as he washes, but we know no more of Caesar than we might expect from an encyclopaedia entry), there is a mismatch of scale, forced upon us by the unorthodox punctuation which runs the two events together. This is not the fictionalization of history, as historical novelists (Yourcenar among them) have allowed us to become accustomed; rather, it refutes the historical novel's harmonization of the narrative discourses of history and fiction, and presents instead their prickly incompatibility.

The rhinoceros which impressed the young Albucius becomes an important influence on Albucius's – and thereby on Quignard's – poetics, through its inclusion among the 'sordidissima', that Albucius makes his principal literary topic. Quignard describes *sordidissima* as 'the most vile words, the most lowly things and the most uneven themes', and will go on to devote the fifth volume of *Dernier royaume* to the subject.[43] Yet its importance to his writing is less a thematic one than a formal one, as is clear from the moment the topic is introduced:

> *The father of Seneca the philosopher asked him one day for examples of 'sordidissima'. Albucius replied: 'Et rhinocerotem et latrinas et spongias' (Rhinoceroses, latrines and sponges.) Later he added to the sordidissima pets, adultery, food, the death of loved ones, gardens.*[44]

The original list of three seems almost comically heterogenous; the extended list becomes more so with its alternation of concrete and abstract nouns and its baffling selection criteria. The motley nature of the list is part of its raison d'être: these are lowly things in part because they are jumbled together in a junk-shop discourse. As with the other key Latin literary term in *Albucius*, the *satura* or potpourri, 'in which most existing literary genres were sliced up and intermingled', the notion of *sordidissima* offers Quignard a Classical antecedent to the rejection of systems, in thought and narrative, that characterizes his own writing.[45] When questioned about his desire to 'demolish the serious' in his writing, his response reveals an aesthetic pleasure in the forms of the *satura* or *sordidissima* for their own sake:

> *'Démantibuler' [demolish] means 'démandibuler'. Dé-mandibuler comes down to stopping the chewing process from working. That leaves the flesh raw, and the pieces whole ... I adore disconcerting parataxes, orderings that don't work, torn-up worlds, Chinese lists, dustbins, attics. I have huge respect for forbidden book deposits, Scheols, second-hand goods shops and other storehouses.*[46]

Quignard's love of miscellanies has as much to do with disorder of presentation as variety of content. The 'Chinese lists' he refers to remind us of Jorge Luis Borges's Chinese Encyclopedia, taken up notably by Michel Foucault as inspiration for *Les Mots et les choses*, which divides animals into a number of absurd categories, including 'belonging to the emperor', 'drawn with a very fine camelhair brush' and 'having just broken the water pitcher'.[47] For Foucault, the fictional taxonomy demonstrates the exotic charm of another system of thought, and thereby the limitations of our own. Quignard's small-scale fragmentations also arise out of a concern for the ordering of information, or the artful disordering of it, which is brought about not only by the arrangement of individual elements, but also by the syntax of the text presenting the information:

> *Just as human love has its figurations, human language has its imagines, its* prosôpa, *its forays which make a breach, which which tear language itself apart. Loggin recommends asyndeton, anaphora, all the broken connections the rhetor has at his disposal. The naked disorder of language disorders the searching thought, while conjunctions fetter momentum or drain away the jet of air.*[48]

Rhétorique spéculative, from which this extract comes, does indeed follow Loggin's stylistic recommendations, as, more or less, do all of

Quignard's essays before and since. Asyndeton and anaphora – the suppression of conjunctions, articles or pronouns and repeated phrases of the type we saw earlier with *pietas* and *castitas* – are commonplaces of his argument. Neither the heterogeneous lists of *Albucius*, nor the fragmented sentence structures advocated here, are specifically *narrative* modes of fragmentation, however, but it is not difficult to find related rhetorical devices within narrative discourse. Temporal liaisons are disrupted by shifts in tense, as in *Ethelrude et Wolframm* (2006), which switches abruptly between past and present tenses mid-scene, sometimes in the recounting of a single action: 'Elle brode [present tense] un nom, sur un mouchoir. Elle le faisait [imperfect] avec application.'[49] *Villa Amalia* flips tenses frequently and seemingly arbitrarily, occasionally several times in quick succession:

> *She puts her hands on her wrists.*
> *Then she put her head on her hands.*
> *She dreams.*
> *She dreamed.*[50]

The suppression of connective vocabulary, and with it causal implications or interpretative glosses, pervades Quignard's writing even in the less explicitly disrupted narratives. The following lines from *Tous les matins du monde*, for instance, may not be fragmented in the sense that the sliced-up stories of Caesar and Cicero were in *Albucius*, but the absence of liaison increases the onus on the reader to infer narrative flow from the terse, self-contained sentences Quignard lays out:

> *When he arrived for his second lesson, it was slender, pink-cheeked Madeleine who opened the entrance gate.*
> *'Because I am going to bathe,' she said, 'I shall put up my hair.'*
> *The back of her neck was pink, with little black hairs ruffled in the paleness. As she lifted her arms, her breasts squeezed and swelled. They headed for Monsieur de Sainte Colombe's cabin. It was a beautiful spring day. There were primroses and there were butterflies. Marin Marais carried his viol on his shoulder.*[51]

What conception of literature is it that leads Quignard to this aesthetic of fragmentation? Quignard's own views on the fragment are expressed in several of his more essay-like works, forming a personal poetics which is itself fragmentary across his oeuvre. Metaphor is Quignard's preferred means to discuss his writing: he compares his style to reconstructed ruins or the spasms of ejaculation in an erotic dream.[52] A passage in the *Petits Traités* accumulates images of transience, suggesting both clarity and dream-like qualities, without exploring the implications of any of the comparisons made:

> *May my readers forgive these fragments, these spasms that I weld together. The breaking wave borrows from the sun a hasty part of its brightness. This abruptness is like a thief's dream. Death too snatches quickly away and gives nothing back.*[53]

Quignard does, however, investigate fragmentation more analytically. His essay, *Une gêne technique à l'égard des fragments* (1986), while ostensibly a study of Jean de La Bruyère, soon reveals its subject to be another avatar of Quignard himself – La Bruyère's taciturnity and solitariness are central to the character study – and the discussion of fragmentation in La Bruyère's *Les Caractères* to be an oblique study of Quignard's own writing style. Quignard claims to have written the essay in an attempt to understand his own mixed feelings towards fragmentary writing. Investigating the hostile reception of La Bruyère's fragments from notable contemporaries like Boileau, Racine and Corneille, he highlights a double difficulty in the form:

> *Its existence saturates one's attention, its multiplication waters down the effect prepared by its brevity. The inability to create an object to be read continuously ought perhaps to be presented in the form of a problem. One should also highlight the lack of satisfaction, both in respect to thought and in respect to beauty, where these scraps and tatters give out.*[54]

Yet despite the dissatisfaction of such shredded discourse, Quignard sees a lucidity in it that faithfully reflects the discontinuity of thought, and the fundamental disjunctions – in birth, sex and death – of human experience. (There are some parallels here with Ernaux's thoughts on the fragments of *Journal du dehors*, discussed in the previous chapter.) Continuous discourse, of which *Une gêne technique* is itself an example, is criticized for a falsely imposed coherence:

*In fact the fragment reveals more circularity, autonomy and unity than
continuous discourse, which vainly covers over its breaks with cunning tricks
that are more or less obvious, sinuous transitions, clumsy cementing, and in
the end exposes constantly to the reader's view its seams, its hems, its* gather-
ings-in.[55]

Beyond this essay, Quignard is often critical of a desire for coherence at any cost: in *Albucius* he is scathing of narrative history:
'historians are afraid and pretend to believe that what happens in
the world of men is coherent'; in the *Petits Traités* he claims the 'the
most beautiful books ... point out holes, fragilities, things forsaken
and fears – something which has been avoided rather than
assuaged'.[56] Despite the reference to beauty, it is not exactly an
aesthetic of fragmentation we are dealing with here, as Quignard's
motives are clearly as much epistemological as artistic. The fact that
fragments express, as Quignard puts it, 'thought provoked, not
thought completed', is particularly important to the successful
incorporation of reflection within fiction.[57] As Jean-Yves Tadié
notes, successful combinations of *roman* and *pensée* in twentieth-
century literature are invariably those which focus more on
questions than answers: 'what weakens certain authors of the *romans
à thèse* is that, giving up on interrogative thought, they have already
made their findings'.[58]

Quignard's discussions of the fragmentary form in *Une gêne technique* hinge on the nature of thought and argument, and take little
account of narrative. Nevertheless, we see the benefits of fragmentation to narrative fiction in the two major virtues Quignard claims for
the fragment: 'the fragment allows one to constantly renew 1) the
narrator's posture, 2) the overwhelming burst of the attack'.[59]
The idea of a renewed narratorial stance is clearly applicable to the
showy polyphony of narration in *Terrasse à Rome*, as well as to
the drastic shifts from cautious historian to spinner of folk-tales in
texts like *La Leçon de musique*. Yet we might also find it in the less
dramatic ruptures of Quignard's other fictions: the new eyes and
new mind of Quignard's amnesiac narrators encourage us to look
afresh at characters and situations, and deter us from taking for
granted a consistent ideological perspective on the diegesis. The
sense of a renewed attack with each break in the text emphasizes
the epistemological aspect, and is particularly effective in the mixed
discourses of an essay-poem-fiction like *Vie secrète*, which argues for a

particular understanding of desire, then follows the argument with a thematically related piece of narrative as if in demonstration.

Fragmentation in narrative and argument may be the distinguishing trait of Quignard's writing, but, it is important to note, it is not a system. The level of fragmentation within and between discourses varies greatly, from the smooth chronologies of the contemporary novels at one end of the scale to the disorienting medley of *Les Ombres errantes* at the other. Within a single text, too, there are competing forces of cohesion and disjunction. We have seen, for instance, the discontinuity of *Tous les matins du monde* on a syntactic level; on the level of the plot as a whole, the novel's cohesion is such that Sylviane Coyault can describe it as 'admirably closed, rigorously centripetal'.[60] Similarly, *Carus*'s rambling discussions resolve into a study of friendship, as the bickering debaters make themselves the topic of discussion; *Vie secrète* gives us eight different, unsynthesized definitions of love from among its stories and arguments, yet creates complexity rather than contradiction out of this profusion; *Apronenia Avitia*'s snapshots of Roman life may lack a perceptible beginning or narrative development, yet they do offer us a form of closure in the final, elegiac fragments, looking back over Avitia's life to learn from experience, and then ending on a melancholy, nostalgic image of youth surrounded by darkness. If Quignard rejects the idea that his oeuvre as a whole can be characterized as 'coherent', he is at least content to label it 'obsessional' for the recurring themes which tie it all together.[61] Fragmentation is by no means an absolute virtue for Quignard; in the case of narrative in particular, he is clear on the necessity of linkage. He describes the human race as 'a species enslaved by narrative', and suggests that the need to connect up our experience of life through stories is instinctive and primordial:

> '*A plot!*' *This is the cry from the moment the cry becomes language. And this is one reason I don't believe in novels without plots. Each of our lives is a continent that only a narrative can land on. And not only a narrative is necessary to accost and combine with one's own experience, but also a hero to assure the narration, a self to say 'I'.*[62]

Echoing Paul Ricoeur, Quignard sees narrative as a representation of 'human' time, the abstraction of chronology rendered into meaningful experience: 'Temporality cannot become human unless it is articulated in a narrative mode. By which I mean that action, the real, a plot, a hunting scene – it's already a verbal narrative.'[63] This respect for narrative cohesion as a means of understanding life tempers Quignard's interest in fragments, and refutes anyone who would make disjunction the essence of his writing. Bruno Blanckeman, for instance, overstates his case when he sees in Quignard 'the refusal of plot when the text is narrative, the refusal of progression when it is argumentative'.[64]

There are other reasons too why Quignard's aesthetic of fragmentation should not be regarded as systematic. For Chantal Lapeyre-Desmaison, in a critique of his work, the very notion of the literary fragment is 'fundamentally asystematic', in both structure and reception.[65] Despite his extensive theoretical writing on literature, Quignard himself makes no particular claim to a new or reconsidered use of fragmentation: in *Une gêne technique*, as we have seen, he shows ambivalence towards the form, and likens his own use to that of a seventeenth-century writer. Elsewhere he seems to suggest that he is doing little more than following the literary *zeitgeist*, claiming that fragmentary writing is now the norm (perhaps due to a Lyotardian suspicion of total systems), and even defining the modern as 'that which no longer tolerates linkage'.[66]

Quignard's lack of an underlying programme to his choice of literary form is a point of difference between his work and that of the *nouveaux romanciers* a generation earlier. As we saw in the Introduction, Michel Butor roams agenerically between novel, essay and poem in territory similar to Quignard's. Quignard's critique of aesthetic coherence is not unlike Robbe-Grillet's: both claim that the desire to unify fragments can be interpreted as a panicked opposition to mortality, asserting order and continuity in the face of chaos and oblivion.[67] Yet, despite such connections, there are none of the revolutionary claims of the *nouveaux romanciers* to be found in Quignard, only a reacquaintance with older forms of writing and thinking. Interviewers are told he does not understand his own creativity: 'I have told you you will get nothing out of me, not about my private life, nor about my creativity, because I can't tell you. I am not a third of what goes on at that moment.'[68] There is no polemic behind his style of writing, no incitement for others to follow his example, not even a consistent body of theory laying out his intentions. His view of the *nouveau roman* is a dim one, as is his view more generally of writing that sets up its own theoretical system in reaction to a previous system:

> *Sartre actually writes – aside from a few feeble American stereotypes – the same novel that Mauriac writes, just as the* nouveau roman *in reality positions itself in the same formal lineage. It's the reign of sameness under cover of a theoretical break, but not a rhetorical one. With the additional tightening of morphological possibilities introduced by the nouveau roman, it has today resulted in total academicism. We know by heart its almost religious prescriptions that starve the novel: the novel within the novel, the disintegration of the action, the sense of dwindling, the silence, the blankness, the waffling dialogue in which poverty of expression suggests depth, a few puns, the loss of characters' identity, the disdain for plot ... I don't know why, but when I get near the rue Bernard-Palissy, a mild and old-fashioned boredom overcomes me.*[69]

Against such academicism, Quignard calls for a 'deprogramming of literature' (a dream he will later admit to finding naive), through which writers might free themselves from sterile debates, constricting theories and intergenerational dialectic.[70] 'Now think only of the energy, of the unmotivated detail, of the play' is the call he makes, rejecting systems as he rejects reason, and neglecting the structure of the ensemble for the pleasure of the detail.[71]

Quignard's narratives are musical narratives. He discusses fiction in terms of rhythm and *tempi*, he refers to music as 'empty narrative', he composes a *ritournelle* to accompany each text he writes and, according to Gilles Dupuis, he can be read musically, in terms of harmony, counterpoint and enharmonic modulation.[72] Quignard's narratives are also narratives of the chase. Narration arouses in us the predator's desire and the prey's fear, he tells us, its path is that of the fleeing prey; narrative's origins are lost in prehistory, in pre-human natural history, in the predator's instinct to chase and kill; happy endings derive from the hunter returning with fresh meat and the story of his successful kill.[73] Yet neither of these models is the system behind Quignard's texts, and neither is given to us in his theoretical writings as a literary strategy. Equally, as we have seen, they are narratives about language – Dominique Viart notes perceptively that the etymologies which endlessly fascinate Quignard's narrators are themselves 'the story buried in the word' – and Quignard's texts are narratives about the self.[74] Perhaps echoing Montaigne, Quignard deprecates *Vie secrète* as personal reflections 'without the slightest collective use', and indeed, the exploration of desire it offers makes little effort to discover perspectives beyond those of the cultivated male heterosexual.[75] But again, none of these overlapping preoccupations is the key to Quignard's work. Just as his texts' jumble of discourses shun hierarchy, so his work refuses to be tied to an overarching stratagem. The avoidance of systems is Quignard's only manifesto.

Quignard's fragmented, multi-discourse texts question the limits of narrative, situating themselves, as he puts it of his latest writing, 'on the fringes of fiction ... on the fringes of noesis. Extraordinarily ageneric.'[76] But there is also one particular narrative put in question by Quignard's practice, and that is the story of the *retour au récit*, with which I would like to conclude this discussion. The concept implies a narrative of twentieth-century literary history, in which French literary fiction tells stories, then, in the post-war years, ceases to do so as the 'adventure of writing' takes over from 'writing adventures', and finally does so again as a new generation emerges from the shadow of *Tel Quel*, Oulipo and the *nouveau roman*. Like any narrative, this one risks setting up a post hoc illusion: the disappearance and re-emergence of storytelling might be viewed as a linear series of cause and effect, a dialectic of reacting generations of French writers with no outside explanations required. We have seen Quignard's disdain for the ruptures and revolutions of twentieth-century French literature. We see in his writing a threefold contradiction of this linear story of French fiction: in time, in geography and in genre, Quignard's work demands a more wide-ranging narrative. Certainly, Quignard may criticize the 'academic' *nouveau roman* and praise those among its contemporaries who inspired him, such as Louis-René Des Forêts, yet the dialogue his work establishes stretches beyond his immediate predecessors.[77] *Vie secrète* lists the models for its own genre-blending form:

> *I'm trying to write a book in which I dream as I read.*
> *I admire utterly what Montaigne, Rousseau, Stendhal, Bataille tried to do.*
> *They mixed thought, life, fiction, knowledge, as if they were a single body.*[78]

And beyond these, Quignard's influences stretch back to the Classical Rome of Albucius and the pre-Chinese Warring States of

Zhuangzi, even to a fascination with the 'narratives' of Palaeolithic cave paintings. As these latter examples attest, the story of Quignard's antecedents is as geographically broad as it is long in duration: the influences of Greek, Roman, Japanese and Chinese writing on his work is strong, and his contemporary engagement beyond French borders is notable, from globetrotting characters like Édouard Furfooz of *Les Escaliers de Chambord*, through tales with foreign settings, like *La Frontière* and *Terrasse à Rome*, to the Cold War geopolitical critique of *L'Occupation américaine*. As European culture becomes more cosmopolitan within itself, Asian and American cultures penetrate deeper into European awareness, post-colonial writers become a stronger literary presence in their former colonizer's culture, and education focuses less on the national story to encompass a wider picture, the idea of French literary history as a self-contained narrative becomes untenable. As much as any current author in French, Quignard is a global author, and his work is a part of world literature. The mixed genres of his work also trouble a narrative that would set him in the lineage of literary fiction alone. Quignard was a poet and essayist before he was a novelist, and throughout his career the essayist has remained at least in parity with the storyteller in his output. An alternative story might easily be constructed of the twentieth-century French essayist, with Quignard alongside Barthes, Kristeva and other theorists who come, in the later part of the twentieth century, to increasingly temper their reflection with narrative.

The best illustration of the way Quignard's writing puts the idea of a *retour au récit* in doubt comes from the relationship between the *Dernier Royaume* sequence and the essay-fables attributed to the fourth-century BCE Chinese sage, Zhuangzi. Taoist writing has long been an influence on Quignard, with references to Laozi and other writers as far back as the *Petits Traités*, and a translation of Gongsun Long among his publications. The influence of Zhuangzi on the *Dernier royaume* volumes is acknowledged by the author, who tells Lapeyre-Desmaison: 'They are no longer *traités* exactly. I'm getting gradually closer to Zhuangzi, whom I've quoted so often in conversation with you. My hope is that it will no longer be possible to untangle fiction and thought.'[79] The connection between the two texts is remarkably close, so much so that critics baffled by the 2002 Goncourt winner, *Les Ombres errantes*, would have done well to turn to Zhuangzi for elucidation. The writings attributed to Zhuangzi are a gnomic mixture of fable, reflection and personal anecdote; the avoidance of social issues and advocacy of a withdrawal from the struggles of life ('wuwei') espoused by Zhuangzi fits well with Quignard's solitary stance. Zhuangzi's rhetorical strategies have clear resonance with *Dernier royaume* and Quignard's wider oeuvre. Like Quignard, Zhuangzi has a liking for poetic non sequiturs and paradoxes, which, like Zen kōans, attempt to side-step logic in provoking the reader into philosophical reflection. Like Quignard, Zhuangzi juxtaposes fragments of narrative – anecdotes of self and others, fables and conversations – with fragments of argumentation, the pieces linked by a common theme but not embedded within a coherent argument, leaving the reader to draw connections and divine meaning. And like Quignard, Zhuangzi is fascinated by language, but holds it as ultimately inadequate to express the mystical truths he aims towards. For both writers, the gaps between fragments and the shifting between discourses are a form of aporia, designating to the reader an epistemological space beyond their words, into which their writing cannot directly penetrate. What these parallels in form and substance show is that it is not enough to figure Quignard's work as a response to mid-twentieth century French experimentalism; it is also a response to writing that is millennia old, from a culture on the other side of the planet, and in a form that refuses all western categories of genre.

Of the five writers on which I have chosen to focus in this study, Quignard is without doubt the one with the most problematic relation to any *retour au récit*, even if the term itself is occasionally applied by critics to his oeuvre.[80] The narrative line of his stories is deliberately disrupted, writing style and point of view may change without warning, narrators appear to lose all recollection of what they have previously narrated, while descriptions and narratorial comments interrupt the flow at unexpected points. Even within the narration of a scene, Quignard's typical syntax, with its lack of connectives and its cavalier use of tense, forces the reader to infer chronologies and causalities that the text does not deign to make clear. What is more, narrative is only one of a number of complex speech-acts employed in Quignard's writing. The sometimes incompatible addressivities of his mingled discourses can leave readers bewildered. Confronted with a text which functions neither as a story, nor as an essay, which is neither history nor fiction, philosophy nor poetry, the reader is unsure of the required attitude of reception: do we suspend our disbelief as for fiction, analyse critically as with an essay, accept on trust as with a work of historical research, or immerse ourselves in the language itself as with a poem? Quignard evidently wishes his readers to do all of these things, to adapt our reading to the occasion, and to discover unfamiliar ways of reading in the clashes and combinations. Yet this is not a methodical deconstruction of storytelling conventions as we find among the experimenters of the previous generation. Quignard's body of work is as multifarious and unsystematic as any of the individual texts within it. The traditional simplicity of the *conte* and the reassuringly well-made life stories of *Chambord* and *Wurtemberg* coexist with the multifaceted narrative of *Terrasse à Rome* and the genre-transcending essay-fictions of *Vie secrète* or *Dernier Royaume*. The aesthetic of fragmentation which we have seen in his syntax, in his narrative, and in his combination of narrative with other discourses, is also present at the level of his oeuvre as a whole, the component parts of which refuse to be rationalized into a unified response to the question of literary form.

Chapter Three
Marie Darrieussecq and the Voice of the Mind

Marie Darrieussecq (b.1969) is the youngest of the five writers, and has at the time of writing barely a decade to her career as a published author. In this short time, however, she has established herself as a significant voice in European literature. Following the *succès de scandale* of her first novel, *Truismes* (1996), which divided critics yet went on to become the kind of publishing sensation not seen in France since Françoise Sagan's *Bonjour Tristesse* (1954), Darrieussecq has produced six further novels, along with several shorter pieces and non-fiction works.[1] The later novels, which will be our main concern here, are very different from the first one, but they have much in common in terms of their themes and style. *Naissance des fantômes* (1998) is the story of a woman whose sense of reality dissolves with the unexplained disappearance of her husband, whom she begins to perceive as a ghost; *Le Mal de mer* (1999) recounts a Parisian mother's flight to the Basque coast with her daughter, and her husband's attempt to trace her. In *Bref séjour chez les vivants* (2001), a family is haunted by the repressed memory of a drowned child; in *White*, ghosts narrate the romance between a heating engineer and a communications operator on an Antarctic base. *Le Pays* (2005) is the story of a writer returning to her roots in a fictionalized Basque country, and Darrieussecq's most recent novel, *Tom est mort* (2007), takes the form of a mother's account of the period following the death of her child.[2] One recurring theme in these texts is that of loss and mourning, given symbolic presence through the ghosts which appear throughout her oeuvre. Geography is another, as characters' sense of their own identity is affected by the homelands they flee or rediscover. The most important theme for our purposes here, however, being the theme with the greatest impact on narrative form, is the workings of the mind: Darrieussecq's novels not only discuss consciousness, drawing on well-researched discourses of psychology and neuroscience to do so, they also attempt to evoke it directly, and many of their most distinctive uses of narrative voice arise as a result of this. It will be the central contention of this chapter that Darrieussecq's unique blend of experimental and traditional techniques of narrative voice is determined by the model of mind her texts seek to represent, setting up a particular challenge to the stream-of-consciousness form and its pretensions to accurately mimic mental function.

The term *narrative voice* betrays structuralism's fascination with linguistics. Its adoption by Genette (as *la voix du récit*) stems from his intention to analyse narrative through the categories of verb declension – tense, mood and voice – with *voice* referring to the active or passive status of the verb.[3] From the start, however, this grammatical sense of the word is sidelined, and the term is naturally assimilated to the speaking voice of a storyteller in order to explore the manner in which the narrator recounts the story to the reader. Genette discusses this under three headings: the time of narration (as we have already seen), the narrative level, concerning stories within stories, and the person, concerning the narrator's position inside or outside the diegesis and his/her involvement in the story. There is something rather arbitrary about Genette's decision to place direct, indirect and narrativized speech elsewhere in his typology, under the 'distance' section of 'narrative mood', since the relationship between the narrator's discourse and that of the characters would seem a better candidate for a discussion of voice even than Genette's chosen issues of when and from where the story is told. Genette himself questions in retrospect the validity of his 'distance' category in *Nouveau Discours du récit*.[4] While my own discussion of narrative voice will not respect Genette's exclusion of these issues, it does preserve the invaluable distinction between voice and perspective that his category of narrative mood provides elsewhere. In Darrieussecq it is particularly important to distinguish the question of 'Who is seeing?' from that of 'Who is speaking?', since her texts set up subtle and unusual relationships between the voice telling us the story and the eyes we are looking through.[5]

Darrieussecq's fictions vary their narrative instance. Her seven novels comprise four retrospective accounts and three present-tense narratives; the short stories have a preponderance of retrospective accounts recounted by their protagonist, but also include third-person and present-tense narratives.[6] There is an interesting progression in complexity in the ownership of the narrating voice as Darrieussecq's career goes on. Her first two novels, *Truismes* and *Naissance des fantômes*, are straightforwardly narrated by characters who declare themselves the writer of the text. The third novel, *Le Mal de mer*, has an impersonal narrating voice from outside the story which focalizes each of the characters in turn. However, from the fourth novel onwards, Darrieussecq's narrating voice can no longer be categorized as either inside or outside the world of the story: first and third persons, narrating from within and without, are alternated or merged in different ways. *Bref séjour chez les vivants* is largely written in fragmented stream-of-consciousness style, as if recording the thoughts that pass through its protagonists' minds. Pronoun usage, however, slips between first and third person as the presence of an external narrator makes itself known amid the mental discourse of the characters themselves. *White* also slips from the narrating voices of the protagonists to external narration, this latter from the troubling perspective of Antarctic ghosts, who are neither outside the world of the story nor truly within it, and who themselves shift from 'we' to 'they' as they lose their hold on the protagonists and the story in the final pages. Lastly, *Le Pays* uses typefaces to clearly demarcate its first and third person narratives, both of which are focalized through the same character, a situation made more complex by the suggestion that both of these voices may belong to its writer-protagonist as author of the text. *Tom est mort* to some extent renounces these complexities, with its autodiegetic narrator writing the past to find peace in the present, but the figure of her husband as reader-in-the-text, critiquing the narrative and influencing its development, demonstrates a continuing interest in issues of voice and perspective.

To explore in more detail the relationship between internal and external narration in Darrieussecq, let us take some examples from *Bref séjour chez les vivants*. In the opening paragraph of the novel, the mother of the family is alone in her garden:

> *She cuts off a nice rose, only two petals have arched out from the bud, it is not yet a bloom, two petals half-open. She is grateful to someone or something she does not know, she gives thanks, for the reprieve of the morning, the flow of her breathing, the enormous, liquid thing that is happiness.*[7]

In the opening section of the novel we find impersonal, heterodiegetic narration of a familiar kind.[8] We are granted access to the character's consciousness via the medium of the 'omniscient' narrator, who offers a description of the character's state of mind in the narrator's own discourse. A certain ambiguity enters at the end of the extract: we are uncertain whether the metaphor for happiness is the narrator's, or, via indirect free style, the character's own. The choice of metaphor, vague, fluid and elemental, is reminiscent of Nathalie Sarraute's tropisms, perhaps testifying to the important influence of the *nouveau roman* author on Darrieussecq's work, which the younger writer acknowleges.[9] Sarraute's project of exploring the 'indefinable movements which slip by very quickly at the borders of our consciousness' has much in common with Darrieussecq's own interest in the mind, and her literary method, contrasting spoken language with unspoken thought, and using dynamic metaphor to evoke the mental processes beneath, also finds many echoes in Darrieussecq's practice.[10]

Later in Darrieussecq's novel, we find that the narrator's discourse has indisputably given way to that of the character. In the second extract, daughter Jeanne considers a possible pregnancy. While pronoun usage remains in the third person (with much ambiguous use of the indefinite pronoun, '*on*'), the colloquial expressions and fragmentary syntax make it clear that this is the character's inner monologue rendered through the guise of the narrator's voice:

> *She'll buy a test tomorrow, no, you need to wait until some time has passed. You ought to feel it straight away. She doesn't feel anything though you have to face up to things: she doesn't feel anything. Sitting on the terrace of the Biela waiting for Jimena. This used to be what, a bike shop. The finest bicycles in Buenos Aires.[11]*

Lastly, in a third extract we see the logical progression from this. As Jeanne, elsewhere in the novel, reminisces about her childhood, the narrator's voice is interrupted by the character's monologue, assumed in the first person:

> *I remember that fairground attraction in Blackpool. She, mum, feeling claustrophobic, staying outside. The three of us, Pierre John and me, why am I thinking about this, where was Anne? sitting on a bench, the Johnson kebab, with three other visitors we were waiting; in the middle of a, what would you*

call it, normal room, a sideboard, a table, pictures, a tea-pot on the sideboard. I remember.[12]

These three ways of presenting thoughts in fiction – through the narrator's voice, the character's voice, or a merging of the two – have been isolated by Dorrit Cohn in her typology of narrative consciousness. Cohn labels the first of them *psychonarration*, which she defines as the narrator's discourse about a character's consciousness; the second is *narrated monologue*, a character's mental discourse in the guise of the narrator's discourse (i.e. in indirect free style); and the third is *quoted monologue*, a character's mental discourse rendered directly, which includes but is not limited to the stream-of-consciousness technique.[13] The three methods, their particular qualities and their interrelations, are the medium through which Darrieussecq's novels express their particular conception of the mind and, as will become clear, they constitute in themselves an essential illustration of this conception.

How might we characterize Darrieussecq's view of the mind? Let us first look at what the writer herself has to say on the matter. Darrieussecq has frequently spoken in interviews about the topic:

> *If you pay attention, not to what you are thinking, but to the form your thought takes, you notice – these are obvious things but we are always forgetting them – that you rarely make complete subject–verb–complement sentences. There are bits of dreams, a fantasy, a memory, songs.*[14]

There are two important implications here for narrative voice. The first is the fragmentary nature of our inner voice's syntax, which is imitable on the page but may cause problems of intelligibility for the reader. The second is the suggestion, in the reference to dreams, fantasies, memory and songs, that the inner monologue alone is not adequate to represent the full variety of mental events which comprise our consciousness. Also to be rendered are the other contents of the mind: the images and sounds which are remembered or perceived, the emotions, sensations or sexuality which impinge on our awareness. Darrieussecq returns to the theme and expands on it in a later interview:

> Bref séjour chez les vivants … *is a book which tries to put the functioning of the brain on the page. I had a little fun too in the field of neuroscience, but it's not at all a scientific book. It begins with the very simple idea that when*

you think, you don't think in sentences, or very rarely. It's very rare to have a complete sentence in your head. You have images, memories, a snatch of music passing through, a vague concept. It's rare for us to formulate them. How can that be put on paper? It isn't stream-of-consciousness, which is already very much a written form. It's really hardly narrative at all, and closer to poetry.[15]

Once again, we have an approach to narrative form which attempts to take it to the very limits of what can be considered narrative, blurring the boundary with another genre entirely. We also see, in her enumeration of mental events, not only the non-linguistic thought mentioned above, but also, implicitly, thought which is pre-linguistic: vague, unformulated ideas which have potential to be expressed through language, but which remain in a state of latency, neither words nor images. Lastly, we see in the reference to neurology that Darrieussecq is interested in the mind as the product of the biological functioning of the brain, rather than as an abstract, immaterial entity.

This figuring of the mind as essentially being, in Francis Crick's words, 'the behaviour of a vast assembly of nerve cells and their associated molecules' is strongly supported by its depiction in Darrieussecq's fiction.[16] The representation is backed by extensive research into popular and technical works of cognitive science, some of which is explicitly referenced in the text, as when, in *Bref séjour chez les vivants*, Darrieussecq models the work of a clinical psychologist character on Jacques Mehler's experiments on infant language acquisition, or quotes Wilder Penfield's research into electrical stimulation of the brain.[17] More pervasive in her fiction is the anatomical terminology of neuroscience, linking thought processes to the areas of the brain from which they emanate, or the neurons and synapses where the electrochemical activity takes place. *Tom est mort* considers the neurology of grief: 'there must be neuronal work in mourning, diversions, dead ends and short-circuits, all the electricity to be reconsidered, synapses to be reviewed'; for the narrator of *Le Pays*, insomnia is 'a red area on a map of the brain' stubbornly maintaining consciousness, and her step-brother's amnesia is seen in similarly physiological terms, 'as if schizophrenia had blocked off areas of his brain, turning arteries into dead ends and nerve-centres into wasteland'.[18] Even *Truismes*, with its uneducated, unintelligent narrator, makes rather incongruous use of the vocabulary of neuroscience: 'That woke me up, so to speak. My neurons went back into place.'[19]

Colette Sarrey-Strack labels Darrieussecq's representation of the self 'anti-cartesian', in the sense that it rejects Descartes's dualist doctrine of an immaterial mind separate from a material body.[20] The above examples confirm this, situating mental events firmly within the physical brain in a way that is unequivocally materialist. Darrieussecq goes further, incorporating the mind not only in the brain, but in the body more generally. Sometimes she exploits literal connections between mind and body, as she does in *Naissance des fantômes* with the hormonal system – 'that shock to the heart, the adrenaline released all at once, an electrical wave which stubs into the ends of your fingers and paralyses your throat' – and the nervous system: 'the fingers through which I could make out, as if with an infrared microscope, the nervous impulses which had burst from the brain'.[21] At other times she draws metonymic comparisons, as in the opening scene of *Le Pays*, which uses the same mechanical and biological terminology to describe both the protagonist's running body and drifting consciousness:

> *I was not thinking about anything ... In my mind masses rolled, joined together or cancelled each other out, formed and broke up. The cogs of my hips, knees, ankles, worked to their utmost, the pistons of my arms pumped, the air coated the depths of my lungs in great jets. The fluids circulated, scrubbing me clean, relieving my tiredness. Oxygen irradiated me, my brain breathed.*[22]

The effect of this is to show the mind in a radically different light from the more familiar models of psychoanalysis. This latter discipline's narratives of the self span an individual's lifetime, reaching back to primal childhood experiences through which to interpret the adult psyche. Freud's famous case study of Sergei Pankejeff, the 'Wolf Man', for instance, explains the state of mind of the adult patient with reference to the posited trauma in his infancy of seeing his father having animal-like sex with his mother.[23] Peter Brooks analyses the case study as a narrative and notes its temporal span, commenting that, like Rousseau's *Confessions*, Freud's case histories look to 'indelible traces of childhood experience in the mature but never quite grown-up adult'.[24] He argues that these psychoanalytic narratives are strongly hermeneutic, comparing them to detective stories in their search of the buried past for an 'origin of all origins' on which the present mental state is founded.[25] (Unlike detective stories, however, this hermeneutic desire is never fully satisfied, as in this case when Freud later suggests the primal scene may have been a retrospective fantasy displacing witnessed animal sex onto the parents, shifting the possible point of origin from the depths of the past to those of the unconscious.)

The psychoanalytic paradigm assimilates well to literature, which frequently looks to a character's early years to explain the formation of adult sensibilities, as in the *Bildungsroman,* and which, according to Roland Barthes, is intrinsically hermeneutic in its narrative structure, stringing its story between the poles of an opening question and a concluding answer.[26] It is very far from the paradigm of cognitive science, of which even the most speculative branches, such as evolutionary psychology, have a much more limited interpretative scope.[27] Darrieussecq's work sometimes appears to embrace such limitations, as when the fateful meeting of two future lovers in *White* is described through the neurology of vision rather than through the thoughts and feelings of the characters:

> *Each photon unpeeling itself from Edmée's outline hurling itself in a straight line at Peter's retinas to recreate, with the memory that is light's own, her image, Edmée's image. And with equal infallibility, her own optic nerves inverting the image left-right, and the lobes of her brain setting it back the right way, zig zag, there's Peter.[28]*

The avoidance of conventional literary analysis of the mind is a general tendency in Darrieussecq's writing. Critics have noted it, including Catherine Rodgers, who suggests Darrieussecq 'refuses psychological explanations, but documents precisely the physical sensations her characters feel', and the writer herself confirms it, describing her work as 'a struggle to manage to speak the real while avoiding commonplaces, and in particular the commonplaces of psychology'.[29]

More importantly for our purposes, though, Darrieussecq's alignment with a cognitive view of the mind can also be seen in the narrative form of her texts. The writer imposes temporal and hermeneutic restrictions on her writing, eschewing many of the liberties afforded to the psychoanalytic narrative. Rather than a macronarrative of the self from childhood cause to adult effect,

Darrieussecq's work recounts micronarratives of the present moment. In novels that sift through the minutiae of their restricted time spans and frequently have recourse to the present tense, she is more likely to recount the surface of the mind – immediate perceptions and physical sensations – rather than its depths.

Darrieussecq's focus on the mind's present moment and surface level solicits the reader's active collaboration in interpreting the story. In *Naissance des fantômes*, the text's central question is why the narrator's husband has disappeared. We detect beneath the surface the narrator's anxiety that she has been abandoned due to the childlessness of the marriage, caused by her inability to bring a pregnancy to term. However, this possibility is never discussed openly by the narrator, nor even considered in her consciousness. Rather, it is up to the reader to recover this suppressed fear from the brief references which skirt around the issue. We see the narrator examine her body in the mirror and note the changes to her figure left by 'my longest pregnancy', but it is her present perception of her body – the weight on her breasts and hips, her darkened nipples – that remain the focus of her narration, rather than leading the story into an exploration of the serial miscarriages implied in her past.[30] Other characters in the novel are more forthright about the narrator's childlessness. Discussing the disappearance, the narrator's friend Jacqueline refers to 'this marriage, and no children', and later calls the husband (in the reported speech within the narrator's first-person account) 'an entity who, without ever giving me a child, had nevertheless lived with me for a certain time'.[31] Again, surface predominates, as the sense of Jacqueline's words fades away to leave the phonetics of their pronunciation: 'these three syllables, *ton-ma-ri*, your husband, which rang more and more phonetically in my ears (a dental occlusive, a labial occlusive, a sonorant liquid'.[32] Only towards the end of the story does the importance of these references start to become clear, as the narrator fantasizes about how she will reconnect to the ghost of her vanished husband: 'I would ask him to describe to me the houses, the streets, the fountains, the sky, and what he had dreamed our children would be like.'[33] Even this reference remains unelaborated, however, and moves quickly into a more abstract discussion of the qualia of perception: 'We would see the same colours, the same shapes, and I would stop wondering if my husband (if cats, birds, fish and flies with compound eyes) really felt and saw what I felt and saw myself.'[34] Darrieussecq is using the self-imposed

cognitive limits of her discourse to designate the boundary she does
not cross, and inviting readers to imagine for themselves the memories that are not recalled and the unconscious thoughts and fears that
are not recovered into consciousness. The *histoire* of an orthodox
psychological novel is transformed by a *récit* that takes its form from a
most unliterary psychological model.

Darrieussecq is at pains to assert that science in her work is in the
service of literature, and not the other way around. We have already
seen her declaration that *Bref séjour chez les vivants*, the novel that
most fully explores the nature of consciousness, is 'not at all a scientific book'. Elsewhere she clarifies her attitude to the science to be
found in her narratives:

> *I've been looking towards science for a long time to find metaphors that work.
> I know a lot of scientists, and I think that we do the same job. We are looking
> for the best possible tool to describe the world. For me that tool is made of
> words.*[35]

Both science and the novelist may share the aim of describing the
world, but the novelist's tool is language in its broadest sense,
including scientific discourse within its polyphonic array, but not
limited by its restrictions. Her emphasis on the metaphorical potential of scientific language demonstrates that the literal truth of the
discourses she employs is not necessarily her sole concern, should
there be a figurative, poetic use that the language will lend itself to.
Darrieussecq herself offers the example of the terminology of
particle physics being used to describe a psychological breakdown:

> *[Science] is quite simply a store of metaphors ... Scientific discourse gives me,
> among other things, all the vocabulary of atomisation. When someone disin-
> tegrates, the world disintegrates around them, and nuclear science gives me
> the words, molecule, particle, atom, neutron.*[36]

Discourses of neurology and cognitive science are not exempt from
this licence. Along with the sober and precise use of such terminology to describe the functioning of the mind-brain, we also find
mental processes described in playfully inappropriate physiological
terms. In *White* a character tries to push a thought out of her head,
'her encephalic membrane as tight as a drum'; in *Naissance des
fantômes* love dissolves 'under the abrasion of my neurons'; *Le Mal de*

mer imagines a beam of light is travelling through a character's brain to project her memories on a screen.[37] Darrieussecq may allow herself the liberty to use scientific terminology incorrectly, but she always makes clear to the reader whether she is employing the terms literally or symbolically, through an obvious comic or poetic element in the latter case. As well as misusing scientific discourse, she is also, of course, free to dispense with it altogether in creating her materialist depiction of the mind, and this she often does, simply by replacing abstract terms with descriptions of physical sensations which emphasize the corporeal aspects of the self, as in this evocation of a child's anxiety in *Le Mal de mer*:

They head towards the ice-cream seller. Her heart thumps as she stands before the colourful tubs, she struggles to read, her heels are hot. The pressure grows on her hand ... she no longer knows what to do about this great hollow in her chest, about the pins and needles stabbing at her heels, or the grasping tension which is climbing up her calves to take over completely.[38]

This 'folk' discourse of the body and senses complements the discourse of anatomical and neurological precision. Both enable the writer to avoid the banalities of conventional literary descriptions of the mind, as she says: 'instead of writing "I felt very afraid" ... I try to find other ways, I try to open new windows onto what fear is, what it is to be alone, what it is to have a body'.[39]

Darrieussecq's view of the mind thus matches closely with the cognitive model. We see this in her use, and in her deliberate misuse, of scientific terminology, and beyond this in the physiological slant of her depiction of states of mind, situating the mind firmly within the brain and body, and dwelling on the borderlines of external perception and physical stimulus, rather than the abstract drives posited by psychoanalysis. Formally we see this adherence in the micronarratives of the conscious moment, displacing the life-long hermeneutic dramas of the psyche which psychoanalysis seeks to explicate. Given all this, it is perhaps surprising to learn that Darrieussecq has herself undergone psychoanalysis, and has recently become a practising psychoanalyst herself.[40] Although she labels her psychoanalytic experiences 'private territory', kept separate from her work as a writer, it is noticeable that *Tom est mort* contains less reference to cognitive models of mind than previous work, and possibly heralds a psychoanalytic turn in her work to come.[41]

We can now return to the issue of narrative voice, and to the typology of consciousness suggested by Cohn. Cohn, as mentioned previously, divides the narrative representation of consciousness into three modes: quoted monologue ('[He thought:] "Am I late?"'), narrated monologue ('Was he late?') and psychonarration ('He wondered if he was late.').[42] How does their usage – typically in Darrieussecq a mixture of all three modes within a single text – reflect the writer's view of the mind? Let us begin with the narrative mode most closely associated with twentieth-century writers' concern for an authentic rendering of consciousness, quoted monologue in its particular guise of the stream of consciousness.

The earliest definition of the stream-of-consciousness as a literary form comes from its self-proclaimed originator, Édouard Dujardin, whose 1888 novel, *Les Lauriers sont coupés*, was an acknowledged influence on Molly Bloom's monologue in the final chapter of Joyce's *Ulysses*.[43] In an essay on his own work, Dujardin describes his style as characterized by 'direct sentences reduced to a syntactic minimum', designed to express 'the most intimate thoughts, which are closest to the unconscious, prior to all logical organization, which is to say, in their formative state'.[44] Later literary theorists have taken issue with this reference to the unconscious. Robert Humphrey redefines the form more neutrally as 'representing the psychic content and processes of character ... at various levels of conscious control before they are formulated for deliberate speech'.[45] Cohn herself argues that, of her three modes, the quoted monologue of stream of consciousness is actually the least suited to evoking the unconscious, since it is the only one unambiguously limited to the mind's linguistic activity.[46] A key aspect of plausible interior monologue is an acknowledgement on the part of the writer of the non-communicative nature of mental discourse: the mind notes, reacts, and considers, but has no need to recount its perceptions and actions to itself linguistically, nor to label the objects of its attention. In consequence of this, the successfully rendered stream of consciousness will have certain fundamental characteristics: its use of pronouns will be cryptically implicit, as thinkers have no need to name the objects of their thoughts; exclamatory syntax will predominate, expressing wishes, fears or other emotive attitudes rather than statements of fact, since exclamation is the most self-sufficient language gesture, requiring no interlocutor; correspondingly, narrative and reportive constructions will be avoided, as thinkers need neither tell themselves stories nor describe to themselves their perceptions.[47] Let us examine a pair of extracts to see how far Darrieussecq's style fulfils these criteria:

> *So hot already, half past eight and that guy parked in our spot, even though it says* privado, *I'll have to call the cops again, and those pansies that I bought because they were blue they're purple and those roses, twenty buds appeared, at least I wasn't ripped off on those plants, swollen to bursting sap rising.*[48]

The passage functions as a description of the environment of the perceiving character, Jeanne in *Bref séjour chez les vivants*, yet it is notable that the passage takes care to enfold visual or other details within an affective discourse. Rather than simply noting the presence of the parked car, we are given an expression of irritation at its position, and it is through this expression that the presence is indirectly communicated to us. Similarly, we are informed of the presence and appearance of the flowers through the character's disappointment or satisfaction with their bloom, and even of the time through an emotional reaction to the heat of the early hour. Implicitness in the use of pronouns is also in evidence when other characters are in question, as in this example from elsewhere in the same novel:

> *The square. Would you call this a square? Such a long time I've been waiting. Someone else could come, someone other than him. Unless he's in disguise. A recruiter. Someone who'd give me something. A mission. Money, right away. What does that matter? We turn a blind eye. A vulgar mind. Just plain vulgar. In the maternity ward, and what will you call this little one? Anne. Anne what? Just plain Anne. The number of times John and mum have told me that, in English or in French.*[49]

Here, in an extract from the novel's opening pages, we see the compromise the writer must make between a plausible rendition of non-communicative mental discourse and the communicative requirements of the novel's own discourse. Darrieussecq introduces us to the character, giving us her name and an idea of where she is and what she is doing, even of the family relationships which attach her to the novel's other characters. Such basic facts of the self are vital to the reader's understanding of the character, but rarely present linguistically in consciousness. Darrieussecq's solution uses the functioning of language itself as a means to present and connect this information. Doubt over the correct term for her location – it is, as later becomes clear, at the Bibliothèque François Mitterrand in Paris – allows her to name it experimentally; linguistic association, through the phrase 'just plain' allows the memory of an anecdote to append itself to the current situation, supplying the reader with her name. As in the previous extract, an emotional stance towards a fact of her situation, in this case, anxiety about a rendezvous, allows the writer to plausibly include information on it, albeit in a fragmented and incomplete way.

In these passages of pure stream of consciousness, Darrieussecq's style is very much in the tradition of the technique's usage. It seems more authentic than Dujardin's, whose monologist has an unconvincing habit of narrating his actions to himself as he performs them, as well as employing a large proportion of complete, well-formed sentences in his monologue:

> *Let's take off our gloves. They must be tossed carelessly onto the table, beside the plate; or rather in my coat pocket; no, on the table; these little things are a matter of manners. My coat on the hatstand; I sit down; oh! I was weary. I shall put my gloves in my coat pocket. Lit up, gilded, red, that sparkling with the mirrors; what? the café; the café I'm in.*[50]

On the other hand, Darrieussecq's stream of consciousness makes more concessions to intelligibility than does Joyce's in *Ulysses*:

> *I like that in him polite to old women like that and waiters and beggars too hes not proud out of nothing but not always if ever he got anything really serious the matter with him its much better for them go into a hospital where everything is clean but I suppose Id have to dring it into him for a month yes and then wed have a hospital nurse next thing on the carpet have him staying there till they throw him out or a nun maybe like the smutty photo he has shes as much a nun as Im not yes because theyre so weak and puling when theyre sick*[51]

The absence of breaks or punctuation in Joyce's text create more of an impression of free-flowing mental association than with Dujardin and Darrieussecq, while at the same time rendering it more difficult to decipher. The static situation of the 'Penelope' section, with

Molly Bloom musing in bed, obviates the need to describe locations or narrate actions, while the position of the section at the end of the novel also frees Joyce from many of the communicative requirements of the previous examples, as Molly's cryptic thoughts frequently allude to characters or events we have had presented to us more clearly in earlier parts of the text.

Dujardin's text is thus the most communicative, and perhaps thereby the least convincing of these streams of consciousness, since, as the single narrative mode of the text, it bears the full burden of describing and recounting to the reader.[52] By the same token, Joyce's seems the purest due to its freedom from these obligations. Darrieussecq exhibits a concern for storytelling which makes her version of the style less radical than Joyce's, but it would seem to fit unproblematically into the category. Why then does she, as we have already seen, reject the label stream of consciousness for her writing? Partly it is a question of fragmentation. Joyce, whom she cites as an influence on her writing, may disregard punctuation, but he retains the rules of grammar, leaving his text divisible into complete sentences, where Darrieussecq's text often consists of isolated words and broken-off phrases.[53] Such minimalist shorthand evokes both the speed and implicitness of mental discourse, and appears plausibly 'less written' than grammatically well-formed utterances. But there is another, more important sense in which Darrieussecq's rendering of the mind might be described as 'less written' than the classic stream of consciousness. Not only does she use fragmentary syntax to suggest a linguistically undeveloped status in the thoughts expressed, she also adapts and hybridizes the technique to express thoughts which are not linguistic in nature at all.

Darrieussecq rejects any link between language and consciousness, saying of her infant son in *Le Bébé*:

> *'End', 'start', 'continuous', 'discontinuous', 'separate', 'together': can it be possible that he has no idea of these concepts? I find it hard to believe in such virginity of the mind. That you need to speak in order to think, that concepts only come with words, seems a poor theory.*[54]

Non-linguistic thought features strikingly in her representation of mind, incorporated into the text in two main ways. Interior monologues are endowed with non-linguistic elements by images inserted directly into the text, and an approximation of the same for sounds.

Pictures of a face and phases of the moon appear in *Bref séjour chez les vivants*, while *Naissance des fantômes* includes a sketch of the narrator's hallucination of spiral stairs within spiral stairs. The optician's chart viewed by Nore in *Bref séjour* is reproduced in the text, and in the same novel, the articles, advertisements and horoscopes read by the characters appear pasted into the novel through changes of font and formatting in the text. Darrieussecq uses a reprinted stave or quoted song lyrics to suggest music the characters are listening to (as did Dujardin), and prefers to evoke noises through striking onomatopoeia – '*RrRrRrRrRrRrRrRrRrRrRrRrRrRr RrRrRrRrRrRr*' is Peter hearing the Antarctic base's heating system struggle into life in *White* – than describe them in conventional terms.[55]

Darrieussecq thus incorporates non-linguistic thought within the stream-of-consciousness form as far as it is possible to do so, and breaches several conventions of serious literary fiction in the process. Beyond aural and visual perception, quoted monologue struggles to incorporate other mental events that are non-linguistic in nature. To resolve this problem, Darrieussecq has no compunction in abandoning pure stream of consciousness in favour of hybrid modes of mental discourse. Narrated monologue is already of use to Darrieussecq as a means of plausibly introducing narration and description into the monologue form. The element of external perspective which comes from melding interior monologue with the discourse of an impersonal narrator allows for information to be communicated to the reader which would be out of place in stream of consciousness. This is demonstrated by the example of narrated monologue quoted at the beginning of this chapter, which inserts the narrator's observation of the character's situation – 'sitting on the terrace of the *Biela* waiting for Jimena' – naturally into the indirect rendition of the character's thoughts. However, the melding of discourses in *style indirect libre* can also serve to create ambiguity around the linguistic or non-linguistic status of the thoughts expressed, if we are unsure about whose words, character's or narrator's, we are reading. Consider the following example from *Le Mal de mer*:

She feels she's thought of everything now. The lamp works, revealing the heather and the craters in the sand beneath the trees. The ten thousand francs are in her pocket; there must be no more worrying, about dropping them, about the wind catching them, about the little one playing with them. The bundle is already a little depleted, they gave her coins back in change for the buns and the orange juice. She walks slowly back up, she has the eggs, the blanket, that's it, that's what they'll do, eat and sleep here.[56]

After an opening which belongs unambiguously to the external narrator, the narrative voice in the remainder of the extract hovers between the narrator's own discourse and the mental discourse of the character incorporated within it. It is through narrated monologue that we see the character chide herself for her anxiety about the money she is carrying, and reach a decision about spending the night on the beach. The text could easily be recast as quoted monologue in the first person ('there, that's what we'll do'), but the mediation of the narrator's voice in the form Darrieussecq has chosen keeps us at a distance from the character's thoughts. It raises the possibility that what we are given is not simply a report of words formulated in the character's head, but rather a verbalization of thoughts which remained at a pre-linguistic stage (as we earlier saw implied in Darrieussecq's comments on the workings of consciousness): anxious mental images of lost banknotes impatiently brushed away, a sudden sense of purpose which might, but need not be, embodied in the exclamatory 'that's it'. To the question, 'Who is speaking?', free indirect style answers that it is narrator and character at once, but since the voice is the narrator's, and the thoughts are the character's, the status of the words themselves remains caught between the two. Before they were taken up into the narrator's discourse, they may well have existed, fully formed, in the character's mind, but the possibility is left open that the narrator's voice is being used to deliver into language an inchoate expression of consciousness, giving us the words that would have been, had the thought surfaced as far as the language centres of the brain.

The third mode of mental discourse, psychonarration, allows Darrieussecq's narrator a more direct and unambiguous means of representing what the brain does not express to itself in language. The following passage, describing Edmée's passage to orgasm during sex with Peter in *White*, demonstrates this clearly:

> I can no longer think *is the last thought formulated by E before she forgets her self, reflexive phrases and syllogisms, and that way that space and time enclose her. Pleasure polarizes and the images flood in, the lake grows,*

spreads, her sex is a point on the lake, an island around which suspension bridges undulate, this is the last image in Edmée's mind when pleasure tears her away, nullifies everything, even the images – she cries out.[57]

'*I can no longer think*' is quoted monologue, which moves to non-linguistic thought in the mental imagery of the island, lake and bridges, which in turn is supplanted by pure sensation. All of these mental events can be relayed to us via the device of the external narrator, who suggests through their combination that complex brain functions like linguistic thought are joined in a mental continuum to basic neural impulses like sexual pleasure. It is perhaps the oldest, most common and conventional means of narrating the mind, but by avoiding the usual terminology with which it labels mental states, and merging it with quoted and narrated monologue, Darrieussecq succeeds in making the style her own.

Darrieussecq would thus appear to be justified in rejecting the term stream of consciousness for her representation of the mind. Stream of consciousness does not originate with Joyce and Dujardin, however, or even in literature of any kind. It was coined by William James, a pioneer of the empirical study of consciousness, and it is interesting to note that Darrieussecq's mind fits closely with James's conception, and indeed much more closely than do Joyce's and Dujardin's 'inner voice' monologues:

> *Now we may think about our topic mainly in words, or we may think about it mainly in visual or other images, but this need make no difference as regards the furtherance of our knowledge of the topic ... It makes little or no difference in what sort of mind-stuff, in what quality of imagery, our thinking goes on. The only images intrinsically important are the halting-places, the substantive conclusions, provisional or final, of the thought. Throughout all the rest of the stream, the feelings of relation are everything, and the terms related almost naught. These feelings of relation, these psychic overtones, halos, suffusions, or fringes about the terms, may be the same in very different systems of imagery.*[58]

Henri Bergson, whose philosophy of consciousness develops in parallel with James's ideas, is equally convinced of the important role of non-linguistic thought. Indeed, he comes to doubt that language has much of a part to play in our mental processes at all, as he suggests in this discussion of creative thought and its conversion into linguistic expression:

if (our) ideas find pre-existing words to express them, this appears to each of them as an unhoped-for good fortune; and, to be honest, it has often been necessary to help luck along and force the meaning of the word to mould itself to the thought. This time the effort is painful and the result uncertain. But it is only then that the mind feels itself or believes itself to be creative. It does not start out from a multiplicity of pre-constructed elements to arrive at a composite whole in which there is a new arrangement of the old. It has been suddenly transported to something which seems both single and unique, which will then attempt to spread itself as best it can over those multiple and commonplace concepts which words give us in advance.[59]

The idea that our thoughts are determined by the categories made available by our language, often known as the Sapir–Whorf hypothesis, and bolstered by various folk-myths about Eskimo words for snow or Native American concepts of time, is now discredited among linguists, bolstering Darrieussecq's suspicions about infant cognition discussed earlier.[60] Thought and language are once again the inner process and the socially developed system, two spheres with complex interaction and incomplete compatibility, that Bergson envisaged. Their relationship is once again at the forefront of studies in the mind, both scientific and philosophical. Darrieussecq's multifarious stream of mental events – words, images, emotions, perceptions and sensations – rendered from whatever perspective and in whatever manner best captures them on the page, offers a vivid evocation of how the mind works that has a sound basis in current theories of cognition.

In Darrieussecq's narratives of consciousness, we see the influence of the modernist originators of the literary stream of consciousness, as well as that of the textual revolution of Nathalie Sarraute. With regard to both, however, her work would seem to step back from avant-garde radicalism: her stream of consciousness makes more communicative concessions than Joyce's and eschews Dujardin's purity to mix in other, more conventional modes of narrating the mind. Her characters are more concrete than Sarraute's, their stories more familiar and comprehensible. But this is not a retreat into tradition; rather, it is a shift from metatextual concerns to a more direct engagement with consciousness as a phenomenon. Where Joyce's inspiration was a literary one, and the spur to Sarraute's innovations was a critique of the Balzacian notion of the literary character, Darrieussecq turns to psychology and neurophilosophy for her model of the self, and creates her style of narrative as a consequence of this. Her micronarratives of the conscious moment, and the motley flow of language, image and sensation through which her characters' minds are narrated are literary innovations in the service of an exploration of consciousness whose principal influences Darrieussecq imports from outside the literary sphere.

Chapter Four
Jean Echenoz and the Uses of Digression

Of the five novelists on which this study focuses, Jean Echenoz (b.1947) is most frequently compared with the experimenters of Oulipo and the *nouveau roman*, perhaps in part due to his position as the most prominent author at *Les Éditions de Minuit* since the *nouveaux romanciers* firmly established the publishing house's avant-garde credentials in the 1950s. Such comparisons are not always apt: when, in 1979, Jérôme Lindon first welcomed the aspiring author to *Minuit*, Echenoz was told, '"You like Robbe-Grillet, of course" ... as if it were obvious, as if my book stemmed naturally from this influence', leaving the writer too embarrassed to admit he has read only one of Robbe-Grillet's novels, and that fifteen years previously.[1] A decade on, though, Echenoz will include Robbe-Grillet in the 'musée imaginaire' of writers who constitute his personal literary milieu.[2] The influence of Oulipo is also acknowledged when he describes Raymond Queneau and the thriller-writer Jean-Patrick Manchette as 'two writers to whom some of us owe, if not everything, at least nearly everything'.[3] But, as the homage to Manchette suggests, Echenoz's literary inheritance is a complex case to unravel. Since *Le Méridien de Greenwich* (1979), the work in which Lindon saw Robbe-Grillet's influence, Echenoz has produced nine further novels. *Cherokee* (1983), *L'Équipée malaise* (1986), *Lac* (1989) and *Nous Trois* (1992) continue the first novel's appropriation and subversion of subgenres of popular fiction. *Le Méridien de Greenwich* and *Cherokee* inhabit the world of *noir* thrillers, *L'Équipée malaise* resembles an adventure story, *Lac* a spy story, and *Nous Trois* changes midway from the print equivalent of a disaster movie to a science-fiction novel. Echenoz's work led early criticism to compare him to a hermit crab, adopting and discarding genres like seashells.[4] While his more recent novels retain links with popular fiction and film – with *noir* crime fiction in particular – Echenoz no longer writes genre pastiche, and his next four novels resist classification. *Les Grandes Blondes* (1995) recounts a television production company's search for a former singing star, Gloire Abgrall, and her homicidal resistance to their approaches. The novel received a sequel of sorts in *Au piano* (2003), in which the afterlife guide of the recently deceased protagonist is Gloire's guardian angel/psychotic delusion from *Les Grandes Blondes*. *Un An* (1997) and *Je m'en vais* (2001) also form a pair, this time more closely entwined as the two plots – a woman's descent into vagrancy in the first, and theft and retribution in the art world in the second – share events and characters across their simultaneous unfolding. Lastly, Echenoz's most recent novel, *Ravel* (2006), represents a new departure in subject matter as the writer becomes biographer of the last ten years of the composer, Maurice Ravel, yet the book remains very much a novel, and in terms of its style very much an Echenoz novel. Aside from these ten novels, Echenoz has also produced a small number of shorter works, notably the novella, *L'Occupation des sols* (1988), and the tribute to his publisher, *Jérôme Lindon* (2001).

Echenoz's commerce with the formalisms of his experimental predecessors and the formulas of genre fiction will both be at issue in the following discussion of the writer's use of narrative form. However, there is one particular feature of Echenoz's writing around which I would like to organize this study of his work, and that is *digression*. The topic of digression is a useful way into Echenoz's writing, partly because its various manifestations are so characteristic of his work, and partly because the notion of digression itself raises questions which are part of Echenoz's own literary preoccupations. If fiction digresses, then what is it digressing from? Is the true course of a narrative the one which it takes, or the one which it ought to have taken? If the latter, how are we aware of this virtual course not travelled? How do our expectations of narrative line and narrative relevance condition our reading experience, and what might be the point or the pleasures in disappointing such expectations? In the discussion that follows, the topic of digression will lead us into several different areas of Echenoz's poetics, and which will take us to the heart of the writer's engagement with the text and his engagement with the modern world it represents.

Digression is a neglected area of narrative form. Randa Sabry, in one of the few existing studies of the phenomenon, refers to an 'almost total lack of interest' among academic critics and theorists.[5] This may be due to the nebulous nature of the concept, or perhaps to its derogatory connotations. Pierre Bayard, discussing digression in Proust, argues that it is unique in rhetoric through being a subjective phenomenon, the presence or absence of which is a matter of the individual reader's interpretation of a passage's relevance to the whole work; moreover, digression inevitably self-destructs as it proceeds, with readers inferring connections and adjusting their conception of the whole in order to reintegrate the excursus into the mainstream of the work.[6] Éric Bordas, exploring the practice in Balzac, notes how often critics (including figures as influential as Erich Auerbach) have viewed digression as an aesthetic flaw. Bordas paraphrases the typical critique as follows: 'Balzac is a bad writer. His inability to master different discourses, among which some have no business in a work of narrative fiction, is one of the clearest proofs.'[7]

Sabry's definition of digression is a broad one: 'A digression occurs when the narration *dissociates itself* from the story (from the action, from the subject), turning away to talk about something else or about itself, and thereby undermines its own orientation towards a pre-determined end (which is not only to direct the story, but to direct it to a successful conclusion).'[8] In Sabry's notion of turning aside, we see the importance of the metaphor which figures narrative as a line. The story progresses towards the conclusion it is aimed at, and any material which does not further its progress to this end is a drift away from the straight line of pure story. Laurence Sterne's *Tristram Shandy* (1759–67) famously illustrates this conception of narrative with a series of sketches illustrating the digressions of each volume of his memoirs as loops and squiggles along a line; the final sketch, a single, unadorned straight line, represents the narrative ideal he claims to aspire to.

What is this straight line of 'non-digressive' narrative, and what does progress along it represent? It is not the line of text, nor the unfolding of the narration, for neither of these differentiate digressive material from relevant. Is it, perhaps, the chronology of the story's underlying *histoire*, the chain of events which connects the novel's opening to its conclusion? For many novels this is the case: each event which brings the story closer to its planned conclusion – a marriage, a death, a revelation – is a step along the line, each element of the text which fails to do so is a step aside. Yet to equate narrative line with chronology is clearly not tenable for all stories. The central third of Balzac's *La Peau de chagrin*, for instance, is an extended analepsis which precedes the novel's opening, yet it is in no sense a digression, being essential to the understanding of the protagonist and the fate which awaits him. And it would be absurd to label detective stories digressive for recounting how the crime was committed at the end of the novel rather than the beginning. Roland Barthes's theory of narrative codes offers a useful corrective. As well as the 'proairetic code' of action, through which the narrative's chain of events is constructed, Barthes also posits a 'hermeneutic code' of understanding. This is defined by Barthes as 'the set of elements which serve to articulate in various ways a question, its answer, and the diverse accidents which can either draw up the question or delay the answer'.[9] The 'question' in the text is loosely enough defined for Barthes's theory to be widely applicable: in *S/Z*'s chosen commentary, on Balzac's *Sarrasine*, Barthes defines the code through the example of the novella's title, and the curiosity induced by the delay before the tale introduces the character of Sarrasine. The conception of the code as a series of hints, decoys, blocks or partial revelations strung through the narrative between enigma and solution represents an alternate linearity to that of chronology and causality. Digression might thus be judged according to the relevance of a given passage to the central question(s) of the text, whether they be a matter of backward-looking curiosity or forward-looking suspense.

Narrative's codes of action and interpretation do not run in parallel; despite Barthes's efforts to unpick them with regard to *Sarrasine*, their entwined thread generally resists dissociation. If a narrative poses the question, 'How will the lovers overcome the obstacles which prevent their union?', then the actions which lead them towards their happy ending or frustrate their progress are simultaneously a process of working through the question towards its answer. In *Reading for the Plot*, Peter Brooks re-entangles Barthes's codes to produce his own definition of plot:

> *Plot, then, might best be thought of as an 'overcoding' of the proairetic by the hermeneutic, the latter structuring the discrete elements of the former into larger interpretative wholes, working out their play of meaning and significance. If we interpret the hermeneutic to be a general gnomic code, concerned*

not narrowly with enigma and its resolution but broadly with our under-
standing of how actions come to be semiotically structured, through an
interrogation of their point, their goal, their import, we find that Barthes
contributes to our conception of plot as part of the dynamics of reading.[10]

Brooks's definition might very well describe the line from which
digression is said to depart. The line is a series of events which are
heading for the novel's concluding state of affairs, and it is also the
accretion of meaning that will make this denouement significant.
Such a view explains why digression must be identified in the
context of the whole work: only once the conclusion is reached can
we see what was leading to our final understanding of the story, and
what was leading us astray.

There are two main ways in which a text might digress away from
this imaginary line, depending on the type of discourse employed.
In one kind of digression the narrative is interrupted by argumentation, as the narrator expounds upon a topic which has arisen in the
story, creating what Genette calls a 'cyst' of non-narrative discourse
within the narrative flow.[11] Bordas considers the practice in the
work of Balzac, the writer who is perhaps most closely associated
with such digressions. Bordas points out that Balzac's commentaries
on his fiction tend to generalize the contents of the novel, demonstrating verisimilitude with an appeal to the reader's own experience
of reality. (We have already seen an example in the second chapter
of this study with the banker's house in *Le Père Goriot.*) While
breaking up the narrative line, these digressions nevertheless build
unity on a thematic level as they explore more abstract implications
of the drama, thus attempting to balance a tension between coherence and progression. Argumentative digression need not
necessarily take its subject matter from the diegesis, however; it
might equally take the form of metafictional commentary on the
telling itself. Such reflexive digressions are less common in the
realist fiction of the nineteenth century (Stendhal being a noted
exception). They abound, however, in the work of the great
eighteenth-century digressionists, Sterne and Diderot, are rein-
vented in the twentieth-century, notably by Gide, to return in force
in the self-conscious writing of postmodern fiction, in which
company we might include Echenoz himself. Metafictional digressions are innocuous enough in first-person narratives: we fully
expect an intradiegetic narrator like Proust's to comment on his

own creativity. In impersonal, third-person narration (Echenoz's preferred mode of storytelling), however, such digressions have the inevitable effect of weakening the realist illusion, as they confront the reader with discussion of the artifices of the text's construction.

Metafictional digressions may be used for comic effect, as when Diderot's narrator in *Jacques le fataliste* enters into burlesque debates with the reader; they can also be a form of deconstruction, an internal questioning and destabilizing of the text, as is the case in *Les Faux-monnayeurs*, where the story's narrator is also its critic. Their presence generally demonstrates the independence of the narrator from the diegesis, since the universe of the text is suspended while the time of narrating goes on.[12] However, they are sometimes used to blur the distinction between what is inside and outside the diegesis, as narrator and 'reader' become characters and the narrated time and time of narration merge, as when, in *Jacques le fataliste*, Jacques and his master are separated and the narrator proposes to the reader: 'let us talk amongst ourselves until they find each other again'.[13] The relationship between narrator and diegesis will prove to be a key concern of Echenoz's own digressive practice.

The second kind of digression is one which does not interrupt the story with non-narrative discourse, but rather, remains within the diegesis. It is a drift away from the narrative line, not in a substantial and self-contained subplot, but rather in wandering into areas of doubtful relevance, which stand aside from the causal chain of events or contribute little to our understanding of their significance. Such digressions might concern minor characters, or subsidiary events. They may also remain with the protagonists and the story's key events, and yet be digressive through eccentric perspectives, inserting descriptive passages at inopportune moments, say, or neglecting what is essential to the plot to focus on background activity. Bayard's theory of the subjectivity of digression has some validity here: ascertaining the presence of these digressions can be a problem, as the narrative line, and the degree of relevance to it, are both to some extent in the eye of the beholder. Fortunately, digressive writing, especially in the comic vein, has a tendency to police its own departures. The two kinds of digression are frequently combined through narratorial comment on the straying storyline. Narrators may apologize for the lapse or assert the author's right to wander; they may obtrusively manage the course of the narrative by hurrying it along or shepherding it back to surer territory. In the picaresque novel, such as *Gil Blas*, the line of narrative trajectory may be so weakly drawn that these digressive episodes become the principal focus of the text, thus rendering the label 'digression' itself a dubious one. These most radically digressive texts question the opposition implied in the term between what is essential to the story, and what is contingent. This question, too, is one with which Echenoz's texts are closely concerned.

One way to mark out for the reader the presence of digressions in the text, and the stylistic intention behind them, is to employ a narrative line with a course that is familiar and predictable. The formulaic narratives of popular genre fiction would fulfil these criteria, offering a storytelling template fixed in the public imagination by the novels, films and television series which repeat the pattern. Echenoz's homages to genre fiction, particularly in his early novels, are explicitly approached with the intention of departing from a template, as the writer explains in an interview on the publication of his third book:

> *My first two books,* Le Méridien de Greenwich *and* Cherokee, *are based on my memories of the roman noir.* L'Équipée malaise *takes after the adventure story, a genre I like a great deal and which offers more flexibility. By mixing ingredients which are adventure settings well-suited to literature and cinema, like Malaysia, a freighter flying a Cypriot flag of convenience, a mutiny, arms trafficking, rubber plantations, you can play ... A system is put in place, starting from which you can cheat.*[14]

The set-up and pay-off structure of conventional thriller plotting is subverted to challenge our expectations. A slow build-up of momentum will lead us suddenly into abstruse side roads, or will perhaps lead nowhere at all, making us re-evaluate what appeared to be significant developments as narrative drift. In *Lac*, we follow for pages the meticulous preparation and elaborate security rituals which lead to clandestine meetings at which nothing of consequence is decided. Genuine developments to the espionage plot – Mouezy-Eon discovers where Chopin is held captive, Seck 'turns' Veber's bodyguards – go unchronicled, while the narrator luxuriates in the *longueurs*, showing us Chopin counting the flowers on the wallpaper in his hotel room or reading his own ID papers to kill time. In *Je m'en vais*, the proairetic and hermeneutic codes of its narrative line culminate simultaneously at the point where the protagonist, Ferrer, finally catches up with the man who has robbed and ruined him to discover (with the reader) that the culprit is his former friend and business partner, Delahaye. The scene, however, plunges immediately into banality and irrelevance:

> *He was dressed as Ferrer would always have liked him to dress at the gallery. The only blot on the picture when Delahaye dropped into an armchair and the turn-ups of his trousers rode up: his sock elastic seemed slack. You look good like that, said Ferrer. Where do you get your clothes? I hadn't a thing left to wear, replied Delahaye, I had to buy myself a few little things here. They have stuff that's not at all bad in the town centre, you wouldn't believe how much cheaper it is than in France. Then he sat up in his chair, adjusted his tie that was a little off centre, probably due to the fright he had had, and pulled up his knee-socks that had sagged down to spiral at his ankles.*
>
> *My wife gave me these socks, he added distractedly, but they won't stay up, you see. They don't seem to stay up. Oh, said Ferrer, that's normal. Socks people give you never stay up. That's very true, said Delahaye with a tense smile, that's very well observed, can I get you a drink?*[15]

Digression and bathos continue to be the watchwords of this 'climax' to the story. When the pair do discuss Delahaye's crime, they quickly bicker into stalemate: 'None of that got us terribly far, so they were silent for a moment for lack of arguments.'[16] Thereafter, the narrator himself appears to lose interest in the characters, becoming distracted into a discussion of tidal flows in the river as they cross a bridge. When, finally, the expected violent confrontation erupts between the two men, after six pages of hiatus (to some extent recuperating the tidal flow passage via the possibility that Delahaye will be thrown into the river), the narrator interrupts the account at its most dramatic moment:

> *We have never taken the time, despite hanging out with him for nearly a year now, to describe Ferrer physically. As this rather lively scene doesn't lend itself to a long digression, let's not take all day over it: let's quickly say that he's a fairly tall man in his fifties, with brown hair and eyes that are green or grey depending on the weather ...*[17]

What is presented as the narrator's negligence is in fact precision. Echenoz has found absolutely the least appropriate point in the narrative to describe his protagonist's appearance, and set the description there. The joke made, we return swiftly to the action, but even this is narrated off-kilter, with narrator and protagonist more concerned about foul language than about the murderous violence. In a final piece of disrespect towards the conventions of the thriller, the chapter is cut off abruptly in the middle of the scene, the resolution of which is despatched in a terse retrospective summary in the following chapter, which itself opens with a deflationary paraphrase of Samuel Beckett: 'Days continued to pass, lacking any alternative, in the usual order.'[18] In all, the essential narrative functions of the episode have not actually been left unfulfilled. The pursuit and revenge plot which has sustained the story through the length of the novel comes to a head in a conventional showdown, which ends the quest and restores stability to the situation: Delahaye is punished and Ferrer's livelihood restored. Where the novel departs from the formula is in its digressions within the *histoire* – delaying the confrontation for a conversation about socks – and within the *récit*, through inappropriate narratorial discourse.

Digressive play with generic formulas can be seen, not only in single episodes of Echenoz's texts, but also in larger-scale narrative structures. To take another pursuit narrative as our example, let us examine how Echenoz recounts the tracking of his heroine, Gloire, by the private detective, Personnettaz, across a hundred pages of *Les Grandes Blondes*. Here, the genre template is freer, as a genuine suspense narrative would be expected to include obstacles and surprises, fast-moving developments and becalmed frustration along the course of the pursuit. Two elements that we would expect from a conventional rendition of such a storyline, however, would be a consistent focus on events which bear directly on the success or failure of the chase, and a coherent development from move to counter-move, from clue to progress as the causal chain of events brings the pursuers closer to their target. In Echenoz's novel, the events in the sequence, as the text allows us to reconstruct them, occur as follows:

1. *Personnettaz agrees to take charge of dealing with Gloire, and to take on Boccara as his assistant. For an instant, he is unwittingly metres away from her as her train passes under the bridge he is standing on (pp. 82–5).*
2. *Gloire flees to Sydney (pp. 90–9).*

3. *[Personnettaz and Boccara travel to Gloire's Breton home and find it empty (unnarrated).]*
4. *Boccara attempts to change the wheel on the detectives' car as they head back to Paris (pp. 100–2).*
5. *[Boccara succeeds, or is given help (speculated upon by the narrator).]*
6. *Boccara discusses his sex life with Personnettaz as the journey continues (pp. 102–4)*
7. *Boccara and Personnettaz attempt to open a safe in Gloire's solicitor's office (pp. 106–8).*
8. *[They succeed, and discover Gloire has travelled to Sydney (unnarrated).]*
9. *Gloire commits murder in Sydney and leaves for India (pp. 109–18).*
10. *Personnettaz claims travel expenses for a ticket to Sydney and has difficulty with the digicode to Boccara's apartment (pp. 121–4).*
11. *[Personnettaz and Boccara travel to Sydney and fail to find Gloire (reported in a single sentence).]*
12. *Boccara discusses his sex life during the journey home (pp. 124–6).*
13. *[Personnettaz traces Gloire to India (unnarrated).]*
14. *Boccara kills time before telephoning Personnettaz, who tells him Gloire's new location (pp. 147–8).*
15. *[Personnettaz and Boccara fly to Delhi (obliquely referenced via the narrator's justification for omitting the episode).]*
16. *Boccara wins prizes and holidays as the airline's millionth customer. Personnettaz returns to Paris alone and takes on Donatienne as his new assistant (pp. 149–52).*
17. *Gloire leaves the Club cosmopolite for Mumbai (p. 163).*
18. *[Personnettaz returns to India with Donatienne and travels to the Club Cosmopolite (unnarrated).]*
19. *Personnettaz discovers Gloire has moved on (pp. 164–70).*
20. *[Personnettaz and Donatienne return to Paris, having lost track of Gloire completely (unnarrated).]*

There are a number of points to note about this narrative sequence. First, even without the eccentricity of the *récit*, the underlying *histoire* is itself lacking in coherence and progression. The chase repeats itself, with only the exotic location and the investigative pairing having changed, and it will continue to repeat itself later in the novel as the investigation begins again from scratch. There is no sense of a developing plot with the pursuers gaining knowledge or gaining ground, merely a series of bursts of activity leading nowhere. Chance regulates the course of events, as when the timing of Gloire's departures makes the detectives eternally a little too late, or when Personnettaz is deprived of his assistant by Boccara's good fortune with the airline. This latter plot device flaunts its improbability so blatantly, presenting itself as a literal one-in-a-million chance, that it breaks the realist illusion to betray the presence of an author manipulating his characters' fates on a whim. There is little coherence to be gleaned from the characters' motivations, either. The story is played out like a game by both the writer and his characters, as Olivier Bessard-Banquy notes of Echenoz's fiction generally.[19] Gloire's global wanderings are spontaneous and random; Personnettaz's commuting between Paris and Delhi is an absurd waste of time and money; the stakes in the whole business are no higher than a potential appearance by Gloire in a 'where are they now?' television show.

It is with the *récit*, however, that this narrative of events becomes seriously unorthodox. The choice of which episodes to narrate, and which the reader must infer in order to fill in the gaps, seems whimsical at best, if not actively hostile towards the reader's desire to follow a narrative line. It appears as if, as Fieke Schoots puts it, the arbitrary is the structuring force of Echenoz's writing.[20] Important hermeneutic developments are omitted, as are major events like the outcomes of two out of the three attempts by the detectives to find Gloire. Instead, we focus on the dead time which occurs between events, or during the forced inactivity of travel. The conversations and actions we are presented with are trivial, such as Personnettaz's difficulties with the digicode, or Boccara's two monologues on his love life, the second of which begins with a confession that the first was 'not even true'.[21] The story is fragmented by the idiosyncratic distribution of scenes and ellipses in the recounting of the sequence (and further divided by scenes involving other characters not included in the list). The missing episodes are brought forcibly to the reader's attention at points where the narrator steps in to manage his narrative: 'But we know she's left Sydney, we already know the journey, so let's deal with this very quickly and get on.'[22] More disconcertingly, the narrator's control over the diegesis appears inconsistent. At the start of the sequence his omniscience allows him to register an event of which no one is aware, the momentary proximity of Gloire and Personnettaz. Yet when the account of the voyage back from Brittany suddenly skips two hours, cutting from a broken-down car to a travelling one, it is the narrator's ignorance which motivates the jump: 'Unless a sensitive soul gave them a helping hand, their conjoined efforts must have succeeded since two hours later they were driving again, headlights full-beam speeding down the fast lane.'[23] The slipperiness of the narrator's status, not knowing or not telling, observing or inventing, adds greater uncertainty to a narrative trajectory which is already treacherous to follow.

The sequence in *Les Grandes Blondes* is not an outright deconstruction of the crime novel's pursuit narrative, however, just as the climax of *Je m'en vais* is not a full-blown parody of a thriller showdown. In both, as in all of Echenoz's fiction, a balance is set up between the traditional pleasures of narrative and the subversive interest to be had from undermining them. When the thread of the pursuit narrative seems in danger of breaking up due to its irrelevancies and omissions, means other than the plot are used to connect its disparate episodes, such as the sex discussion continued over two separate journeys, or Boccara's heavy cold in the safe-opening scene, a result of his struggle to change the wheel in freezing rain. Blanckeman suggests that the familiarity of Echenoz's borrowings allows him to treat many of the essentials of the genre plotline as redundant information.[24] Trusting his readers to know how thrillers work, he is able to economize on the basic mechanics of character motivation and plot development and spend time flitting around the margins of his diegesis. Echenoz himself compares this practice to jazz improvisation:

Something happens with jazz. The work I was able to do a while ago on genres may have something to do with the jazz standard, a classic tune that is taken up over and over by all kinds of musicians who found in it a melodic, harmonic, seductive, interesting, fertile unity, and each one will treat it in his own way, glorifying and sabotaging it at the same time. I have great admiration for Thelonius Monk in particular, who would constantly return, as well as to his own compositions, to major standards like Just a gigolo and would corrupt them to destroy and glorify them all at once, to expand them. Sabotage in order to expand is a formula I'd happily adopt as my mission. Or destroy to embellish. Create as many obstacles as possible with regard to a fixed form to destabilize, break, weaken and torture it, but not with perverse intent, rather to turn it round a little. You also find in jazz elements of syncopation, breaking off, missteps, traps, rupture and dissonance, which are very precious to me when applied to writing.[25]

As with the jazz standard, Echenoz's model remains recognizable within its improvised reworking, and its own aesthetic value can still be appreciated through the new stylings which distort its form. There is an essential difference here from some of the more radical deconstructions of genre formula undertaken in the previous generation, such as Robbe-Grillet's *Projet pour une révolution à New York*, which dismantles the workings of its popular-fiction model entirely, destroying any possibility of reading for the original pleasures of the genre. Echenoz's novels still retain a narrative line, hermeneutic and proairetic codes largely intact, even if our path may depart from it and the focus of our interest may be elsewhere.

In previous chapters we have seen the use of narrative form to explore the subjective experience of time, traverse the boundaries of discourse or render the functioning of the mind in language. Next to these, Echenoz's fiddling with the rules of mass-market fiction may seem lacking in literary ambition. The writer is indeed sometimes accused of being gratuitous; Jean-Louis Ezine, in an article in the *Nouvel Observateur*, calls his novels vacuous and insipid, sapped by their own pervasive irony.[26] Ezine is in a minority of critics, however: more typical is the reaction of Pierre Lepape, who hailed him early on as 'the most significant writer of the 1980s', a reputation that his subsequent work has consolidated and enhanced.[27] There is more to Echenoz than genre parody, and more to his use of narrative form than deliberate misuse of pulp-fiction formulas. Jean-Claude Lebrun's characterization of Echenoz's writing shifts the focus of interest away from the narrative formulas that Echenoz's digressions depart from, to highlight the unexpected areas these digressions lead us into:

> Almost as soon as it begins, each book of Echenoz's starts to pitch and yaw and seems not to want to hold the intended course, but as it goes it begins to cross paths with all this jumble of flotsam which tend to become progressively the real focus of interest ... When we reach the end, what lasts and predominates is not a sense of scattering or incoherence, however, but much rather that of an extremely rigorous system, or perhaps of a constellation in which every part, large or small, down to the tiniest particle of stardust, is subject to the same imperious law of gravitation.[28]

This flotsam may be literal objects (and Lebrun has in mind particularly the everyday items which distract the attention of narrator
and characters in the manner of Delahaye's troublesome socks,
above), but we might also extend the metaphor to include other
literary artefacts – characters, episodes, descriptions and commentaries – which are encountered seemingly by chance, and yet, as we
shall see, can provide structures of their own in the text, independent of the plot. For Blanckeman, Echenoz's digressive play is
not simply parodying specific types of familiar fiction, but manipulating at a more fundamental level the 'narrative matrices' found
across all forms of storytelling.[29] It is these aspects of Echenoz's work
– the new perspectives gained from digression and its effect on the
basic functions of narrative – which take his use of narrative form
beyond the parodic and into more complex areas of literary representation. Of course, popular genre fiction is not Echenoz's only
inspiration for the narrative structures of his writing. His later
novels distance themselves from such work, often taking on more
sombre trajectories such as a descent into homelessness (*Un an*) or
a tragic decline through neurological disease (*Ravel*). As we have
seen, however, even in his earliest work the course of the narrative is
sometimes inspired by influences which trump even Quignard's in
their distance from the French literary tradition, since they are not
literary at all in nature. To the syncopations and missteps of jazz
improvisation, we might also add a number of other cultural influences, which, like jazz, play a dual role of thematic elements within
the diegesis and shapers of the narrative structure itself. Television
is one such: snatches of programmes appear in the background of
Echenoz's scenes, often in ironic counterpoint to the 'real-world'
action. The channel-hopping cuts between characters and situations that characterize much of Echenoz's work, the dropped
storylines and fragments of other lives we will not pursue, suggest a
perfusion of television into the fabric of the text itself: for Emer
O'Beirne, in a study of the phenomenon, Echenoz's narratives
demonstrate how 'the culture of zapping has transformed our experience of narrative'.[30] Equally the *bande dessinée* thought bubbles
that appear above people's heads in *Nous Trois* hint at a deeper relationship with comic strip narratives, and with Hergé's *Objectif lune* in
particular, in the construction of that novel.[31] Most evident of all,
however, in theme and structure, is, without question, the cinema.
Film is a constant point of reference for Echenoz, from the cod

philosophizing over the great movie blondes in *Les Grandes Blondes*, to the unlikely afterlives of Doris Day and Dean Martin as service personnel in purgatory in *Au piano*. It is also an integral part of his narrative structure, as when the narrator's voice evokes an imaginary camera's eye, viewing events 'in tracking shot', 'wide shots' and 'medium shot', or blurs the boundaries between film and the reality of the diegesis by fooling the reader into taking one for the other.[32] Techniques of film editing are mimicked in Echenoz's arrangement of material. In *Ravel*, the detailed account of Ravel's journey to America which takes up nearly all the first half of the novel contrasts sharply with the rapid series of vignettes of the composer's concert tour of America that follows, making the latter sequence strongly reminiscent of film montage (especially given its accompanying 'music').[33] More widely in Echenoz's oeuvre, the influence of cinematic cross-cutting is perceptible in the 'continuity editing' which connects chapters dealing with different characters, locations or time periods. In a typical example from *Je m'en vais*, the final words of the seventh chapter are a reference by Delahaye to Arctic sunrise, which then 'cuts' to a description of this very event, six months later, in the opening line of the eighth.[34] Borrowing another medium's narrative grammar gives Echenoz's fiction a further remove from reality – it seems almost that we are reading the story of a film – and gives it greater licence to venture into the unexpected and implausible. Paradoxically, it renders Echenoz's work less suitable for film adaptation than it might otherwise have been, since it is the inappropriate juxtaposition of film and prose narrative techniques which create the unusual perspectives and ironic humour. The lack of success of *Cherokee* (Pascal Ortega, 1991) and *Un an* (Laurent Boulanger, 2006) at the cinema should make future directors approach Echenoz's work with caution.

To investigate Echenoz's manipulation of matrices of narrative, we must move beyond the mishandling of genre conventions and the transposition of non-literary narrative structures, and explore the basic characteristics of narrative, on the large and small scale. What of the Aristotelian fundamentals, the unified beginning, middle and end, in which an incentive moment leads through complication to a point of climax, which then unravels to a resolution which restores stability? Beginnings and endings in Echenoz are a particular focus of his digressive play, being as they are points of high uncertainty in the narrative line, where the plot has yet to get underway, or where its forward impetus is supposedly played out. The openings of Echenoz's novels often focus on characters or events which will prove marginal to the ensuing narrative, thus setting up certain expectations for the story to come, only to deliberately disappoint them. *Lac* has the most striking example of this, devoting two chapters to the character of Vito Piranese, dwelling on his life story and his lost love, Martine, before his path crosses that of Franck Chopin, who will prove to be the novel's real protagonist, and Piranese is summarily dismissed from the story. The first chapter of *Je m'en vais* begins by introducing the hero, Ferrer, but two pages later is describing in detail the front door, and the photo of a dead matador pinned to it, belonging to a character, Laurence, whose exit from the story will be as rapid as her entrance is marked. Stylistically, too, we may be wrong-footed by Echenoz's openings, as when *Les Grandes Blondes* begins its narration in the second person – 'You are Paul Salvador you are looking for someone' – in the manner made famous by Michel Butor's *La Modification*, only to discard the conceit as a throwaway comic flourish –'but you aren't Paul Salvador' – a few lines further on. Endings continue on past the point of resolution to trouble the regained stability of the diegesis. *Nous Trois* joins together its earthquake and space-shuttle epics with the single thread of Meyer's obsession with Lucie, a woman he twice loses and twice discovers again by chance. When romance finally blossoms in zero gravity, the story appears to have reached its culmination, underlined when, back in Paris and six pages from the end of the novel, the couple move in together. But the story does not end here. Instead, the narrator telescopes weeks of their relationship into a few lines in order to continue past the happy ending into boredom, dissatisfaction and an incipient break-up.

Between these unfocused openings and endings, narrative structures are equally capricious and unpredictable. There are disorienting changes midway through, as with *Nous Trois*, which transplants its characters to a whole new literary subgenre for its second half. Narrative trajectories wander with their aimless protagonists. Like Gloire in *Les Grandes Blondes*, *Un an*'s Victoire leads the story through haphazard travels that would be picaresque, were they not so bleak and futile:

> *She carried on picking at random on her map ... It would produce a saw-tooth wandering without much control: if it happened that someone made a*

detour to help her on her way, it would happen too that she had to adapt to
someone's destination, the one balancing out the other. Her itinerary thus
showed little coherence, having certain similarities to the shattered course of a
fly trapped in a room.[35]

Echenoz's narratives of frenetic, directionless activity are suited to
the symbolism of the buzzing fly, strikingly employed also in the
entomological espionage of *Lac*. His characters journey from place
to random place, they rebound between a succession of shallow,
short-lived relationships, or they are simply buffeted along by events
in complex schemes that exceed their understanding and bring
them little benefit. These twisted itineraries of narrative are further
confused by characters and episodes that seem to stand apart from
the story, like Odile Otero in *L'Équipée malaise*, or the baby-listener
débâcle that takes up a chapter of *Je m'en vais*, and sliced up by a
narrative structure that, until Echenoz's most recent work, insisted
on alternating or otherwise interspersing chapters between two or
more parallel stories.[36]

Echenoz's digressive practices are not all about introducing incoherence, however, and a closer look at some of the techniques
mentioned reveals some interesting paradoxes. We have already
seen how 'continuity editing' stitches together disparate episodes by
a thematic link between the close of one and the opening of
another. When in *L'Équipée malaise* (to take a new example), the
scene shifts between chapters from the would-be rescuers of Justine
to her kidnapper, it is not an emphasis on this shared plotline that
binds the chapters, but rather the arbitrary fact that captor and
rescuer are both reading news articles about small European states
in the same edition of a newspaper.[37] The narration connects,
while the plot beneath remains fragmented. In linking together
episodes via irrelevant details, while the significant connections of
the *histoire* are ignored or non-existent, Echenoz's narration both
compensates for his fragmentary storytelling (preserving it from
incoherence), and draws attention to it, by highlighting coincidence over causation.

Closure, like continuity, can also be provided by means other than
the line of the plot. Circularity is a frequent characteristic of
Echenoz's novels, with the story's end signalled by the protagonist's
return to their starting point, either literally, as is the case with
Victoire in *Un an*, or figuratively, as with Chopin in *Lac*. Interestingly,

certain characters in Echenoz's novels appear to have no function in the diegesis other than to put in an appearance at its beginning and end, reinforcing the sense of a closed circle without having contributed anything to the story which has brought us here. The portrait-painter, Max, in *Nous Trois*, is one such character, figuring centrally in the first and last chapters and barely mentioned in-between, as are Laurence in *Je m'en vais* and Vito in *Lac*. Rather than being entirely gratuitous, as they may have seemed at first, these characters are now seen to serve an aesthetic function, signifying within the formal structures of narrative by book-ending the plot, even if they play no meaningful role within it.

Within the body of the text, recurring 'irrelevancies' in theme and structure strike the same balance between digression and cohesion. Laurence's matador photo, for instance, receives a strange echo when the narrative, for no reason linked to the plot, chooses to dwell on the spectacle of an unknown young man playing at bull-fights with the Atlantic waves at Biarritz.[38] There is no further connection between the scenes – Laurence's photograph is seen through Ferrer's eyes, the young man through Delahaye's – and if there is any symbolic meaning in the trope, perhaps designating the struggle between Delahaye and Ferrer, then it is obscure and unde-veloped. Rather, the impression we have is once again of a purely aesthetic device: a pair of digressions communicate across the length of the novel, drawing the story together in the manner of a musical leitmotif, devoid of semantic content.

Un an is suffused with such leitmotifs, overlapping systems of echoes which punctuate the narrative and provide a sense of aesthetic order to the story of a disordered life. The odour of dogs and the presence of dogs in cars link up Victoire's hitch-hiking experiences, as the succession of cars she travels in proceeds system-atically through the possible permutations of the two variables. Stylistic echoes connect the descriptions of the two bicycles Victoire avails herself of on her travels, with the list of the former's gleaming accessories mirrored in a catalogue of the latter's decrepitude, and both lists topped off with an ironic touch of pathetic fallacy: 'And the sun was shining' for the first, 'and the rain was falling' for the second.[39] Golf balls make intermittent appearances through the story, their mysterious sound at first troubling Victoire, then shat-tering Delahaye's car window, affording Echenoz the opportunity to dwell on the 'little white citrus-skinned spheres', then collected in the drawer of Victoire's wardrobe, and finally, after a long absence from the text, resurfacing in a whimsical description of horse-chestnuts, whose spiky casings are seen as 'negative golf balls'.[40] As neither golf balls nor conkers play a role in the plot, the suspicion arises that the inclusion of the former was largely motivated as a set-up for the jokey representation of the latter. All three sets of connections are limited to the narrator's discourse: they are not elements intrinsic to the *histoire*, but rather contingent on the narrator's choice of language to draw connections that would otherwise pass unnoticed.

Echenoz's earlier, more overtly metafictional novels sometimes feature outright parodies of narrative coherence within the text itself. His first novel, *Le Méridien de Greenwich*, features near the end a literal 'figure-in-the-carpet': Abel finds that the apparently meaningless patterns on an ornamental rug, 'without connections or continuity between them', resolve when viewed from above into the image of an ark, which appears as 'a perfect sum, a catalogue of nature and culture set in order with care'.[41] The revelation is partly an ironic accompaniment to Abel's discovery that the novel's complex drama of rival factions vying for a mysterious invention has all been orchestrated from above with the express intention of having each faction wipe out the other. It also has wider resonance for the novel, offering contrasting tongue-in-cheek symbols of the narrative as a unified, integrated whole or 'a jumble of unrelated items' reflected in the carpet symbol which is itself borrowed from another text.[42] The two novels that follow, *Cherokee* and *L'Équipée malaise*, both make gentle mockery of the idea of narrative as progress towards a predetermined destination through the device of the fortune-teller. The protagonist of each novel has their fortune told early in the narrative in a way that accurately foreshadows the path of the story to come. In *L'Équipée malaise*, the unfeasibly detailed and accurate prediction even foretells the aesthetic structures of the coming narrative with its opening line: 'everything will go in pairs, always more or less in pairs'; the principle of 'binarity' which governs the ensuing story, from its paired characters and events to its preoccupation with mirrors and doubles, has been widely noted by critics.[43] *Cherokee* pushes the parody further by inserting into its opening chapter the following prediction to the protagonist, Georges, the subsequent fulfilment of which is made all the more miraculous by the fact that Georges is asleep at the time the words are spoken: 'You are going to meet somebody, she breathed softly into his ear. And you will go on a journey, a short journey. And then you will make lots of money.'[44] The prediction is, of course, a deliberate cliché, with the implication that these lines are the generator for the plot upon which we are about to embark. In the event, the novel proves to hold a dizzying profusion of characters and plotlines, yet we cannot escape the fact that, reduced down to its most basic outline, Georges's story is essentially about a meeting, a short journey, and finding a lot of money.

The final point I wish to make about digression and coherence in the large-scale structures of Echenoz's texts concerns the connectivity between narratives. I am referring to Echenoz's 'twinned' novels, the simultaneously conceived *Un an* and *Je m'en vais*, and the looser pairing of *Les Grandes Blondes* and its later sequel-of-sorts, *Au piano*. In many ways, the paired narratives are mutually reinforcing and enriching. *Au piano* fleshes out the character of Gloire's 'guardian angel', Béliard, from *Les Grandes Blondes*; *Je m'en vais* resolves the mysteries left hanging by *Un an* of Ferrer's 'death' at the opening, and the claim by the resurrected Ferrer at the denouement that Delahaye, whom we have met five times in the course of the novel, has been dead all along.[45] Equally, *Un an* answers some burning questions from *Je m'en vais*, such as the identity of the young woman Delahaye picks up between Auch and Toulouse, the belated recognition of whom causes him such anxiety, as well as several questions which are barely posed, such as the cause of the 'muffled footsteps' heard by Delahaye in the hôtel Albizzia, which are made by a fleeing Victoire.[46] Through their imbrication, these two novels recuperate each other's digressions. The narrator's interest in describing Delahaye's choice of hotels as he lies low under his new identity appears less gratuitous once we see how his itinerary intertwines with Victoire's, and how, for her, the characteristics of each hotel mark a precise stage on her decline into poverty. Victoire's return near the end of *Je m'en vais*, seen from Ferrer's perspective, is a humdrum episode. To the reader of *Un an*, where the same events form the bewildering shock denouement, they are a vital element in the two novels' shared narrative, and their very banality in the later novel is a irony to savour. As with the internal connections we discussed earlier, there are also links between texts which create coherence through 'parallel irrelevancies' without a role in the plot. *Au piano* and *Les Grandes Blondes* both contain the consoling thought, expressed by different characters both known by the name 'Paul Salvador': 'I might have ended up in Manila, selling individual cigarettes'; both novels describe ceiling fans reflected in restaurant spoons, which seem like spiders to Gloire and insects to Max.[47] Such gratuitous connections are winks to the careful reader, for the rest of us to pass over none the wiser.

The relationship between the paired novels is not simply one of mutual coherence building, however; the narratives also interfere with one another destructively. *Au piano* flags up the inconsistencies in the two texts' representation of Béliard – from murderous homunculus to urbane, full-sized human – through his 'explanation' that, as a trainee in the previous story, 'they make you be small, mean and nasty'.[48] *Je m'en vais* may resolve the mystery of Ferrer's and Delahaye's 'deaths' in *Un an*, but it only renders Delahaye's behaviour in the latter novel more mysterious: we still do not understand how or why he should track Victoire down on three separate occasions to tell her lies, nor why his attitude should be so different when they meet by chance on the road to Toulouse. This latter episode is the only one to be narrated in detail in both texts, and the considerable differences between the versions is troubling: *Je m'en vais* recounts a diatribe by Victoire against Delahaye's use of the ungrammatical expression, 'vous allez sur Toulouse?', allowing Delahaye to recognize her voice. In the earlier novel, focalized through Victoire herself, the expression is not used and Victoire does not speak.[49] The discrepancy not only destabilizes the *histoire*, but also raises questions about the status of the *récit*. Is this an exercise in unreliable points of view in the manner of Nathalie Sarraute? Does it represent an incapacity, or a carelessness, in the 'omniscient' narrator? Or is it a demonstration of the fictionality of the text, exposing the void beneath the language, should anyone be tempted to look there for what 'really happened' in the story?

The most drastic effect of the later novel in each pairing, however, comes in their retrospective reordering of the terms of the narrative. Both *Un an* and *Les Grandes Blondes* hold elements of the fantastic, hesitating – as Tzvetan Todorov puts it – between rational and supernatural explanations for the events of the story.[50] *Un an's* Twilight Zone ending throws the narrative into a limbo of uncertainty, raising the possibility that Victoire has been consorting for the past year with a ghost. The narrator of *Les Grandes Blondes* sets out the terms of its own hesitation explicitly: 'At best, Béliard is an illusion. At best he's a hallucination produced by the young woman's deranged mind. At worst he's a kind of guardian angel, or at least related to that congregation. Let's imagine the worst.'[51]

In fact, the narrator's *parti pris* of treating Béliard as an independent being is a deliberately quirky narrative perspective on a diegesis that can comfortably accommodate Béliard's presence without recourse to the supernatural. Prior to his entrance, the narrative has already established Gloire as psychotic and delusional, and nothing about her 'guardian angel' encourages us to see him as anything but a hallucination – a reading all but confirmed by his shockingly uncharacteristic appearance in Sydney, goading Gloire into murder in a moment of panic. The games the narrator plays by focalizing his narrative through Béliard's perspective, or asserting Béliard's physical effects on the world when focalized through Gloire, push the conceit to its limits without ever venturing into the impossible.

Both sequels wreck this careful balance, wrenching the narrative of the earlier novel towards their own understanding of the shared diegesis. They do so in opposite directions: *Je m'en vais*, with its convoluted explanation of faked funerals and peculiar heart conditions, drains *Un an* of the uncanny. *Au piano*, with its matter-of-fact assertion of the business of purgatory and reincarnation in which Béliard is employed, drags *Les Grandes Blondes* unwillingly into the realm of the marvellous. Each shift is an arbitrary one: the sequels could equally well have proved the presence of the supernatural in *Un an* and its absence in *Les Grandes Blondes* and left entirely valid readings. It is also a shift that fails to register fully, as the fixity of the second novel is unable to impose itself on the earlier one with total authority. The odd coincidences and inexplicable behaviour of Delahaye in *Un an* are not to be quashed by the thriller logic of *Je m'en vais*, just as the undecidable status of Béliard in *Les Grandes Blondes* is not resolved by a second incarnation which is deeply at odds with the homicidal pixie of the first. Christine Jérusalem labels Echenoz's first pair of novels 'a false diptych', the parts of which complicate and obscure each other as much as they cohere and reinforce, and the same might be said of the second pair.[52] Echenoz's own metaphor for their relationship – 'they cross paths, like two cars, they cross paths and don't recognize each other' – is an evocative choice for two trajectories of narrative which will not combine into a single thread.[53]

Digression is not only a matter of the large-scale structures of the plot. It can also be an issue in the small scale of paragraphs and sentences, and it is to these that we now turn our attention. What place is there in Echenoz for that most archetypal of digressions, the interruption of narrative by argumentation? As mentioned, this is the practice particularly associated with Balzac, and perhaps Hugo, in which the narrative flow is suspended while the narrator discourses upon a matter arising from the story. Balzac's digressions are highly varied: they may inform or opine (or do the latter in the guise of the former); they may appeal to the reader's knowledge of human nature or French society to validate the story recounted; they may be a succinct maxim, a discursive clause within a sentence of action or description, or an essay of several hundred words. The 'Physionomies Parisiennes' section of *La Fille aux yeux d'or*, which takes up a third of the novel, prefacing its drama with a bestiary of Parisian types, is arguably a triumph of digression over the narrative which gives rise to it – even putting in doubt which gives rise to which.

Despite the presence of an intrusive narrator in all of Echenoz's work, who frequently interrupts narrative with argumentation, the extended digression is not to the writer's taste. The longest example in his oeuvre amounts to 168 words, and owes more to Diderot than to Balzac. It occurs in *Au piano*, as Max attempts to pursue a woman he believes may be his lost love, Rose, through the metro system. As hope fades and the absurdity of a tube-train chase is made manifest, Max gives up scanning the station platforms he passes, and instead examines firstly his fellow passengers, and then his ticket, at which point the narrator's own discourse interrupts:

> *Max soon preferred to look at his ticket.*
>
> *As not much is going on in this scene, we could fill it by discussing this ticket. There are lots of things to say about these tickets, you see, about their secondary uses – tooth-pick, nail-cleaner or paper-knife, pick or plectrum, bookmark and crumb-sweeper, slipway or straw for illegal substances, a folding screen for a doll's house, a tiny notebook, a souvenir, something to hold a phone number that you scribble for a girl in case of emergency – and their various fates – folded in half or quarters lengthways and then likely to be*

*slipped under a wedding ring, a signet ring, a watch strap, folded into sixths
or even eighths like a concertina, torn into confetti, peeled in a spiral like an
apple, then thrown in the metro bins, on the metro floor, then thrown outside
the metro, in the gutter, in the street, at home to play heads and tails:
magnetic strip heads, 'urban sector' tails – but this is perhaps not the moment
to go into all that.*[54]

The status of the digression as an interruption of the narrative by
other discourse is rendered dubious by Echenoz's employment of
the same conceit we saw earlier in *Jacques le fataliste*. In suggesting that
his digression fills in a dull moment in the story, the narrator affects
to believe that the time of narrating is dependent on narrated time,
as if he were commenting on real-time events. The passage gives the
impression of a conversational opening from the narrator to the
reader, in the topic management of its opening and closing lines, and
in the casual, colloquial tone of its language. This tone also suggests
an assumed familiarity on the reader's part with the subject matter:
Echenoz is exploring with the reader their shared territory of the
minutiae of everyday metropolitan living. The uses and fates of
metro tickets include the comically imaginative, but these are very
much outnumbered by the everyday. Much of the list is, in fact, so
ordinary as to be beneath notice – we ignore tickets in gutters, we
unconsciously fold them into concertinas – and there is a reminder
in Echenoz's list of Perec's fascination with the *infra-ordinaire*, or of
Robbe-Grillet's determination in his first novel to interest us in a
tomato segment.[55] The passage holds a mixture of order and
disorder: the list seems random at first, but is divided into two
symmetrical parts, and in its final terms comes to resemble poetry in
its rhythmic repetitions. Most interesting is the question of relevance.
The text seems at pains to emphasize the irrelevance of the passage:
in embarking on it, the narrator presents it as a spur-of-the-moment
decision motivated only a touch of boredom with current narrative
events; the colloquial language reinforces the idea of a narrator
making it up as he goes along. The substance of the digression is
relentlessly trivial, and this is underscored by a final line which seems
to apologize for the narrator's lapse (ironically, since the narrator
has already 'gone into' the topic more than is reasonable) and hurry
us back into the story. Yet this impression is deceptive, since this
passage will prove to be not at all irrelevant. Looking back from the
novel's end, we might even consider it the symbolic heart of the story,

prefiguring the 'urban sector' to which Max is assigned in the after-life ('what's with this stupid name taken off the old metro tickets', fumes Max as he learns the verdict) and the coin-flip randomness with which this fate is chosen over the paradise of the Park, as Béliard admits a few lines further on: 'there's always something a little bit arbitrary about the decisions'.[56]

Many of these characteristics are typical of narrators' interruptions in Echenoz: their apparent spontaneity, their focus on the unimportant and the everyday, and their resulting air of irrelevance which may in fact be a trap for the unwary. *Ravel*'s innocuous digression on the shapes of signatures as the composer leafs through the transatlantic steamer's *livre d'or* returns to the reader's mind in the story's later stages, as Ravel begins to lose control of his motor functions and lives in fear of being asked to sign his name in public.[57] A discussion of the simoun wind and a Moroccan sandstorm scene in *Nous Trois* become meaningful when the sand deposited in France is later postulated as a presage of earthquakes.[58]

Not all such digressions are recuperated by the plot, of course, and many of the narrator's interruptions are simply comic asides, such as the discussion of the 'avian ideology' of Malaysian bird-life in *L'Équipée malaise*, or generalizations on modern life, as when a telephone call in the same novel is preceded by the narrator's thoughts on the variety of international dialling tones.[59] One thing all the digressions have in common, however, is a foregrounding of the narrator and a manipulation of the narrative flow. Nowhere is this manipulation more obvious than when the narrator chooses to expound on a subject because of its absence from the story rather than its presence, as happens in *Un an*:

> *This road is far from the beaches, you can't see the sea, and you're sorry about it. You'd like to see the waves be born, swell and overturn, see each of them over and over again offer their version, their interpretation of the ideal wave, you could compare their speed, their conception, their succession, their sound, but no, Victoire got off the coach at about three o'clock in Mimizan.*[60]

Discussing this passage in interview, Echenoz has recourse once again to the metaphor of jazz as he describes how geography forced him to improvise and distort his original intention to describe a sea view, which proved non-existent when he came to check his heroine's route on a map:

I have to redo it all in the conditional, to express the frustration of not being able to describe the waves, to imagine the description that might have been made of them ... It's as if the rhythm section imposed a different tempo. You're then necessarily in a state of contradiction, and you need to profit from that contradiction. That makes you work with a different and greater interest than if you followed your initial inclinations. You do violence to yourself, to the story, to other people ... It upsets things, which is a major interest of literature.[61]

Good-natured violence to the narrative is a hallmark of the narrator's interventions. He hustles the narrative along – 'Let's keep moving now, speed up' – and obtrusively shepherds the reader's viewpoint: 'let's accompany them to their vehicle ... let them leave. Let's go back to Paul's.'[62] He addresses his characters directly – 'But it will work much better, Maurice, it will work a hundred thousand times better than *La Madelon*', Ravel is told as he composes the *Bolero* – and criticizes their actions: 'Personally, I'm starting to get a little fed up with Baumgartner.'[63] He will even buttonhole his readers, again in a manner highly reminiscent of Sterne and Diderot, anticipating our reactions – 'you foresee the worst, understandably' – making assumptions about our knowledge – 'quite a lot of people you wouldn't know ... others you've perhaps heard of' – and at one point making mock accusations against us for falling into the trap set by his deceptive narration: 'I know you, though, I can see you from here. You thought Max was another one of those ladies' men, one of those good old womanizers ... Well not at all.'[64]

Discussing this aspect of his writing, Echenoz includes his addresses to the reader as part of a broader play with pronoun usage, which he defines in opposition to the systematic experiment found in texts of the previous generation:

Systematically opting for the second person, as you find in Butor's La Modification *or Perec's* Un homme qui dort *doesn't interest me as a system. But of course I like those opportunities, making use of the first, second or third person singular or plural in the same way that you would film a scene with three cameras. Also, since the book will sooner or later meet a reader, it seems normal to me to address him, to call him 'tu' or 'vous' – most likely 'vous', actually – only to abandon him immediately for an overall view. To avoid any precise formalist project.*[65]

These grammatical movements and straying viewpoints are another kind of wandering in Echenoz's narrative which have a strong kinship with the wanderings of a narratorial digression. Another passage from *Au piano* offers us an effective demonstration:

> *The next day, around half past twelve, Béliard came to fetch Max with the idea of getting you out to meet people, he explained. It wouldn't be good for you to stay alone in your corner, you mustn't stay cut off from everyone, it's always good to interact. It would thus be the first meal that Max would have outside his room, on leaving which they came across Doris in the corridor. She was standing there, apparently hanging around in the sector without much to do, as if she were only waiting to run into Max. And although the latter, as we've said, had never been what you might call a womanizer, had never been sensitive to the more or less subliminal appeals that might be addressed to him, because he was never sure enough of himself to consider them as such, it seemed to him that Doris was looking at him more precisely, was smiling at him more pointedly. Even her make-up and her walk, more supple and dance-like than usual, were different from on previous occasions, as if something, well I don't know. But what can you be thinking. What are you starting to imagine.[66]*

The opening sentence of the extract slides from the impersonal discourse of the narrator into Béliard's direct speech. The point of transition is indeterminate: at 'came' we are, grammatically, with the narrator, by 'you' we are with Béliard, the anomaly of which makes the reader do a double-take. The end of the sentence is back with the narrator, then another sentence of direct speech, then, at 'it would thus', the narrator resumes control. Echenoz's typical disregard for the punctuation of speech leaves all of these transitions unmarked: only the tone and sense of the discourse allows us to assign a voice to it as we read further into the sentence. Even with the narrator, we are still not on stable ground, however. We slip disconcertingly mid-sentence from scene-setting to event, from conditional to past historic. The scene proceeds with an external view of Doris, focalized through Max, but our perspective shifts again when the narrator refers to himself in the first-person plural: his reminder to the reader, 'as we've said', brings the communicative act of storytelling to the fore, only to return us once again to the past historic of the diegesis by the sentence's end. The final shift takes us from the third person of the narrator's account to the first, then second person of Max's internal monologue, again at an undecidable point between the incompatible pronouns, 'him' and 'I'. The discourse interference is exacerbated here through the already close alignment between narrator's and protagonist's points of view. Sympathetic to his hero, and focalizing his narrative through Max's thoughts and perceptions, the narrator's identity already blurs to some extent with that of his character, with the result that, in style and substance, the intervening discourse could easily belong to either of them, and a ghost of the narrator's chiding voice remains even when Max is clearly the originator of the thoughts in the final sentences.

All of this may not be digression in the classic sense, but these wandering discourses and viewpoints not only reflect the narrative straying of digression proper, but also create an environment within the narrative discourse itself in which the unexpected and undisciplined can flourish: this is truly, as Echenoz says, discourse with which to tell a story which might head off in any direction.[67] *Nous Trois* represents Echenoz's most extreme venture with narrative perspective, baffling and amusing us with its marriage of two incompatible viewpoints, the impersonal third-person narrator and the autodiegetic first-person account. The first-person narrator, DeMilo, disappears from the scene for much of the novel, yet continues to narrate the experiences of the novel's true protagonist, Meyer, as if a conventional impersonal narrator, focalizing through Meyer's mind and apparently omniscient of the diegesis through which Meyer moves. The incongruity of the narrative instance is brought home to us in the last section of the novel, where DeMilo and Meyer meet to become fellow astronauts and rivals for Lucie's affection. The narration, however, chooses to privilege its focalization through Meyer over the narrator's own viewpoint, leading to unsettling double perspectives like the following:

> *Meyer leafed through it [an article on the aftermath of the Marseille earthquake], thinking he recognized a shop front on the route of one of the funeral processions, a shop glimpsed in the opaque dust as he had just left the shopping centre with Mercedes. He closed the magazine as I appeared at the far end of the corridor, adjusting the cuffs of my jumpsuit.*[68]

Despite this being ostensibly DeMilo's voice we are reading, we are privy to the thoughts and perception of Meyer, we see Meyer's own discourse in the use of the nickname 'Mercedes' for Lucie, whom

DeMilo has never known by this name and, most disorientingly, we remain with Meyer's viewpoint even when the narrator enters, as seen in the external presentation and the perspective implied in the expression, 'at the far end of the corridor'. The text offers no elucidation of this impossible amalgam of subjective and impersonal narration, which refuses to be rationalized into, say, dual narrators, or a fake 'omniscience' on the part of the first-person narrator. Echenoz's own tongue-in-cheek explanation is that the text is a third-person narration within which one of the characters happens to have the 'right' to use the first person, which hardly sets matters straight.[69] It is little surprise that this impossible narrator, Echenoz's playful creation, should himself play games with his narration, keeping us in the dark for most of the novel that the characters Lucie, Mercedes and 'the doctor' are all the same person, a trick the writer repeats with Delahaye/Baumgartner in *Je m'en vais*. As with the ellipses we saw in the sequence from *Les Grandes Blondes*, it is again demonstrated that Echenoz's erratically wandering narration may leave us with treacherous holes as well as irrelevant excess.

As a final point on Echenoz's errant language, we should note a related piece of grammatical misconduct. As well as playing with pronouns to create startling effects in point of view, the writer also enjoys playing with tenses to create dislocations in narrative time. Echenoz's 'gearbox' of time-shifting verb tenses has attracted much critical attention.[70] Michel Volkovitch, in a study of the writer's tense usage, argues that unpredictable tense changes are part of Echenoz's strategy to create a vision of 'an eminently unstable world'.[71] Colin Nettelbeck notes that even when Echenoz is using the *passé simple*, he does so with an ironic attitude towards this most conventional storytelling mode, noticeable particularly in the comically mannered imperfect subjunctives which arise in improbable clusters or unlikely colloquialisms.[72] While the *passé simple* is the fundamental narrative tense for all Echenoz's novels save *Ravel*, its dominance over the narration is never assured. There are sudden moves into the present tense for moments of vivid immediacy when events happen quickly. Conversely, the present tense also appears in moments where nothing happens at all, and static narrative approaches the status of description. Other verbs weaken our connection with the narrative present, as extensive use of the pluperfect and the future tense or conditional mood send us backwards or forwards in time, as in this example from *Au piano*:

At around six o'clock he heard Alice come in, but did not stop working: he would spend the end of the afternoon getting right certain nuances of the two movements, Presentiment *followed by* Death, *from Sonata 1.X.1905 by Janácek, after which he would go up to find Alice busy in the kitchen. Oh, he would say, fish. Yes, Alice would reply, why? No, nothing, Max would say, setting the table, I like fish, where did you put the fish knives?*[73]

The sonata movements drolly reference the opening-page announcement of Max's impending death which has coloured our reading of the novel so far. But the temporal dislocation which follows is a smaller, subtler affair. The conditional construction leaves the narrative present at the point of Alice's return, to narrate the rest of the afternoon as Max's future, its status indeterminate between a firm assertion on the part of the narrator and an unfulfilled intention on the part of the character. Yet the continuation of the passage becomes absurdly specific. The dialogue in direct speech (itself, we might note, something of a digression in its banality) contradicts the implication of unfulfilled intention in the verbs, while also ruling out other possible interpretations of the conditional mood, such as a suggestion of an oft-repeated daily routine. A little piece of narrative has been cast adrift from its rightful place in the *passé simple* of the narrative's present moment, setting the episode in an unnatural light, and breaking the rules of narrative discourse for the pleasure of transgression. Through techniques like this, Echenoz's texts are once more straying from the narrative line, breaking away from the moving point of our progress through the story's chronology by presages of what is to come and belated accounts of events already past.

As with the large-scale wanderings of the plot, in the details of discourse we see similar techniques used to similar ends. There is a playfulness, and a caprice, in Echenoz's use of narratorial argumentation, of obtrusive narrative management, and of deviations of perspective and chronology caused by inventive use of verbs and pronouns, just as there is an unashamed delight in the arbitrary course of the *histoire* and its eccentric rendering in the *récit*. Echenoz's play is a reaction against orthodoxy, and the reader's familiarity with this orthodoxy is a precondition for its effectiveness: the element of parody can be appreciated only by those familiar with its model. It is a measured reaction, however. Echenoz shuns the systematic and radical deconstruction associated with the *nouveau roman* and its acolytes, such that, just as his plots retain to some degree a causal thread leading to a conclusion with some degree of closure, so his intrusive narrators disrupt but do not destroy the narrative line, and his grammatical misdirection never allows us to lose our grip on the when and where of the story for very long.

More than was the case with the other three writers we have examined, Echenoz's use of narrative form is, as we have seen, metafictional in intent. For Ernaux, Quignard and Darrieussecq, structures of narrative are influenced by considerations that are not in themselves entirely literary in nature: Ernaux attempts to capture lived and remembered experience in different qualities of narrative; Quignard searches for forms that will bypass the strictures of logical argument for his meditations on love and history; Darrieussecq seeks to render the verbal and non-verbal functioning of consciousness in narrative. Echenoz's idiosyncrasies, though, have as one of their primary references the conventions of literature, be they the specific traditions of a particular fictional genre or more fundamental conventions of storytelling. He may not adopt the doctrines and constraints of the experimentalists, yet he remains in their lineage through his particular interest in the possibilities of the telling, no matter what the tale. That such wildly differing subject matter as Ravel's biography, a space-shuttle mission and a *noir* thriller should each produce texts suffused with the same, instantly recognizable Echenozian style, formed from the same techniques of narrative manipulation, is evidence that the content of his novels does not determine their form. Rather, the ostensible subject of the story is rivalled for position as the main focus of the narrative by the topic of fictionality itself: the possibilities of the story are sometimes less interesting to the writer than the possibilities of storytelling.

However, Echenoz's digressive fictions are not to be seen as writing about writing without meaningful reference to reality. There is a consistency to certain areas of his wandering – the journeys he narrates between settings, the dead time he recounts between events, and the objects he describes along the way – which accumulates into a vision of contemporary life, and one in which the digressive nature of its presentation is an important element. Consider the voyages which Echenoz's novels take such an inordinate amount of time recounting, by steamer in *Ravel*, by metro in *Au*

piano, by aeroplane in *Les Grandes blondes,* or in motorway traffic in
Cherokee. These are not simply a perverse foregrounding of the
'connectives' of narrative over the significant events at either end of
the journey (although this is certainly part of the reason for their
prominence, particularly in cases where the journey proves ultimately pointless).

They also form an exploration of the *non-lieux,* to
borrow Marc Augé's expression for public spaces of transit, which
feature so strongly in modern urban life, yet which receive little of
our attention, taken in life as in fiction as pragmatic staging-posts to
get us to the main event.[74] There is a critical edge to Echenoz's
focus on his characters' constant hurrying about, usually for unconvincing motivations and invariably to little success. This negative
slant, poised between derision and melancholy, becomes an implicit
critique of a culture perpetually on the move, rootless and rushing,
which rarely counts the time expended in transit or measures it
against the gains achieved. Similarly, the dead time of Echenoz's
narratives, in the insomniac nights, lonely weekends or enforced
idleness, are more than just the negative of thriller logic, which
skips uneventful periods to bring us to the next dramatic confrontation. In dwelling on these interludes, Echenoz emphasizes the
emptiness and solitude of his characters' lives, an emphasis which
proliferates through his texts to become a general pronouncement
on modern life. An account of Personnettaz's daily routine in *Les
Grandes Blondes* makes the point clearly in its closing lines:

> *He pulled on some clothes without thinking of whether they matched, vaguely
> planning to buy some shoes one of these days – these must easily have forty
> thousand on the milometer. But beyond that possibility, nothing else to do
> today, no more or less than yesterday. And nothing drains a person like idle-
> ness behind the Place de la République, in an opaque two-roomer on the rue
> Yves-Toudic.*[75]

The objects which distract the narrator along the way, from golf
balls to metro tickets, also play a dual formal and referential role, as
do the other sights and sounds – the noise made by walking in
corduroy trousers, the trajectories of bubbles in beer, a conversation
between supermarket cashiers – which make up what Viart calls the
'marginal, fragmentary notations pulled from everyday reality', for
which, he claims, the story itself is no more than a pretext.[76] As well
as exercising the seldom-used right of narratorial freedom to ignore

the significant and focus on the incidental, these descriptive byways catalogue our urban European environment and lifestyles at the turn of the millennium, often almost literally, with the narrator plunging enthusiastically into extensive lists of items to be found in handbags, glove compartments, gutters, and elsewhere. Echenoz's background in sociology has, by his own account, been influential on this aspect of his writing: 'I did a few years of sociology at university, I always want to mark situations by objects, by discourse systems, by types of exchange.'[77] His working method is to extensively document all aspects of his fiction – he claims to include around one per cent of the background information he gathers in the finished novel[78] – allowing the narrator's curiosity to lead him away from the story on occasion and into a brief torrent of facts about, say, the specifications of transatlantic steamers, or the farming of rubber plantations.[79] Davis and Fallaize note an echo of Barthes's *Mythologies* in the trawl through items with telling significance to the society that produced them, although rather than analysing and demystifying the products of consumer culture, Echenoz simply displays them for our enjoyment, his off-beat descriptions and improbable anthropomorphism rendering the everyday anything but mundane.[80]

A significant number of the signs of the times which distract our narrator are connected by their artificiality. There is the clichéd, formulaic dialogue of game-show hosts and news reporters, brief snatches of which are heard in passing and cut off mid-flow by the text.[81] There are the fake places, like the ersatz place of worship that is the airport 'spiritual centre' in *Je m'en vais*, the artificial lake that gives *Lac* its title, built to complement the soulless luxury of the chain hotel which overlooks it, or the imitative purgatory of *Au piano*, cobbled together from familiar replicas of these same luxury hotels and restaurants, of solicitors' offices and hospital operating theatres, and surrounded by innumerable reduced-size pastiches of the dream homes of all cultures scattered through the park. And there are the fake things and fake situations, like Byron Caine's counterfeit machine in *Le Méridien de Greenwich* and the 'real artifices' of Schmidt's absurd outfit in *Au piano*, which draws so heavily on the clichés of disguise as to leave Max suspecting it is not a disguise at all, or like the shuttle blast-off in *Nous Trois* which turns out to be a simulation and the robbery in *L'Équipée malaise* which is revealed to be a televised reconstruction.[82] The preponderance of fakery has led to inevitable comparisons with the ideas of post-modern theorist Jean Baudrillard, who posits modern society as being a state of 'hyperreality', in which reproduction and imitation efface the authentic to become simulacra, copies of copies of a non-existent original.[83] There is a hollowness to Echenoz's artificial worlds, which chimes with the emptiness of his characters' lives and the futility of their activity. At the same time, this artifice connects the substance of Echenoz's novels back to their form, with its pastiche of genre fiction and its fickle mimicry of narrative conventions. In these asides and digressions, the in-between voyages and becalmed interludes, Echenoz is undermining the novel as we expect it to function, turning away from the linear progress of the plot into the side roads of curiosity. What we discover down these side roads, however, is not just a metafictional critique of traditional storytelling, but an incisive portrait of our shallow, image-ridden society and the busy, empty lives we live within it.

Echenoz has been called the most representative writer of French fiction's supposed 'retour au récit'.[84] On the evidence of this study, such a label is not earned by distance from or rejection of the metafictional experiments of *Tel Quel*, Oulipo and the *nouveau roman*, with all of whom Echenoz has more in common than the other writers we have seen so far. If the label is valid, then it is due to his connection with, rather than his separation from, the previous generation. Like Ernaux, Echenoz was marked by the experimental era in his early attempts to write. He tells *Lire* magazine:

> The novel – the novel form – didn't have a very good press at the time [the late 1970s], we were swimming in theory instead. People didn't talk much about writing novels, fictions, they talked about producing texts. Exploded punctuation, deconstructed narration, etc., it was highly interesting. Alone in my corner, I produced quite a few texts myself. And then, at some point, I must have had enough, I told myself: I'm not going to produce another text, I'm going to try to write a novel.[85]

Echenoz's published writing may not have the exploded punctuation of Sollers's *Paradis*, or the deconstructed narration of Simon's *Les Corps conducteurs*, yet on both counts, as we have seen, his practice is far from orthodox, and has characteristics in common with both writers. He avoids theorizing his work, discussing it with modesty and humour in interviews, and producing, in 'Pourquoi j'ai pas fait poète', the antithesis of a *nouveau roman* polemic, using comic self-deprecation to avoid serious analysis of his own creativity.[86] Echenoz's work retains the imprint of an earlier, more radical approach to the novel: he has learned from their theories, and been given freedom by the new ground opened up by their more extreme practice. He has returned to the story, not through abandoning this heritage, but through employing it in his 'quiet destabilizing' (to use Schoots's term) of the traditional novel, which balances its metafictional interest with a concern for the pleasures of representation and storytelling.[87]

The practice of digression is emblematic of this relationship to literary experiment. It is a deviation from the norms of storytelling, which may lead us to better perceive and question these norms, but it is a deviation which ends by returning us to the narrative line. Echenoz's narrative subversions do not aim to overturn narrative conventions or destroy the traditional pleasures of following a story: they are diversion, not revolution. There is a sporadic element to digressive writing, which makes it unsuitable for totalizing aesthetic systems, but ideal for inventive, throwaway ideas and narrative mischief. Viart suggests that Echenoz writes 'to disturb narratology', impishly undermining the rules and categories set out by the structuralists in the same way that Doubrovsky's *autofiction* sets out to play havoc with the Lejeunian concept of autobiography.[88] The disturbance is not coherent enough to found a new aesthetic of narrative, yet the absence of programme is in itself a liberty. The *nouveaux romanciers'* doctrines limited and homogenized their individual outputs; Echenoz remains as free to write like Balzac as he is free to write like Butor, while of course retaining the option to write like no one else at all. Echenoz finds his place in the vanguard of contemporary French literature, not through radical aesthetic rupture and renewal, nor from serious engagement with the political, psychological or philosophical spheres, but from a recombination of some of the old pleasures of fiction that the experimenters sometimes neglected with some of the new possibilities that their novelistic revolution afforded.

Chapter Five
Patrick Modiano and the Problem of Endings

Of the five authors in this study Patrick Modiano (b.1945) has the longest career as a published writer, beginning with *La Place de l'étoile* in 1968, and has maintained a high literary profile ever since, combining critical acclaim with popularity among the reading public.[1] The twenty-three novels and non-fiction narratives he has so far produced, up to *Dans le café de la jeunesse perdue* in 2007, regularly exceed 150,000 copies in sales; his 1978 Goncourt winner, *Rue des Boutiques Obscures*, sold 470,000.[2] With his other literary prizes including the Prix Fénéon (1968, for *La Place de l'étoile*), the Grand prix du roman de l'Académie Française (1972, for *Les Boulevards de ceinture*), and the Grand prix de littérature Paul-Morand (2000, for his oeuvre to date), he is, even more than Pascal Quignard, at the centre of France's literary establishment. His work reaches broader audiences through his work as a screenwriter for Louis Malle and Jean-Paul Rappeneau, through his children's fiction, as well as through a number of other side-projects, including two collaborations with the illustrator Pierre Le Tan.[3]

Of the twenty-three texts which concern us most closely here, seventeen are subtitled 'roman' and one, the slightly shorter *Fleurs de ruine*, as 'récit'. Of the other five, three, *Livret de famille*, *De si braves garçons* and *Des inconnues*, combine several short narratives under a common theme, and two, *Dora Bruder* and *Un pedigree*, announce themselves as non-fiction, being biography and autobiography respectively. Within and across these different genres, however, the most noticeable aspect of Modiano's writing is its homogeneity. It is a characteristic the author himself acknowledges, admitting on the publication of *La Petite Bijou:* 'I've had the impression for over thirty years that I'm writing the same book – the impression that twenty books published separately in fact form only a single book.'[4] Critics also note the obsessive return to the same themes, the interchangeable characters, and the recurring structures of narra-tive. From the first novel, *La Place de l'Étoile*, we have the first-person retrospective narration by a male narrator exploring his Jewish iden-tity in a menacing atmosphere of anti-Semitism, centring on the Occupation. The second, *La Ronde de nuit*, retains many of these features, while beginning to straighten out the *nouveau-roman*-influ-enced narrative chaos of the first novel into the limpid, classical style and structure that characterizes his later work, and introducing several more elements which will become staples of his writing, such as the precisely mapped Parisian setting, the troubled relationship with absentee parents, the sinister milieu of *demi-monde* or *haut pègre*, largely based on the Rue Lauriston gang with whom Modiano's father was associated, and the perspective of melancholy nostalgia from a time of narrating many years after the events described.[5] By the third novel, *Les Boulevards de ceinture*, the tone is set. The narrator moves between levels of time from a time of narrating approximating Modiano's time of writing, to a primary narrative level years before (here, featuring the narrator's father, a clandestine Jew under the Occupation, his shady associates, and a beautiful and elusive young woman), and, beyond that, to earlier, more nebulous memories which shape the narrator's sense of self and his relationship to his father. The action of the primary narrative level is held within a larger structure of a quest into troubled memory in search of resolution to abiding mysteries and thereby a more stable identity. The ending of the novel presents this quest as, in part at least, a failure, with the investigations inconclusive, and the narrator advised in the closing line that he would do better to think to the future.

The above describes in essence what Akane Kawakami will dub 'the Modiano novel', a uniformity of style, structure and theme, which, she suggests, 'create[s] an effect comparable to that of a popular subgenre, eliciting from the reader the chain response of recognition, anticipation and subsequent fulfilment or disappoint-ment'.[6] Kawakami considers possible reasons for this uniformity, examining whether Modiano's repeated references to his oeuvre as a single book might be taken literally, positing the deliberate creation of his own subgenre, enriched by an expanding network of intertextual echoes, or seeing in the repetition a postmodern suspi-cion of originality, and a renunciation of the modernist demand for rupture and novelty. Less charitable interpretations are noted elsewhere, with John Flower, for instance, pointing out that

Modiano's repetitions have been seen as 'a sign of imaginative weakness' or even 'a conscious exploitation of a formula that guarantees high sales'.[7] Whatever the reason, all of Modiano's subsequent novels can be read as variations on the theme. The first-person male narrator inquiring into his own past will appear in all but three of the subsequent texts, the exceptions being an experiment with impersonal third-person narration (*Une jeunesse*), and three ventures into the use of a female narrative voice (*Des inconnues*, *La Petite Bijou*, and part of *Dans le café de la jeunesse perdue*). The Occupation and the Holocaust are a central concern in *Livret de famille*, *Remise de peine*, *Voyage de noces*, *Fleurs de ruine*, *Chien de printemps*, *Dora Bruder* and *Un pedigree*, and have a symbolic presence in many others, as when, in *Villa Triste*, the Jewish narrator flees the 'round-ups' ('rafles') taking place in Paris during the Algerian war.[8] The shady father will recur in *Livret de famille*, *Remise de peine*, *Fleurs de ruine*, *Un cirque passe*, *Dora Bruder*, *Accident nocturne* and *Un pedigree*, with a similarly troubled relationship to a mother who also resembles Modiano's own appearing in *De si braves garçons*, *Vestiaire de l'enfance*, *La Petite Bijou* and *Dans le café*; the remaining novels without exception give prominent roles to morally ambiguous father-figures and/or menacing *demi-mondains* resembling those of the Rue Lauriston gang. A mysterious and beautiful woman will be the object of the narrator's fascination in many novels; she will usually vanish (*Dimanches d'août*, *Un cirque passe*), less often reappear again later (*Du plus loin de l'oubli*, *Accident nocturne*). All of Modiano's protagonists are rootless and drifting – disorientation is a frequent characteristic, as is a persistent sense of emptiness – and all are seeking fixity through their investigations into the past, looking for 'solid ground under the shifting sands' as the narrator says in *Accident nocturne*, an image Modiano repeats on his own account in the autobiographical *Un pedigree*.[9] As the novels slip between up to four different levels of time, narrators express pessimism about unifying the self by recapturing the past. Yet, over and over in the novels, we encounter a brief episode in which a dream-like state of altered consciousness gives the narrator the impression that different time-periods are merging, and he can re-enter the world of his memories. In *De si braves garçons*, we read: 'this whole evening spent with them in the half-darkness of the terrace was imprinted with the sweetness of a dream. And again, along the empty streets of Neuilly, I thought I heard the clatter of horseshoes and the rustle of leaves from twenty years ago.'[10] These short-lived sensations of 'the transparency of time' contrast with, and sometimes offer consolation for, the lack of resolution to the investigation into memory which drives the plot.[11] At the endings of Modiano's novels, the people searched for often prove to be dead or untraceable, and the settings of the remembered drama have vanished through demolition and redevelopment. The story uncovered has generally reached an ending of a sort, but questions remain unanswered, and those answers we have received are often not entirely consistent with one another. The narrator him-/herself is left feeling unfulfilled by the inconclusive end, ruefully acknowledging the hopelessness of the task, or even expressing regret at having ever taken on the quest, as is the case with Ambrose Guise in *Quartier Perdu*, whose closing words are: 'I too, from this day forward, would like to remember nothing.'[12] Inconclusiveness is one of the most reliable structural aspects of each new Modiano novel to appear, such that the author's regular readers quickly become accustomed to the expectation that they are being led towards an ending, but not towards a conclusion.

The uniformity of Modiano's work is clearly demonstrated by the similarity even of novels with radically different premises. *La Petite Bijou*'s female narrator takes on a similar search into her hazy past to that of her male precursors, recounts it in similar terms, and reaches similar results. The short stories in *Des inconnues* and *Livret de famille* condense similar themes and structures to present the novels in miniature. Most strikingly, the biographical study of Holocaust victim Dora Bruder in the eponymous work, and the memoir of childhood, *Un pedigree*, fit seamlessly into the fictional oeuvre. In both, we are once again presented with a search into the past to fix an identity, based around the streets of Paris and on reproduced letters and documents (genuine in this case) in an atmosphere where rootless, neglectful parents and the menace of the Occupation loom large. In both, the ending foregrounds a sense of inadequacy: the facts of the autobiography have failed to recapture the essence of experience, and the facts of the biography remain elusive.

In truth, the similarity of Modiano's fiction and non-fiction is less remarkable than it might appear. All of Modiano's fiction is to some extent *autofiction*, to borrow Doubrovsky's term once again. As biographical studies by Thierry Laurent and Dervila Cooke suggest, and

Modiano's own *Dora Bruder* and *Un pedigree* confirm, the author's personal experience has always been the basis of his fiction, with the events, relationships and preoccupations of his life transformed to varying degrees in successive novels.[13] As with Annie Ernaux, Modiano's oeuvre moves from apparent fiction to self-declared autobiography, meaning that interesting new light is sometimes cast on earlier narratives by the reappearance of 'fictional' elements from them in a later, non-fiction text. This also, of course, has implications for the analysis of narrative form in Modiano, as structures which might appear to have been arranged for aesthetic reasons may later prove to be determined by real events, as we shall see.

In Modiano's defence against the charge of repetitiveness, even the harshest critic would acknowledge the subtlety and importance of the subjects to which he returns constantly. The entwined themes of memory and identity, how the former shapes the latter, and how memory's failings lead to the fragility of the self, are a topic that twenty-three novels are far from exhausting. The melancholy poetry of Modiano's style, and the haunting indeterminacy of his settings and characters, contribute to a justly celebrated oeuvre. For our own purposes, the homogeneity of Modiano's work offers us the opportunity to conclude this series of author studies with a venture into the furthest reaches of narrative theory, an area, indeed, where the discipline itself threatens to break down as a distinct subsection of literary theory. For if Modiano's works lend themselves to the label of the 'Modiano novel', their endings are just as much 'Modiano endings'. Structurally and thematically, they always have a number of features in common with other texts in the writer's oeuvre, being to an extent predictable to the experienced Modiano reader, and highly distinctive among literary fiction in general. This makes them well suited to a study of the functioning of closure, a treacherous topic in narrative theory, for which the complex interconnections of structure, sense and symbol challenge any notion that form might be extracted from a work to be discussed separately from 'content' and, more troublingly, make us question whether anything in the functioning of endings can be usefully generalized beyond the particularities of an individual text.

Despite being one of the oldest topics in poetics, closure has received scarcely more attention than digression in modern narrative theory.

For Aristotle, as we touched on while discussing Echenoz, the plot of tragedy could be broken down into a complication, during which incidents follow on from the play's opening to a turning point, a change of fortune for the protagonists, after which the plot's unravelling ('λύσις' is the Greek term, root of the English word 'analysis') proceeds to the play's end through the logical consequences of what has gone before.[14] In the recent study of narrative, however, many of the major theorists, including Genette, Wayne Booth, Gerald Prince and Mieke Bal, have little interest in the subject, perhaps due to its categorical slipperiness, being neither a matter wholly of poetics, nor of hermeneutics. If narrative theory is a branch of poetics, then it is concerned with explaining how texts function. In order to do so, it begins with certain assumptions about what the text means – what its effects are – and proceeds from this point to examine how these effects are produced. Thus, if we are exploring how a *récit* presents an underlying *histoire* –the basic premise of many works of narrative theory – then we will need to take an idea of the nature of this *histoire* as our starting point. Studies of literature with a more interpretative, hermeneutic bent will approach from the opposite direction, searching for the meaning or effect of the text from a basis which includes assumptions about its poetics.

Issues of closure, however, defy either approach. The ending of a plot is obviously at least partly a matter of poetics, and indeed attempts have been made to extrapolate general rules about the narrative architecture that produces closure, most famously by Vladimir Propp in his *Morphology of the Folktale*.[15] Propp's method simplifies and divides plots into archetypal 'functions', which are then shuffled and allocated among equally simplified character-types. It is an approach that proves fruitful in analysing the progress and conclusion of folk tales, but apart from these and strongly formulaic genre fiction, it is of little use.[16] In literary fiction, closure is not simply a matter of attaching the predicted final term to a series of familiar elements. Narrative line, as I argued in the previous chapter, is both a succession of events and an accretion of meaning, and in literary fiction neither of these is composed of stock features. We can judge how far the ending of a particular story constitutes closure, according to the relationship between the events and meaning of the final plot segment and those that preceded it. However, in literary fiction, there is no fixed formula of villains to vanquish and princes to marry, nor are we in the halfway house of, say, classic detective fiction, where the structure is formulaic (the unmasking of the culprit and explanation of the crime), but its semantic content is not (since not *any* solution will provide closure). In literary fiction, almost by definition, no generalized formula can decide the level of openness or resolution in the ending, since the unique attributes of the preceding narrative have made the requirements for closure equally unique. Even more than with the issue of digression, then, we are departing from narrative theory in its purest form, since here we are dealing with a matter of the whole text rather than extractable discourse, and of its meaning as much as its technical structure. Armine Kotin Mortimer, at the start of her study of closure, announces that her strategy is a refusal to distinguish between the two senses of the word *fin*: she views closure as a matter of the novel's purpose as well as of its end point.[17] There is a similarly useful polysemy to the English word *conclusion*: closure is as much the logical inference from the narrative's premise as it is the end term of the narrative's sequence.

What are the findings of those literary theorists who do venture into this territory? There is unanimity that the study of closure must entail leaving behind the quasi-scientific objectivity found in other branches of narrative theory. J. Hillis Miller criticizes the structuralist tradition for attempting to 'decode' narrative as if parsing grammar, while neglecting interpretation.[18] His own deconstructionist view of closure is that our analysis must end in aporia, since 'no narrative can show either its beginning or its ending' as it presupposes continuation beyond its limits; its apparently closed-off ending is always vulnerable to reopening by means of a sequel.[19] (While my own study will resist the temptation to follow Miller by declaring the issue intrinsically undecidable and leaving it at that, the question of a re-opening of an earlier text by a later one is a matter to which we shall return.) Kotin Mortimer also distances herself from any attempt at objectivity, by declaring closure to be produced collaboratively between text and reader.[20] In order to study the phenomenon, she proposes, we must acknowledge that we are not analysing the text, but analysing a reading of the text. Clearly, we are far from the kinds of issues with which we began this study, where the chronologies of narrative or the ownership of narrative voice could be specified with confidence.

Frank Kermode's classic study, *The Sense of an Ending*, for which closure in fiction is only one element of a wide-ranging exploration of ending, neglects the technicalities of narrative structure to focus on the 'humanization' of time created in the interval between a story's beginning and end.[21] He symbolizes this with the example of how the listener's mind converts two identical beats from a clock into a tick and a tock, an opening and a close connected by an interval of expectation, and contrasts this with the following interval, from tock to tick, which we do not invest with significance. From this illustration he posits that literature deals, not simply with chronological time, but with 'a significant season ... poised between a beginning and an end', which he labels *kairos*.[22] This idea of the humanly significant interval can be discerned behind many theories of closure. Peter Brooks suggests that our mode of reading fiction can be characterized as the 'anticipation of retrospection', a confidence that what we are reading will prove to have been meaningful once we discover its end point.[23] Jonathan Culler's 'double logic' of narrative form, which we encountered in the chapter on Ernaux, similarly invests the time span between a story's beginning and ending with connective force. Culler's view is that the acknowledged 'forwards' logic of cause and effect within the story recounted is complemented by a hidden, 'backwards' logic in its plot construction, which takes the story's meaningful conclusion as its starting point, and works back through the narrative ensuring the way is prepared. In Culler's example, Oedipus kills his father Laius and marries his mother Jocasta, and is therefore revealed to be guilty at the close of the play, but in the second logic of tragedy, Oedipus's guilt is a precondition of the drama (otherwise it will not be a tragedy), and therefore Laius must be revealed to be his father and Jocasta his mother.[24]

D. A. Miller takes issue with the idea that closure governs the whole text, citing as evidence the two very different endings Dickens wrote for *Great Expectations*.[25] Miller figures narrative in terms of instability and quiescence: what is narratable is in some sense unstable. The opening of a narrative shows a situation out of balance – a wrong to be righted, a lack to be filled – and narration can be sustained until the situation is restored to stability in one way or another, returning us to the non-narratable.[26] For Miller, there is something make-believe about closure: it is a repression, not an absence, of the narratable to give the impression that the suspended significations of the narrative can ever be truly fixed. The traditional novel (Miller's examples are taken from nineteenth-century Realism) dispels the disquieting undecidability of the narrative-in-progress with an implicit guarantee that matters will be fixed by the ending, a guarantee which, since Modernism, literary fiction has withdrawn from its readers. As Marianna Torgovnik points out, however, the open ending beloved of more recent literary fiction, Modiano's included, can be as conventional or formulaic as any. She cites a number of works in which the open ending seems a consequence of 1970s literary fashion, a ready-made stylistic flourish rather than a necessary outcome of the narration or the subject matter.[27]

Torgovnik is one of the few theorists of closure to attempt a methodical dissection of her subject, including definition and taxonomy, and her study offers us some helpful terminology for use in discussing Modiano's work.[28] She suggests that closure is essentially 'a sense that nothing necessary has been omitted from a work', and divides endings into five structural types. The most satisfactorily closed endings demonstrate *circularity* or *parallelism*, depending on whether they refer back to the opening of the narrative or points along its length. Such returns may imply stasis, but they may also show thematic contrasts between the beginning and the end to demonstrate, say, a character's growth. *Incompletion* mimics the previous procedures, but with the omission of some elements necessary for a full sense of closure. Two other forms of open endings are the *tangential* ending, introducing a new topic, or *linkage*, the 'to-be-continued' ending of the *roman-fleuve*. Torgovnik's varieties of openness are helpful distinctions, but it is unfortunate that her conception of closure boils down to a return to earlier parts of the text. Closure indeed requires an *outcome* of something seeded earlier in the story, but it is surely useful to distinguish endings which are simply a development from earlier stages from those which are genuinely a move back towards the opening situation, as is the case with, say, *L'Éducation sentimentale*. Torgovnik's typology also calls to mind the limitations of the structural approach in this area of narrative theory. Perhaps what is important in categorizing closure is not so much the *shape* of the ending, but the success or failure (or Pyrrhic victory) of the protagonist in resolving the problems that formed the premise of the story, a hermeneutic issue that her strictly narratological approach avoids. The ending of *L'Éducation sentimentale* would read rather differently had Frédéric returned to Nogent-sur-Seine with Mme Arnoux at his side, for instance. All these theories of closure, along with certain ideas that we have encountered in previous chapters, like the question-response plot structure of Barthes's hermeneutic code, will be of use to us as we attempt to unravel the functioning and interpret the sense of Modiano's distinctively half-closed endings.

Let us begin with an examination of Modiano's endings in isolation, before integrating them into a more holistic view of the text. Here are the final paragraphs of Modiano's most celebrated novel, *Rue des Boutiques Obscures*:

> *I don't know how long I stayed beside that lagoon. I was thinking about Freddie. No, he was certainly not lost at sea. He had probably decided to cut his last ties and must be hiding on an atoll. I would find him eventually. And then, I had one last step to take: visit my former address in Rome, Via delle Botteghe Oscure, 2.*
>
> *Evening fell. The lagoon was gradually extinguished as its green colour was absorbed. Grey-purple shadows still chased across the water in vague phosphorescence.*
>
> *Without thinking, I had taken out of my pocket the photos of us that I had wanted to show Freddie, and among these, the photo of Gay Orlow as a young girl. I hadn't noticed before that she was crying. You could tell by her frown. For a moment, my thoughts took me far from that lagoon, to the other side of the world and a seaside resort in southern Russia where the photo was taken, long ago. A girl is coming back from the beach at dusk, with her mother. She is crying for no reason, because she would have liked to carry on playing. She moves away. She has already turned the corner of the street, and aren't our lives as quick to melt away into the evening as that child's sorrow?*[29]

We note first of all that the novel ends in close-up rather than overview, to use two more of Torgovnik's terms: we remain in the scene of narrated time, rather than pulling out to an epilogue from the perspective of the time of narrating. Yet this is not exactly a Jamesian final scene, cut off abruptly in mid-flow. The narration in these final lines comes adrift from the narrated moment, looking first to the future in a projected continuation of the narrator's search, and then to the past, in a reverie on a photographic image. Both time-shifts further contribute to a blurring of the scene by their semi-imaginary nature. The backward glance brings the photo to life, and the moving image then becomes the basis for a general comment on life. The forward glance evinces a confidence which the pattern of narrative so far demonstrates as misplaced, and the locations it mentions, an unspecified south sea atoll, the dream-like rue des Boutiques Obscures, seem to set the proposed continuation in an unreal space.[30] The confidence of Guy Roland (the narrator) is further undermined by the retrospective status of the narration: why does he not bring us up to date with the progress or outcome of these projects? We can only suspect that they have come to nothing.

Both the drift towards dream-space and the ill-omened silence from the time of narrating are forces of closure, serving to counteract the 'to be continued' of the protagonist's plans. The scene itself contributes to this: it is a static scene at the other end of the world from the narrator's home, as if his investigation has reached its furthest point. It is almost literally a fade-to-black, as night engulfs the lagoon, which is the kind of rhetorical end-signal that Viktor Shklovsky dubbed 'illusory ending'.[31] The final image, combining dusk, departing figures, and the end of the child's play, echoes the scene before the protagonist, with a further air of finality from its status as a photograph of time long past. Ending is also signalled in the move from description to symbolism with the child's tears, captured in what Philippe Hamon has called a 'clausule', a terse maxim that caps a narrative by evoking themes which resonate through its length.[32] Here the *clausule* shifts the emphasis further still from the proposed continuation of Roland's search: in presenting human life as a fleeting sorrow, something quickly lost and perhaps not even worth recapturing, the narrator may be expressing despair at the human condition or acceptance of it. Whichever interpretation we choose, it is an attitude which suggests Roland's heart is no longer in the continued struggle to rediscover his former identity. It is given weight by its positioning in the final line, and more so by its present-tense verb, making it the only significant element of the novel's end which we can attribute to the later, narrating self rather than the narrated self at the lagoon, as if it were summing up what the events of the novel as a whole have taught him about life.[33]

How typical is the ending of *Rue des Boutiques Obscures* with regard to Modiano's other work? It is, in fact, very representative of the 'Modiano ending', having important aspects in common with all of his other novels. All of Modiano's novels end in 'close-up' on a final scene, often set apart from the narrative by a chronological shift.[34]

The two major elements of the *Rue des Boutiques Obscures* scene, the glimmers of light in surrounding darkness, and the receding human figure, are favourite closing images of Modiano, and recur throughout his oeuvre. *De si braves garçons* ends on an image of moonlit grass shining with 'pale green phosphorescence'; *Vestiaire de l'enfance* closes with distant fireworks sparkling silently in the night sky; the last line of *Du plus loin de l'oubli* refers to a sign on a closed business, 'glowing like a night-light, for no reason'.[35] *Villa triste* and *Livret de famille* both end on a view of someone vanishing into the distance, as does the penultimate chapter of *Fleurs de ruine* and the first story of *De si braves garçons*. Many of these images are explicitly linked to broader themes of loss and memory, as with the small epiphany on the 'transparency of time' in *Vestiaire de l'enfance*, or the comment accompanying the departure in *Livret de famille* that the narrator's baby daughter in his arms 'did not yet have a memory'. *Clausules* are also much in evidence elsewhere. In two cases the novel's title becomes the final words of the novel: signifying lost contentment in *Dimanches d'août*, or the damaged lives of the boarding-school pupils in *De si braves garçons*. Symbolic images, sketched in a few words, are common. *Voyage de noces* makes a metaphor out of the returning tide for the feelings of emptiness and remorse that engulf both protagonists; a rock falling into the sea in *Une jeunesse*, and a casting-off from a collapsing jetty in *Un pedigree* both form closing metaphors for a burdensome past left behind.

The tension we see at the end of *Rue des Boutiques Obscures* between markers of closure and a narrative that posits itself as still in progress is typical of the relationship between Modiano's plots and their endings. An examination of the plot of *La Petite Bijou* will make this relationship clearer. Expanded from one of the short stories of *Vestiaire de l'enfance*, *La Petite Bijou* revisits familiar Modiano territory of an investigation into a troubled past and a difficult parental relationship, carried out by a first-person narrator seeking an affirmed identity and an exorcism of old ghosts, although, in this case, both the narrator and the parent in question are female. In the novel, the narrator's childhood is reawakened when, as an adult, she believes she has caught sight of the mother who abandoned her. Although she trails the woman home, and later lingers outside her apartment, she ultimately fails to make contact with her, leaving her identity in doubt. Further memories are evoked as she becomes a nanny for the neglected daughter of disreputable parents, and as she finds an alternative mother-figure in an older woman friend. In the end, though, when she wakes to new life after a suicide attempt, many questions remain unanswered about the mother's past actions, the unknown woman in the present, and the fragments of childhood which have returned in vague and ambiguous memories.

Readers' expectations (and for the moment, let us consider the expectations of the 'untrained' reader who is not yet familiar with the rules of the Modiano novel) of the course of the coming narrative and its ultimate resolution are strikingly set up from the very start of the story. Here are its opening lines:

A dozen years had passed since I was last called 'la Petite Bijou' and I was in the Châtelet metro station at rush hour. I was in the crowd following the endless corridor on the moving walkway. A woman was wearing a yellow coat. The colour of the coat had attracted my attention and I was looking at her from behind, on the moving walkway. Then she walked along the corridor signed 'Towards Château-de-Vincennes'. Now we were standing still, pressed against each other on the stairs, waiting for the barrier to open. She was next to me. Then I saw her face. The resemblance of this face to my mother's was so striking I thought it was her.[36]

The novel begins with only inches separating the narrator (later named Thérèse) from the woman who appears to be her mother, then struggles to close this gap with a genuine meeting and a resolution of their broken-off relationship. The opening scene is not a recognition scene: Modiano presents a carefully balanced doubt, and the following pages continue to finesse the question, offering the reader first 'the certainty it was her', then the suggestion that the mother may have died 'long ago in Morocco'.[37] It seems a classic case of narrative structured according to the Barthesian hermeneutic code: an enigma has been formulated, and the narrative develops through the clues and red herrings towards the resolution which will assuage our curiosity. Indeed, the narrative does appear to be developing in accordance with Barthes's theory: we seize as evidence the unknown woman's family name of Boré, suspiciously close to Borand, the name of the man who may have been Thérèse's father. At other points, Thérèse's state of mind shakes our faith in her perceptions, raising the possibility of wilfully mistaken identity, as when she projects her own story onto that of the Valadier family for whom she works: 'Véra Valadier's voice had changed ... Perhaps she was thinking of that near future – the years pass so quickly – when her daughter would be grown and she, Véra, would haunt the corridors of the metro for eternity, dressed in a yellow coat.'[38] As each possibility is explored, the narrative seems to be moving towards settling the question, as Thérèse finds the woman's home, learns about her from the concièrge, shares her story with others, and climbs the stairs to the woman's apartment. The subsequent failure to settle the question leaves the hermeneutic thread dangling, in a way that might seem frustrating in a more traditional narrative. Can a story which builds its narrative around questions, then leaves them unanswered, properly be called a story at all? The same might be asked of the equally unresolved subplots: the Valadiers, who vanish, leaving nothing but mystery; the secrets of Thérèse's mother's wartime life; or the narrator's relationship with her pharmacist woman friend, which suggests the possibility of a traditional happy ending in the two women travelling, or even moving in together, only to leave the prospect hanging.

However, if we look more closely at how the narrative of *La Petite Bijou* develops and finishes, it becomes clear that the story is not just a tick without a tock. Even without prior experience of Modiano's penchant for inconclusiveness, the reader is unlikely to consider *La Petite Bijou* incomplete, due to structures of narrative which shape it into a satisfying, in many ways quite conventional story, despite the unanswered questions at its heart. Looking more closely at the enigma of the woman who may be the narrator's mother, we see that it is structured very differently from the enigma at the centre of a traditional mystery narrative. What might be said to be its hermeneutic climax comes when Thérèse reaches the woman's front door, with the intention of ringing the bell, before losing her nerve and fleeing the building. In fact, this scene is not even halfway through the story; in the remainder of the novel, the narrator makes no further visits to the woman's home district and no attempt to contact her. The recounting of the scene itself is at odds with its ostensible hermeneutic role. The physical situation, with the narrator barred by a closed door and the woman perhaps not even home, is a regression from the earlier situation, observing her through the glass of a phone box or a shop window, which is itself a step back from the initial situation, pressed up against her on the metro staircase. The hermeneutic thread of narrative is being counteracted by a symbolic one of increasing distance. And even at the crucial moment, the hermeneutic crux is not the focus of the narrative: rather than asking whether the woman in the apartment is or is not the narrator's mother, the text drifts into childhood memories of a closed door and a failure to make contact:

> *I stood at the door without ringing the bell. Often, when I would come home alone to the big apartment near the Bois de Boulogne and ring, no one would open the door. So I would go down the staircase and phone from a café a little further down the avenue. The owner would look at me kindly, the customers too. They seemed to know who I was. They must have asked about me. One day one of them said, 'it's the girl from number 129'. I had no money and they didn't make me pay for the call. I would go into the phone booth. The telephone on the wall was too high for me and I had to stand on tip-toe to dial the number: PASSY 15 28. But no one would reply ...* [39]

This displacement away from the initial question and into other questions about the narrator's past and present selves, to which the identity of Mme Boré is largely irrelevant, becomes apparent as we proceed through the story. Later in the novel it is made clear that the unknown woman is not so much the object of Thérèse's search as the trigger for a re-evaluation of her own identity:

> *'I have the impression your childhood memories weigh on your mind, he said. It was since the evening when I'd seen the woman in the yellow coat on the metro. Before, I'd hardly given them a thought.* [40]

Displacement is one of the key narrative mechanisms at work in Modiano's open endings. Our initial hermeneutic focus on concrete questions which prove insoluble shifts on to other, more nebulous questions of the self, which by their nature have no clear-cut answer, but which nevertheless are at least partly settled at the denouement. In this case, Thérèse is moved by her encounter with the woman in the yellow coat to revisit her own childhood in memory, and thereby to understand her present sense of pain and abandonment. This new direction in the narrative line is once again driven by our curiosity, but our expectations of closure are much more modest. Closure there certainly is, however, at least in the psychoanalytic sense of the term, as the narrator disinters her repressed anger against her mother and works through it to emotional understanding and what sounds like forgiveness in the regretful fantasy of her mother's lost letters from Morocco:

> *The letters that were sent to me from Morocco must have been left unopened ... They had the wrong address, or a simple spelling error on their envelopes, and that had been enough to send them astray, one after another, in an unknown sorting office. Unless they had been sent back to Morocco, but there was nobody there any more. They had got lost, like the dog.*[41]

With Thérèse's near-death and rebirth, as we have seen, mirroring symbolically the turned page of her obsession with the unknown woman, it is clear that both the openness and the ending have been fashioned carefully. Nothing is neatly tied up, and we are no nearer to resolving the initial mystery than we were on the first page, yet within this melancholy atmosphere of unfinished business, there is narrative structuration at work to round off the reading experience with a sense of closure.

Wherever we look in Modiano's oeuvre, we see searches renounced, unanswered questions displaced by others less clear-cut yet more tractable, and new starts in life which consign past pre-occupations to history. Of course, loose ends abound. Characters vanish without trace, like Sylvia in *Dimanches d'août* or Jansen in *Chien de printemps*. Re-established chronologies leave gaps unaccounted for, such as the aftermath of the failed border crossing in *Rue des Boutiques Obscures*, or Dora Bruder's two *fugues* in the non-fiction text. All of Modiano's work holds characters with secrets: sometimes these are menacing figures from the criminal underworld whose dealings are darkly hinted at, like the shady characters of *Remise de Peine* or *Les Boulevards de ceinture*, sometimes they are victims for some unknown reason in the thrall of such characters, like Marie in *Vestiaire de l'enfance* and many of Modiano's other female leads. Such mysteries incite the narrators into their *recherches*, and determine that these *recherches* will be, to some extent, failures. Yet wherever there is such a failure, the reader is granted hermeneutic compensation through a change in the narrative's priorities. In *Fleurs de ruine*, we quickly become aware that the initial mystery of what went on between M. and Mme T. in 1933 behind closed doors in the rue du Fossé-Saint-Jacques can never be cleared

up, but in the course of the novel attention drifts via linking characters to the narrator's parentage and the narrator himself, leaving
the question of the T.s' suicide seeming less urgent. In *Dimanches
d'août* the displacement seems almost to be one of literary genre; as
Sylvia's kidnap comes to seem unresolvable, the semantic charge of
the event itself shifts away from mystery and towards the tragedy of
loss. The narrator's focus on the intrigues around the stolen
diamond blurs, and nostalgic reminiscences about the narrator's
past relationship with Sylvia come to the fore, culminating in a final
remembered idyll of August Sundays at the beach before the trou-
bles entered their lives. Conversely, when resolutions do come, they
fail to bring with them the expected satisfaction. Guy Roland and
Ambrose Guise shy away from the traumatic past events which their
research restores to memory. Exceptionally, the narrator of *Du plus
loin de l'oubli* rediscovers the woman who vanished from his life
fifteen years earlier, but their reunion is anticlimactic, underlining
the irretrievable nature of their past together. For the habitual
reader of Modiano especially, such disappointments serve to further
weaken the hermeneutic desire established at the novels' openings.

Other narrative strategies foreshadow the novel's inconclusiveness to limit the reader's expectations of closure. In *La Petite Bijou*,
for instance, on two occasions the narrator evokes distant voices
from unknown speakers, first on the foreign radio stations to which
Moreau-Badmaev listens in the darkness and later on crossed lines
as Thérèse calls her mother's old telephone number. The distance
and anonymity of these voices, and the lack of communication in
both cases, must remind the reader of Thérèse's struggle to re-enter
into communication with her mother and her own past, and the
mood they cast over the main narrative can only be one of
pessimism. Elsewhere in Modiano's oeuvre, demolished buildings
play a similar role, signalling to the reader the unrecoverable nature
of the past before the protagonist has grasped this, as in the
opening of *Villa Triste*, which begins: 'They knocked down the hôtel
de Verdun.'[42] The very reality of the remembered past is sometimes
called into question. In *Voyage de noces* memory merges with dreams:
'Like that envelope. Had it existed in reality? Or was it just an object
that was part of my dream?'[43] In *Dimanches d'août* it blurs with
fiction: 'It was no longer very real. Even the blood which had
spurted from his lip and covered his chin did not seem to be real
blood but a film effect.'[44] Such strategies doubly undermine the

hermeneutic drive behind narrative, by suggesting at once that clear answers are unlikely to be found in such fallible material, and that the very search for truth may be inappropriate if the quality of memory is more like a dream or a film than a historical archive.

When the denouement comes, formal or symbolic means may supply an alternative sense of an ending to that which a neater plot resolution might have offered. Torgovnik's circularity and parallelism are common structural features. *Les Boulevards de ceinture* ends with the narrator's return, years later, to the Seine-et-Marne village where the primary narrative took place, to find only a photo of its major players in a bar and the barman's vague speculations as to what became of them, just as a return to his old boarding school by the adult narrator will close the schoolboy tales of *De si braves garçons*. *Du plus loin de l'oubli* offers parallelism in its ending with the possibility that the narrator is about to discover Jacqueline for the third time, after a second interval of fifteen years.[45] Combined with the symbolic closure to be found in the images and *clausules* of the type which we saw in the final lines of *Rue des Boutiques Obscures*, such closed structures create a powerful sense of the narrative's return to stasis, which the unanswered questions do little to disturb. With previous experience of the 'Modiano novel', readers' familiarity with displaced questions, renunciation of quests that prove too difficult or traumatic, and the narrator's sense of moving on into a new stage of life, will enhance the satisfactions of an inconclusive ending which was our expected destination.

Mention of the effect of the wider oeuvre on the reading of a particular text brings us back to J. Hillis Miller's point about the provisional nature of closure. For Miller, an implicit 'could be continued' remains in all narrative endings, which may be realized in the form of a sequel, retrospectively weakening the sense of an ending in the earlier text. None of Modiano's novels have sequels in the conventional sense, yet each new text will overlap with and expand upon the universe of its predecessors in a close textual relationship analogous to a narrative continuation. There is even an aspect of development as Modiano's oeuvre goes forward. Narrators in more recent novels are generally older than in the earlier ones, shadowing the ageing author; early preoccupations with the Occupation, Jewish identity, the father and his associates, become less central, and themes of lost love and lost youth gain prominence with a shift from the 1940s to the 1960s as the principal backdrop. These connections between works become particularly interesting when we revisit the same material via a new genre. *Voyage de noces* closes with a slightly modified version of the 1941 newspaper clipping which will open the non-fiction *Dora Bruder*: a desperate *petite annonce* placed by the parents of a teenage girl on the run. In the later work, Modiano explains the genesis of the former in his obsession with the unknown story behind the clipping:

> *It seemed that I would never manage to find the slightest trace of Dora Bruder.*
> *So the lack that I felt gave me the impetus to write a novel,* Voyage de noces,
> *as good a way as any to continue to focus my attention on Dora Bruder, and*
> *perhaps, I told myself, to elucidate or guess something about her, somewhere*
> *she had been, a detail of her life.*[46]

Thus, seven years after its original publication, *Voyage de noces* becomes the first volume of a diptych, in which the runaway girl's story is rendered both through fantasy and through fact, creating an interesting parallel with another study of a childhood during the Holocaust, Perec's *W ou le souvenir d'enfance*.[47] The case of Ingrid Teyrsen (Dora Bruder's fictional alter ego in *Voyage de noces*) is closed at the end of the story by the *petite annonce*, which explains to the narrator her secret trauma. When the case is reopened in *Dora Bruder*, the clipping becomes the author-narrator's starting point, and our understanding of the earlier text is altered by the knowledge of the historical truth at its heart: Modiano himself notes how an insignificant passage in the earlier book becomes charged with meaning when he discovers an unwitting link to Dora's real story.[48]

The most striking reopenings of Modiano's narratives, however, are highly personal ones, as material from his fiction reappears in autobiography. *Un pedigree* is a patchwork of elements from the whole of Modiano's previous oeuvre, now presented as being as much reminiscence as creativity. Names recur, like Stioppa, Gay Orloff and McEvoy, attached to people similar but not identical to their previous fictional incarnations.[49] We revisit locations like the ruined chateau of *Remise de peine* or the Annecy boarding school of *Des inconnues* (which transforms it from a boys' to a girls' school).[50] And we return to incidents from the fiction, like the vice-squad interrogation that opened *Un cirque passe* or the performance to an empty theatre of

Vestiaire de l'enfance.[51] One novel which seems particularly affected by this revisiting is *Accident nocturne*, published two years before *Un pedigree*, with which it has a large number of similarities. In both, the narrator recalls the childhood incident of a pet dog being run over on the rue du Docteur-Kurzenne; in both, this is associated with another road accident, in which the narrator is hit by a van while walking home from school.[52] The texts have names (such as Morawski) and places (such as Sologne) in common, and common portraits of a father who sees his son only through intermittent rendezvous in cafés and a mother who leaves her son in the care of a young woman.[53] The narrator's decision at the denouement of *Accident nocturne* to abandon his obsessive research and live in the present is belied by the very similar search carried out in the author's own name in his next book, which, incidentally, also presents its research into memory as an attempt to have done with the past in order to move on. It remains to be seen whether, for Modiano, such a form of closure can ever be more than temporary.

The problem of ending in Modiano is that his texts resist classification, being both closed and open, both classically satisfying and dangling with loose ends. The problem of ending for narrative theory is that closure depends on meaning as much as form, and indeed renders it difficult to distinguish between the two. These are not, in fact, two distinct problems, but one and the same. The endings of Modiano's texts have closed and open aspects, not from an arbitrary aesthetic choice on the writer's part, but because of what his novels *mean*: the ending they reach is determined by the conclusions at which they arrive.

Modiano's novels are studies of memory and identity, and studies of how identity is informed by memory. Our present self is to a large extent the product of memory, not only because an awareness of our past gives us understanding of how we came to be who we are, but also because memory is at the centre of our inner life, supplying our dreams and imagination, and shading our current perceptions with connotations from past experience. Remembering in Modiano is a mental struggle which is never wholly successful. Voluntary memory brings back fragments of clarity jumbled with vague images, uncertain facts and gaps of forgetfulness, as illustrated by this recalled tableau in *Fleurs de ruine*:

We were left alone in the living room for a few minutes, and I am trying to bring together as many details as possible by an effort of memory. The French windows which gave onto the boulevard were half-open due to the heat. It was number 19, boulevard Raspail. In 1965. A grand piano at the back of the room. The sofa and the two armchairs in the same black leather. The silver coffee table. A name like Devez or Duvelz. The scar on her cheek. Her unbuttoned blouse. A very bright light from a spotlight or a torch. It lights up only a small part of the scene, an isolated moment, leaving the rest in shadow, for we will never know how events unfolded and who exactly these two people were.[54]

Modiano's verbless syntax emphasizes the disjointed nature of the recalled impressions, which fail to cohere into a full description. The metaphor of the beam of light is very reminiscent of Proust's view of voluntary memory, 'this kind of patch of light, cut out against indistinct darkness'.[55] However, unlike in Proust, the more powerful involuntary memory, which compensates for the failings of voluntary memory, remains frustratingly elusive in Modiano: 'The more I looked at its white façade, the more I felt I had seen it before, a fleeting sensation like the shreds of a dream that escape you when you wake, or reflected moonlight.'[56]

With the unreliable functioning of memory in Modiano and the distressing nature of the events to be recalled, the narrators suffer the predicament of straining to piece together a past which may only bring them pain. Kawakami suggests the passive nature of Modiano's protagonist-narrators and their lack of clear personality traits makes them a kind of degree-zero narrator, striving 'to gain – or to regain – a basic but essential sense of their own transient identities'.[57] This incomplete personality is very much emphasized by the texts themselves. Sometimes it is the narrator's key characteristic and the narrative's driving force, as with the amnesiac narrators of *Rue des Boutiques Obscures* and *Quartier perdu*. Often it is in the recurring theme of a void at the heart of the self, evoked through symbols like the statue-less plinth of *Vestiaire de l'enfance*, or discussed in detail, as the narrator does in the same novel:

The feeling of the void invaded me, even more violent than usual. It was familiar to me. It would take hold of me, as others are taken by bouts of malaria ... Out of everything I may have felt during the years I was writing my books in Paris, this impression of absence and emptiness is the strongest. It is like a halo of white light that prevents me from making out the other details

of my life at that time and which muddles my memories. Now I know the way
to get beyond this dizziness. I have to repeat to myself softly my new name:
Jimmy Sarano, my date and place of birth, my work schedule, the names of
the colleagues at Radio Mundial I'll meet that day, the outline of the chapter
of The Adventures of Louis XVII *that I'm going to write, my address,*
33 Mercedes Terrace, in short, I have to grasp onto all these landmarks in
order not to be sucked up by what I can only call: the void.[58]

Modiano's narrator-protagonists are not whole people. They are cut
off from a past which they nevertheless yearn to recapture and be
reconciled with. But memory is an inadequate tool to achieve these
aims, and their other investigations – searching archives for documents or revisiting locations – are a derisory substitute. By the end
of their stories, the past has to some extent been brought to light
and the tale has been told to the satisfaction of the reader, or at least
of the initiated reader whose personal horizon of expectations is
adapted to the Modiano novel. Yet, as we have seen, gaps remain in
the story, and the narrative's failure to provide closure is the
narrator's failure to unify past and present into an unimpaired identity. The basic philosophy of Modiano's work is that the past is not
fully recoverable, and the self cannot therefore be made complete.
This view of human nature naturally finds its expression in the
open-ended narrative – indeed, it is difficult to imagine how such
an outlook could be successfully expressed in a more traditionally
structured story. The form of the narrative is itself part of the means
of expression of the writer's worldview, as the petering out of the
investigation, and the dangling threads at the end of the story,
demonstrate the unrecovered self more vividly than any discussion
of the theme within the work.

Once again, then, in Modiano we have seen an employment of narrative form which refuses the *lisibilité* of classic or conventional fiction,
but which is nonetheless a step back from the radicalism of Claude
Simon's generation of French writers. Once again, the use of narrative form is determined by the novel's human drama to a greater
extent than was the case in many experimental novels of the 1950s,
1960s and 1970s. Modiano is less interested in questions of narrative
representation and its relationship to reality, than he is in finding the
form to complement his understanding of the human condition.

This positioning within the literary sphere is very much a deliberate one, and Modiano, more than any of the writers we have seen
so far, is keen to define his own position in opposition to that of the
experimenters. He describes the *Tel Quel* group as 'Martians' and
decries the *nouveau roman* as having 'no tone or life'; he declares he
has no interest in any 'experimental school' nor in 'literature for its
own sake, research into writing'.[59] Rather, Modiano sees his literary
heritage coming from writers in the early twentieth century, whose
humanistic concerns connect more closely to his own, even if his
generation no longer produces the sustained, monolithic works
through which they expressed them:

> *I often feel that people in my generation have a weakness compared to those of*
> *the previous generation: our powers of concentration are less strong. The*
> *previous generation managed to create a global work, a kind of cathedral. I*
> *think of Proust or Lawrence Durrell, his Alexandria Quartet. These people*
> *lived in a world where you could concentrate more, while for people in my*
> *generation, it's fragmentary. You might manage to make something global,*
> *but out of fragments, if you like …*[60]

The image of a novelist who has been largely untouched by the
metafictional turn in literary culture during his early development
as a writer is encouraged by the author, and agreed upon by certain
critics, such as Colin Nettelbeck, who sees in Modiano a cultivation
of the old-fashioned (writing his novels by hand, labelling novel-
writing itself a 'retro' occupation in the information age), and in his
melancholy themes of slow, quiet disintegration a lineage that stems
from Verlaine and Valéry.[61] Kawakami considers this image to be
somewhat deceptive, arguing that Modiano's writing is essentially
postmodernist through its elements of parody, especially of the
detective story, its preference for the popular over the elitist, and its
'gently and ironically experimental' aspects in such areas as its shuffled chronologies, its empty narrators and its 'unreality effect' from
an over-abundance of opaque names and details.[62] But can
Modiano be said to have taken direct influence writers like Alain
Robbe-Grillet (as Kawakami also claims he has)?[63] There are
certainly parallels: novels like *Le Voyeur* or *La Maison de rendez-vous*
offer us open endings with inconclusive investigations, unusual
chronologies and questions around the issue of identity. Yet it would
be misleading to make too much of such similarities between

oeuvres that are very different in their techniques and preoccupations. Perhaps the most important legacy of the experimenters' generation for Modiano's work is their reshaping of the literary landscape into which he emerged, and their refashioning of the tastes and expectations of the readership to whom he is speaking. Modiano's open-ended quest narratives play more dangerous games with readers' expectations than pre-war novelists had dared to attempt. Henry James's later novels may break off mid-scene, but do so only at a resonant line of dialogue uttered at a point when the drama has reached its natural conclusion. Even Gide, who gives to his character Édouard the line, '"Could be continued", it is with these words that I should like to end my *Counterfeiters*', is rather more conventional in the ending of his own version of the novel.[64] As Armine Kotin Mortimer points out, besides Édouard's writing, all the major plotlines of Gide's novel have been tidily closed off, through circularity, death, a return to reason or a resolution of problems.[65] Gide invites the reader to see his ending as a refusal of closure, thereby resisting a basic falsification in literature's representation of life, yet, by current standards, his practice is by no means as open as it might be, or as his metafictional commentary might suggest.[66] Modiano's novels leave many more questions unanswered and pathways unexplored than Gide's, and what is more, do so within the framework of investigation narratives that raise a much stronger expectation of and desire for hermeneutic resolution. Yet Modiano can seem to us the very opposite of radical experimentalism, gaining mainstream commercial success and a critical reputation as a classic storyteller. This can partly be ascribed to the homogeneity of his oeuvre, of course, which over time becomes comfortably familiar, but is also, without a doubt, due to his presence in the wake of the radical generation, who expanded the limits of fiction and thereby enlarged the middle ground.

The Return to the Story

In an interview marking the publication of *La Possibilité d'une île* (2005), Michel Houellebecq, France's best-selling literary novelist and the only writer of his generation to achieve major fame beyond the French-speaking world, told the *Nouvel Observateur:* 'You must believe that I count myself in the tradition of those French writers who ask questions of today's world and do not renounce Balzacian narration.'[1] Frédéric Beigbeder, author of similarly provocative and successful critiques of contemporary mores, recalls in his 9/11 memoir, *Windows on the World*, meeting Alain Robbe-Grillet, then aged 80, near the scene of the attacks:

> '*Why come to New York to write about it ?' the great novelist asks, stroking his white beard. 'When I write a novel set in Berlin, I don't go to Berlin to write it.'*
>
> '*It's because I'm writing the Old Novel. I leave the new one to young people like you.*'[2]

Like the five writers of this study, they are unashamed to draw attention to the traditional aspects of their work, and distance themselves from the aesthetic of rupture espoused by the experimenters' generation. Their work, however, is unmistakably part of the post-experimental culture that exploits the new norms of formal innovation for its own purposes. Houellebecq's *La Possibilité d'une île* (2005), for instance, divides the narrative between its contemporary protagonist and 'commentaries' by three far-future clones of himself who read through his text at the same time as we do. His *Extension du domaine de la lutte* calls for new narrative forms to represent contemporary life:

> *This gradual obliteration of human relations is not without certain problems for the novel. How indeed might one undertake the narration of those fiery passions, lasting several years, sometimes making their effects felt over several*

generations? The least you can say is that we are a long way from Wuthering Heights. *The novel form is not designed to represent indifference or nothingness; we need to invent a flatter, more concise and dreary mode of expression.*[3]

Beigbeder's Old Novels equally owe some of their liberties to the New. *99 francs* (2000) narrates each of its six sections through a different person of the verb, before finally dissolving into a stream of advertising slogans; *Windows on the World* itself combines fiction, essay and autobiography, as well as poetry and other non-novelistic discourses, in sections timed minute by minute through the morning of 11 September, even at one point mimicking the shape of the World Trade Center in the columns of text. Yet neither of these writers would call himself an experimental novelist, nor would their readers and critics, by whom these narrative flourishes often pass uncommented, dream of doing so. The palette of narrative techniques has expanded and the avant-garde innovations of fifty years ago now sit comfortably in mainstream fiction. They are no longer innovations, and they are no longer either the *raison d'être* behind the writing of the novel they find themselves in, or its principal characteristic apparent to the reader.

In our case studies, we have seen writers who retain a strong interest in the possibilities of narrative, and who remain inventive in the manner in which they present their stories. Ernaux uses the dual timelines of narrative – that of the time of narrating and that of the narrated time – to explore the different effects of the story recounted when the relationship between these timelines alters. At the same time, she exploits the chronological division for her own feminist and socio-historical purposes, dividing herself into a present writer and a past everywoman in order to generalize from her experience. Quignard fragments his narratives and mixes them with poetry and essay-forms as he circles the inexpressible in his meditations on time, love and art. He is the only writer of the five whose work might truly be called experimental, yet he is distanced from the earlier generation by his hatred of systems, his returns to ancient literatures from other cultures, and his acknowledgement of the continuing need for connectivity and coherence, be it in the classic realism of his most famous novels, or in the themes of melody and hunting which symbolize the central human importance of narrative in his more reflective writing. Narrative form in

Darrieussecq is informed by her particular conception of how the mind works, and a desire to represent consciousness vividly and immediately on the page. What results is a reinvention of the stream of consciousness that brings it closer to the original psychological definition of the term, and an innovative narrative discourse that recounts the surface impressions of the mind instead of analysing its depths. Echenoz wears his influences from the experimental generation more openly, yet favours irreverent play over adherence to doctrines. His digressive, unpredictable narratives retain a metafictional element in their parody of literary conventions, yet are more a celebration of the possibilities of storytelling than a critique of its founding assumptions. Modiano, finally, gains immense success with novels that are less straightforward than his reputation suggests. His typical fade-out endings, leaving his plots to a large extent unresolved, refuse one of the most fundamental aspects of narrative: its development towards a natural conclusion. That such novels can nevertheless situate themselves in the mainstream of fiction suggests how the experimenters' legacy has changed expectations of the novel.

Through the five studies we have seen the uses of narrative theory in analysing the way stories work, in describing how narrative incorporates time and how its chronologies interact, in noting the types of narrative and non-narrative discourse employed and identifying the boundaries between them, or in unpicking the use of focalization and narrative voice which determine the perspective from which the reader apprehends the story. But we have also seen the limits of the discipline in circumstances where formal elements of narrative become inextricably bound up with the interpretation of the story, as when the topic of digression forces us to decide what is significant in a narrative and what is tangential, or when the issue of closure proves the structure of a story and its meaning are not always clearly distinct from one another. Narrative theory is an invaluable tool, but it is clear that, as a self-contained discipline set apart from conventional literary criticism, it is incapable of giving us access to some of the most fundamental aspects of narrative structure. Literary analysis will always be an art as well as a science, and when the impersonal methods of 'narratology' falter, more traditional and subjective modes of interpretation are required to take us deeper into the workings of the text.

Three of our five writers visibly performed their own *retour au récit* in the early days of their writing careers, with Modiano's *La Place de l'étoile*, Echenoz's *Le Méridien de Greenwich*, and Ernaux's unpublished *Du soleil à cinq heures* all bearing the mark of formalist influence, from which they proceeded to distance themselves in subsequent texts. Their shifts are roughly contemporaneous with other returns carried out in late career by experimentalists like Sollers and Robbe-Grillet, or in mid-career by writers who have a substantial oeuvre in both camps, of which Le Clézio is perhaps the best-known example.[4] All five of the case studies insert themselves into a literary landscape in which formalism and radical experiment have become rare, in which schools and movements have been replaced by flourishing individualism, and in which the form of the telling has been reintegrated with the story to be told. French authors today appear less interested in questions of narrative representation and its relationship to reality, than they are in finding the form to complement their theme, be it the nature of time or their understanding of the human condition. Where certain writers of the previous generation might deliberately choose a banal, clichéd or pastiched *histoire* to be transformed by the dazzling innovations of the *récit*, now the use of narrative form is far more likely to be determined by the novel's human drama. The adventure returns to prominence over the writing. Far from signalling the end of the creative use of narrative form, however, the *retour au récit* continues to foster new ways of telling stories. They are perhaps less radical than formerly, but they are also less gratuitous, as the new possibilities afforded by the experimenters' generation, shorn of their restrictive doctrines, are exploited by contemporary writers in the service of their view of the self and of the world.

Notes

Introduction

1 'Retour à l'Histoire (H majuscule), retour aux histoires (h minuscule), retour au sujet (après la description de tant d'objets), retour à la "création", retour à "l'œuvre", retour aux personnages, à l'intrigue, au récit. Nous avons désormais toutes les libertés', Maurice Nadeau, 'L'État des lieux' (editor's introduction), *La Quinzaine littéraire*, 16 May 1989, no. spécial, 'Où va la littérature française?', 3–4 (p. 3).

2 'Tout le monde est à peu près d'accord, en effet, pour un "retour au récit", mais le récit n'est pas un lieu de rendez-vous sans ambiguïté pour ceux qui ne l'ont jamais quitté, d'une part, et pour ceux, dont je suis, qui en sont un peu sortis pour aller voir, du dehors, de quoi il était fait, et ce que l'on pouvait en faire encore', *La Quinzaine littéraire*, 8.

3 'Ce qui caractérise le plus profondément peut-être la nouvelle littérature postmoderne, c'est la renarrativisation du texte, c'est l'effort de construire de nouveau des récits', Aron Kibédi-Varga, 'Le Récit postmoderne', *Littérature*, 77 (February 1990), 3–22 (p. 16).

4 '[R]éinvestissement dans une tradition élargie, qui embrasse à la fois Faulkner et Proust, Diderot et Sterne', Jean-Claude Lebrun and Claude Prévost, *Nouveaux Territoires romanesques* (Paris: Messidor, 1990), p. 43.

5 'Au long de cette décennie, l'on assiste néanmoins, dans le domaine romanesque, à un retour en grâce du récit et de la fiction. Ceux-ci ne sont plus alors perçus comme d'artificielles et gratuites constructions divertissantes (telles que les avaient fustigées les nouveaux romanciers), mais comme l'animation d'un univers imaginaire où il serait possible d'interroger et de ressaisir le sens du monde', Jean-Michel Maulpoix, *Histoire de la littérature française – XXe siècle, 1950/1990* (Paris: Hatier, 1991), p. 406.

6 Dominique Viart, *Le Roman français au XXe siècle* (Paris: Hachette, 1999), p. 125 ('Retours au récit'); Anne Cousseau, 'Postmodernité: du retour au récit à la tentation romanesque', *Études sur le roman du second demi-siècle*, cahier no. 1 (2002), 5–17; Dominique Combe, 'Retour du récit, retour au récit (et à Poésie et récit)', *Degrés: Revue de Synthèse à Orientation Sémiologique*, 111 (Autumn 2002), b1–b16.

7 Marie-Claire Bancquart and Pierre Cahné, *Littérature française du XXe siècle* (Paris: Presses Universitaires de France, 1992), p. 443; Yves

Baudelle, 'Les Grandes Lignes de la littérature française depuis 1945', in Frank Baert and Dominique Viart (eds), *La Littérature française contemporaine: questions et perspectives* (Leuven/Louvain: Presses Universitaires de Louvain, 1993), pp. 35–46 (p. 37); Bruno Blanckeman, *Les Récits indécidables: Jean Echenoz, Hervé Guibert, Pascal Quignard* (Villneuve d'Ascq: Presses Universitaires du Septentrion, 2000), p. 14; Olivier Bessard-Banquy, *Le Roman ludique: Jean Echenoz, Jean-Philippe Toussaint, Éric Chevillard* (Villneuve d'Ascq: Presses Universitaires du Septentrion, 2003), p. 33; Henri Godard, *Le Roman modes d'emploi* (Paris: Gallimard, 2006), pp. 413–35.

8   Colin Davis and Elizabeth Fallaize, *French Fiction in the Mitterrand Years: Memory, Narrative, Desire* (Oxford: Oxford University Press, 2000), p. 14.

9   '[C]ette période où, d'une manière générale, on assiste au reflux de la poussée avant-gardiste des trois décennies précédentes, et en particulier de celle, extrême et extrémiste, des années soixante-dix. Le Sollers de *Nombres*, de *H*, ou de *Lois*, se détend et s'assagit dans *Femmes* ou *Portrait d'un joueur*. Robbe-Grillet se fait autobiographe tout en continuant à passer par la fiction. Une nouvelle génération d'écrivains hérite des expériences romanesques récentes et cherche en même temps à s'en démarquer', Pierre Brunel, *Glissements du roman français au XXe siècle* (Paris: Klincksieck, 2001), p. 31.

10 'Les pratiques expérimentales et textualistes qui dominent la scène littéraire à la fin des années 70 sont parvenues à leurs plus extrêmes limites. La notion même du "roman" s'y est perdue au profit de celle, plus générale, de "texte" ... De tels livres confinent à l'illisibilité et n'atteignent plus le public. L'idéologie du "nouveau" pousse à la surenchère et finit par ne plus proposer d'autre légitimation que son aspect innovant, indépendamment même de ce qu'il peut avoir à dire. Toute ésthétique qui se déclare d'avant-garde pose la nécessité d'une rupture avec les "formes anciennes". En finir avec ces surenchères suppose de rompre avec une telle pratique. C'est l'événement majeur des deux dernières décennies du siècle', Viart, *Le Roman français au XXe siècle*, pp. 113–14.

11 Jean Ricardou, *Pour une théorie du nouveau roman* (Paris: Seuil, 1971), p. 32.

12 '[I]l semble que l'on achemine de plus en plus vers une époque de la fiction où les problèmes de l'écriture seront envisagés lucidement par le romancier, et où les soucis critiques, loin de stériliser la création, pourront au contraire lui servir de moteur', Alain Robbe-Grillet, 'A quoi servent les théories' (1955), in *Pour un nouveau roman* (Paris: Minuit, 1961), pp. 7–13 (p. 11).

13 Michel Butor, 'Réponses à *Tel Quel*', in *Essais sur le roman* (Paris: Gallimard, 1992), pp. 173–84 (p. 176); first published in *Tel Quel*, 11 (Autumn 1962).

14 'Le soupçon, qui est en train de détruire le personnage et tout l'appareil désuet qui assurait sa puissance, est une de ces réactions morbides par lesquelles un organisme se défend et trouve un nouvel

équilibre. Il force le romancier à s'acquitter de ce qui est, dit Philip Toynbee, rappelant l'enseignement de Flaubert, "son obligation la plus profonde: découvrir la nouveauté", et l'empêche de commettre "son crime le plus grave: répéter les découvertes de ses prédécesseurs"', Nathalie Sarraute, 'L'Ère du soupçon' (1950), in *L'Ère du soupçon* (Paris: Gallimard, 1956), pp. 57–79 (p. 79).

15 'Open a dictionary at the words "potential literature". Nothing there. A regrettable omission', François Le Lionnais, 'La Lipo (le premier manifeste)', in Oulipo, *La Littérature potentielle* (Paris: Gallimard, 1973), pp. 15–18 (p. 15).

16 Ibid., p. 17.

17 '[C]ontraintes, programmes ou structures alphabétiques, consonnatiques, vocaliques, syllabiques, phonétiques, graphiques, prosodiques, rimiques, rhythmiques et numériques', François Le Lionnais, 'Le Second Manifeste', in Oulipo, *La Littérature potentielle*, pp. 19–23 (pp. 19–20).

18 Hélène Cixous, 'Le Rire de la Méduse', *L'Arc*, 61 (1975), 39–54.

19 '[D]étermine et surtout, mot d'époque, surdéterminera toute l'histoire du roman français jusqu'à aujourd'hui', Jean-Pierre Salgas, '1960–1990: Romans mode d'emploi', in Yves Mabin (ed.), *Le Roman français contemporain* (Paris: Publications de la Ministère des Affaires Étrangères, 1993), pp. 5–37 (p. 10).

20 '[C]'est bien un *roman*, en ceci que le procès narratif y est à la fois radiographié et porté au-delà de lui-même. C'est un roman qui vise à rendre impossible l'exploitation romanesque et ses effets mystifiants', Philippe Sollers, 'Introduction: écriture et révolution', in *L'Écriture et l'expérience des limites* (Paris: Seuil, 1968), pp. 5–7 (p. 6).

21 '[V]oix fleur lumière écho des lumières cascade jetée dans le noir chanvre écorcé filet dès le début c'est perdu plus bas je serrais les mains fermées de sommeil et le courant s'engorgea redevint starter le fleuve la cité des saules soie d'argent sortie du papier jute lin roseau riz plume coton dans l'écume 325 lumen de lumine en 900 remplacement des monnaies 1294 extension persane après c'est tout droit jusqu'à nos deltas ma fantaisie pour l'instant est de tout arrêter de passer les lignes à la nage brise matin feu lacs miroirs ...', Philippe Sollers, *Paradis* (Paris: Seuil, 1981), p. 7.

22 Alain Robbe-Grillet produced three volumes of 'romanesque' autobiography: *Le Miroir qui revient* (1985), *Angélique, ou l'enchantement* (1988) and *Les Derniers Jours de Corinthe* (1994); Sarraute's *Enfance* was published in 1983, and Duras's *L'Amant* the following year. Sollers's *Un Vrai Roman* appeared in 2007.

23 Fieke Schoots, *Passer en douce à la douane: l'écriture minimaliste de Minuit* (Amsterdam: Rodopi, 1997), p. 101.

24 This study will borrow Genette's terminology for the three key elements of narrative he discerns: *histoire* for the events of the story as they might be summarized, regardless of the perspective or chronological order of their recounting; *récit* for the narrative discourse through which the events of the *histoire* are presented to us; and

narration for the recounting itself by the narrative voice. Gérard Genette, 'Discours du récit: essai de méthode', in *Figures III* (Paris: Seuil, 1972), pp. 65–282 (p. 72).

25　'[L]e récit n'a jamais été absent des ouvrages de texture romanesque, jusque dans les pires heures de la littérature expérimentale des années 1970. Tout au plus le souci narratif s'effaçait-il devant d'autres priorités', Bessard-Banquy, *Le Roman ludique*, p. 33.

26　'[V]ieilles recettes du roman balzacien', Nadeau, 'L'État des lieux', p. 4.

27　'Ils acceptent la portée critique des réflexions dont il a été l'objet'; 'un dialogue *critique* avec le passé culturel', Viart, *Le Roman français au XXe siècle*, p. 114.

28　Eli Flory, 'La Rentrée littéraire au banc d'essai', *Le Magazine des livres*, September–October 2007, 4–11 (p. 4).

29　Editorial, *La Quinzaine littéraire*, 1–15 October, 1978, 4.

30　'[L]e produit d'une étude de marché et d'une stratégie commerciale fondée sur une énorme effort de promotion.' Yves Baudelle, 'Les Grandes Lignes de la littérature française depuis 1945', in Frank Baert and Dominique Viart (eds), *La Littérature contemporaine: questions et perspectives* (Leuven/Louvain: Presses universitaires de Louvain, 1993), pp. 35–46 (p. 40).

31　See, for instance, Dominique Rabaté, 'Résistances et disparitions', in Guichard and others, pp. 9–46 (p. 11).

32　Lebrun and Prévost, *Nouveaux Territoires romanesques*, p. 14; Flory, 'La Rentrée littéraire', p. 5.

33　Tzvetan Todorov, *La Littérature en péril* (Paris: Flammarion, 2007).

34　Pierre Jourde, *La Littérature sans estomac* (Paris: L'Esprit des péninsules, 2002), pp. 13–24.

35　Lebrun and Prévost, *Nouveaux Territoires romanesques*, p. 30.

36　Bruno Blanckeman, *Les fictions singulières: étude sur le roman français contemporain* (Paris: Prétexte, 2002), p. 6.

37　Fieke Schoots, *Passer en douce à la douane: l'écriture minimaliste de Minuit* (Amsterdam: Rodopi, 1997), and Warren Motte, *Small Worlds: Minimalism in Contemporary French Literature* (Lincoln, NE: University of Nebraska Press, 1999) discuss the phenomenon.

38　Pierre Brunel, *Où va la littérature française aujourd'hui?* (Paris: Vuibert, 2002), p. 233.

39　'Pourquoi la littérature respire mal', in *Préférences* (Paris: José Corti, 1961), pp. 71–104 (p. 77).

1 Annie Ernaux and the Narrating of Time

1　Ernaux labels her style 'écriture plate' in *La Place* (Paris: Gallimard, 1983), p. 24.

2　Lyn Thomas, *Annie Ernaux: An Introduction to the Writer and her Audience* (Oxford and New York: Berg, 1999), p. x.

3　Ibid., pp. 134, 136.

4　Isabelle Charpentier, 'Anamorphoses des réceptions critiques d'Annie Ernaux: ambivalences et malentendus d'appropriations', in

Fabrice Thumerel (ed.), *Annie Ernaux: une oeuvre de l'entre-deux* (Arras: Artois Presses Université, 2004), pp. 225–42 (p. 226).

5   '[U]ne forme de critique – qui ne peut être qualifiée de polémique, tant elle est dépourvue d'idées et d'arguments – convoquant le corps, le mode de vie, l'origine sociale et l'appartenance de l'écrivain au sexe féminin pour néantiser son livre', Annie Ernaux, Preface to Thumerel (ed.), *Annie Ernaux*, pp. 7–10 (p. 8).

6   'En aucun cas, on ne lira ces pages comme un témoignage objectif sur le "long séjour" en maison de retraite, encore moins comme une dénonciation', Annie Ernaux, *Je ne suis pas sortie de ma nuit'* (Paris: Gallimard, 1997), p. 12; *Une femme* (Paris: Gallimard, 1987), pp. 23, 106.

7   Warren Motte, *Small Worlds: Minimalism in Contemporary French Literature* (Lincoln, NE: University of Nebraska Press, 1999), p. 57.

8   Fabrice Thumerel, 'Avant-propos', in Thumerel (ed.), *Annie Ernaux*, pp. 11–36 (p. 13).

9   The texts in question are *La Place* and *Une femme*.

10 Chloë Taylor Merleau, 'The Confessions of Annie Ernaux: Autobiography, Truth and Repetition', *Journal of Modern Literature*, 28 (2004), 65–88 (p. 75); Siobhán McIlvanney, *Annie Ernaux: The Return to Origins* (Liverpool: Liverpool University Press, 2001), p. 176.

11 'C'est toujours la chose à dire qui entraîne la façon de le dire, qui entraîne l'écriture, et la structure du texte aussi ... Je ne pourrais pas dire vraiment que je cherche à rénover la forme du récit, je cherche plutôt à trouver la forme qui convient à ce que je vois devant moi comme une nébuleuse – la chose à écrire –, et cette forme n'est jamais donnée par avance', Annie Ernaux and Frédéric-Yves Jeannet, *L'Écriture comme un couteau: entretien avec Yves Jeannet* (Paris: Stock, 2003), pp. 53–4.

12 Annie Ernaux, Michèle M. Magill and Katherine S. Stephenson, 'Entretien', in Michèle M. Magill and Katherine S. Stephenson, *Dit de femmes: entretiens d'écrivaines françaises* (Birmingham, AL: Summa, 2003), pp. 73–88 (p. 83).

13 *Se perdre* (Paris: Gallimard, 2001), for instance, contains numerous references to Proust, including pp. 86, 97, 112, 184, 200, 264, 286, and one to Beauvoir on p. 355. Beauvoir is also discussed in *Les Années* (Paris: Gallimard, 2008), pp. 95, 125, and several other texts. Camus appears in *Les Armoires vides* (Paris: Gallimard, 1974), p. 156 and *Ce qu'ils disent ou rien* (Paris: Gallimard, 1977), p. 81.

14 '[J]'avais une vision solipsiste, antisociale, apolitique, de l'écriture. Il faut savoir qu'au début des années soixante, l'accent était mis sur l'aspect formel, la découverte de nouvelles techniques romanesques', *L'Écriture comme un couteau*, p. 75.

15 Annie Ernaux and Pierre-Louis Fort, 'Entretien avec Annie Ernaux', *The French Review*, 76 (2003), 984–94 (p. 991); *L'Écriture comme un couteau*, p. 97.

16 Ernaux mentions her *nouveau roman* lectures in *Se perdre*, p. 71.

17 '[L]a certitude – largement partagée, un cliché désormais – qu'on ne peut pas écrire après eux comme on l'aurait fait avant, et que

l'écriture est recherche et recherche d'une forme, non reproduction. Donc pas non plus reproduction du Nouveau Roman ...', *L'Écriture comme un couteau*, p. 97.

18 '[J]'accorde maintenant au langage une fonction comme le Nouveau Roman, c'est à dire, se débarrasser d'idéologies ... La recherche est sur deux fronts, c'est l'écriture moyen d'action sur le monde, mais l'écriture est une production humaine comme le reste ... c'est une institution ... donc si on se sert de l'institution, ça va remettre en cause. L'écriture peut être sexiste, l'écriture est idéologique', Ernaux, Magill and Stephenson, pp. 83–4.

19 Alain Robbe-Grillet, 'Sur le choix des générateurs', in *Nouveau Roman: hier, aujourd'hui II: Pratiques*, ed. by Jean Ricardou and Françoise van Rossum-Guyon (Paris: UGE, collection '10/18', 1971), pp. 157–62 (p. 160); 'mais je ne suis quand même pas dans ces romans-là, de toute façon!', Ernaux, Magill and Stephenson, 'Entretien', p. 83. Other declared influences on Ernaux's writing include Céline, Flaubert, Sartre, Perec and Sarraute (Ernaux and Fort, 'Entretien avec Annie Ernaux', p. 991). She also demonstrates an awareness of autobiographical writers past and present, citing Rousseau, Michel Leiris and Serge Doubrovsky, and declares an interest in literary theory, mentioning Barthes, Genette, Goldmann, Blanchot and Starobinsky (*L'Écriture comme un couteau*, pp. 90–2). Her writing is strongly influenced by sociological theory, in particular Pierre Bourdieu, whose terminology of dominant and dominated social classes is much in evidence in Ernaux's own social critique.

20 *La Place*, p. 29; *Les Armoires vides*, p. 12.

21 'Faut-il se déterminer toujours par rapport au "roman"? Ce qu'on appelle roman ne fait plus partie de mon horizon ... Les prix littéraires continuent de consacrer le roman à tour de bras – ce qui est moins une preuve de sa vitalité que de son caractère institutionalisé – mais quelque chose d'autre est en train de s'élaborer, qui est à la fois en rupture et en continuité avec des oeuvres majeures de la première moitié du XXe, celle de Proust, de Céline, les textes surréalistes ... Dans les propos courants sur les livres, le mot "roman" circule avec un sens de plus en plus étendu. Il y a des défenseurs hystériques de la "fiction". Mais au bout du compte, le label, le genre, n'ont aucune importance, on le sait bien. Il y a seulement des livres qui bouleversent, ouvrent des pensées, des rêves ou des désirs', *L'Écriture comme un couteau*, pp. 55–6.

22 Genette, 'Discours du récit', p. 228. The time of narrating is not to be confused with 'narrative time', Genette's *temps du récit*, which refers to the order, speed and frequency with which events are rendered in the text, relative their putative chronology in the world of the story (*temps de l'histoire*).

23 Genette, 'Discours du récit', pp. 233–4.

24 *Narration antérieure*, in which future events are recounted, and *narration simultanée*, in which the two times coincide, are the other possibilities, both of which are also found to some extent in Ernaux.

25 'le désir de montrer le temps réel de l'écriture du livre, sans les préparatifs, les abandons, de l'entrée définitive dans le projet jusqu'à son aboutissement', *L'Écriture comme un couteau*, p. 127.

26 Ibid.

27 *Une femme*, pp. 21, 43, 103.

28 'Toutes les heures, je fais des ciseaux, de la bicyclette, ou les pieds au mur. Pour accélérer', *Les Armoires vides*, p. 11.

29 The titles underscore this companion status, since *'Je ne suis ...'* is a quotation from *Une femme*, and the initials of *Se perdre* invert those of *Passion simple*, which are themselves the initials of the lover himself.

30 *Journal du dehors* (Paris: Gallimard, 1993), pp. 88–90; *Se perdre*, pp. 247–62, 310.

31 *Se perdre*, p. 102.

32 *Ce qu'ils disent ou rien* is the only one of Ernaux's texts to displace its narrator from the author's working-class origins, moving to a more middle-class background in which the *café-épicerie* does not feature.

33 *Une femme*, p. 105; *La Place*, pp. 113–14. The final anecdote in *La Place* concerns a former pupil of Ernaux's, whom she discovers working in her local supermarket, having dropped out of college. The first line of this concluding paragraph dates the encounter as occurring 'in October last year'. Immediately below the paragraph, the dates 'novembre 1982–juin 1983' mark the time of writing.

34 'Dans la semaine qui a suivi, je revoyais ce dimanche, où elle était vivante, les chaussettes brunes, le forsythia, ses gestes, son sourire quand je lui avais dit au revoir, puis le lundi, où elle était morte, couchée dans son lit. Je n'arrivais pas à joindre les deux jours. Maintenant, tout est lié', *Une femme*, p. 103.

35 'Je ne peux pas décrire ces moments parce que je l'ai déjà fait dans un autre livre, c'est-à-dire qu'il n'y aura jamais aucun autre récit possible, avec d'autres mots, un autre ordre des phrases', ibid., p. 73.

36 *Lisibilité* ('readerliness') is a term coined by Barthes to denote writing that, among other characteristics, obsessively connects, completes and unifies. See *S/Z*, in *Oeuvres complètes*, ed. by Éric Marty, 5 vols (Paris: Seuil, 2002), III, pp. 119–345 (p. 206).

37 Alison S. Fell, 'Recycling the Past: Annie Ernaux's Evolving *Écriture de Soi*', *Nottingham French Studies*, 41 (2002), 60–9 (pp. 62–4).

38 'Je sens que le récit m'entraîne et impose, à mon insu, un sens, celui du malheur en marche inéluctablement. Je m'oblige à résister au désir de dévaler les jours et les semaines, tâchant de conserver par tous les moyens – la recherche et la notation des détails, l'emploi de l'imparfait, l'analyse des faits – l'interminable lenteur d'un temps qui s'épaississait sans avancer, comme celui des rêves', *L'Événement* (Paris: Gallimard, 2000), p. 48.

39 '[N]aturellement pas de récit, qui produirait une réalité au lieu de la chercher', *La Honte* (Paris: Gallimard, 1997), p. 40.

40 'Je ne fais pas le récit d'une liaison, je ne raconte pas une histoire (qui m'échappe pour la moitié) avec une chronologie précise, "il vint le 11 novembre", ou approximative, "des semaines passèrent". Il

n'y en avait pas pour moi dans cette relation, je ne connaissais que la présence ou l'absence. J'accumule seulement les signes d'une passion, oscillant sans cesse entre "toujours" et "un jour", comme si cet inventaire allait me permettre d'atteindre la réalité de cette passion', *Passion simple* (Paris: Gallimard, 1991), p. 31.

41 Nelson Goodman, 'Twisted Tales; or, Story, Study and Symphony', in W. J. T. Mitchell (ed.), *On Narrative* (Chicago: University of Chicago Press, 1980), pp. 99–115 (pp. 114–15); first published in *Critical Inquiry*, 7 (1980–1), 103–19.

42 'Je ne savais pas vers quoi je filais, comme dans les romans-feuilletons, et même dans *L'Étranger*, je me souviens, il y avait écrit, c'était comme quatre coups brefs qui frappaient sur la porte du malheur, mais je ne pouvais pas me le dire puisque je ne me doutais de rien, de savoir la suite maintenant ça me fausse tout', *Ce qu'ils disent ou rien*, p. 81.

43 'Ces dangers et ces limites, donc, sont à peu près les mêmes que l'on rencontre dans tout discours rétrospectif sur soi. Vouloir éclaircir, enchaîner ce qui était obscur, informe, au moment même où j'écrivais, c'est me condamner à ne pas rendre compte des glissements et des recouvrements de pensées, de désirs, qui ont abouti à un texte, à négliger l'action de la vie, du présent, sur l'élaboration de ce texte ... Ce que je redoute, en parlant de ma façon d'écrire, de mes livres, c'est, comme je vous le disais, la rationalisation *a posteriori*, le chemin qu'on voit se dessiner après qu'il a été parcouru', *L'Écriture comme un couteau*, pp. 16–17.

44 'Et aussi ce rêve troublant: une petite fille en maillot de bain a disparu (et est retrouvée ensuite, morte?). Il y a reconstitution avec la petite fille, *vivante*, qui part se promener. Le fait qu'elle soit vivante à nouveau va permettre de savoir ce qui s'est passé. Mais c'est très difficile, parce qu'*on connaît l'issue*. (Très juste.) Rêve qui est l'image du romanesque, de l'écriture: on connaît la fin', *Se perdre*, p. 363.

45 Jonathan Culler, *The Pursuit of Signs* (London: Routledge, 1981), p. 198. For Culler, the double logic is primarily concerned with the question of whether the *histoire* invents the *récit* or vice versa. Here, the issue is more one of the selection of events than their invention, but the basic premise holds: is the shape of the narrative determined by the events of Ernaux's life, or is the selection of events determined by the requirements of the narrative itself? We shall return to Culler's theory later in this study, in the chapter on Modiano.

46 '[L]es événements se produisent dans un sens et nous les racontons en sens inverse', Jean-Paul Sartre, *La Nausée* (Paris: Gallimard, 1938), p. 65.

47 *Journal du dehors*, p. 8.

48 'Je m'aperçois qu'il y a deux démarches possibles face aux faits réels. Ou bien les relater avec précision, dans leur brutalité, leur caractère instantané, hors de tout récit, ou les mettre de côté pour les faire (éventuellement) "servir", entrer dans un ensemble (roman, par exemple). Les fragments, comme ceux que j'écris ici, me laissent

insatisfaite, j'ai besoin d'être engagée dans un travail long et construit (non soumis au hasard des jours et des rencontres). Cependant j'ai aussi besoin de transcrire les scènes du R.E.R., les gestes et les paroles des gens *pour eux-mêmes*, sans qu'ils servent à quoi que ce soit', *Journal du dehors*, p. 85.

49 *'Je ne suis pas sortie de ma nuit'*, p. 12. The complete sentence seems to conflict with what Ernaux has written elsewhere about intermittent narration, and so deserves to be quoted in full: 'Being unaware of what was to follow – which characterizes all writing perhaps, and certainly mine – took on in this case a frightening aspect.' ('Cette inconscience de la suite – qui caractérise peut-être toute écriture, la mienne sûrement – avait ici un aspect effrayant.') Ernaux here maintains a distinction between the 'effrayant' diary narrrative and retrospective narration, but claims an element of 'inconscience' to both, a statement which contradicts her remark quoted earlier on 'l'image du romanesque, de l'écriture: on connaît la fin' (see above). Ernaux admits there are 'inévitables contradictions' (*L'Écriture comme un couteau*, p. 13) in her ideas on writing across a thirty-year career. Her remark here reminds us that, while the material may be fixed in advance in retrospective autobiography, the selection and representation of it may be an adventure that unfolds as the writing of the text proceeds.

50 'Longtemps, j'ai pensé que je ne le publierais jamais. Peut-être désirais-je laisser de ma mère et de ma relation avec elle, une seule image, une seule vérité, celle que j'ai tenté d'approcher dans *Une femme*. Je crois maintenant que l'unicité, la cohérence auxquelles aboutit une oeuvre – quelle que soit par ailleurs la volonté de prendre en compte les données les plus contradictoires – doivent être mises en danger toutes les fois que c'est possible', *'Je ne suis pas sortie de ma nuit'*, pp. 12–13.

51 '[D]ans le stupeur et le bouleversement que j'éprouvais alors', ibid., p. 13.

52 'Sans doute pourrais-je attendre avant d'écrire sur ma mère. Attendre de m'être évadée de ces jours. Mais ce sont eux la vérité, bien que je ne sache pas laquelle', ibid., p. 110.

53 'En face de nous, une femme décharnée, spectre de Buchenwald, est assise, très droite, avec des yeux terribles. Elle relève sa chemise, on voit la couche-culotte appliquée sur son sexe. Les mêmes scènes à la télé font horreur. Pas ici. Ce n'est pas l'horreur. Ce sont des femmes', ibid., p. 25.

54 'De plus en plus maigre. A chaque visite, il y a toujours un détail qui me bouleverse, focalise l'horreur. Aujourd'hui, c'était ces grandes chaussettes brunes qu'on leur met, montant jusqu'aux genoux, et qui, trop lâches, retombent sans cesse. Mon geste étrange: relever sa blouse pour voir ses cuisses nues. Elles sont atrocement maigres', ibid., p. 98.

55 'Un peu gigolo: il me boit une demi-bouteille de Chivas, me réclame le paquet de Marlboro entamé. Mère et pute, je suis les deux. J'ai

toujours aimé tous les rôles'; 'Je lui ai rapporté des cigarettes Marlboro, une cartouche en free-tax. Il en extirpe un paquet aussitôt (il n'avait donc pas de cigarettes sur lui? habitude de se servir chez moi) et il n'oubliera pas la cartouche en partant'; 'J'aime qu'il vienne sans cigarettes – exprès? – et me demande s'il peut emporter le paquet. Moi: "Prends l'autre aussi." "Oui?" Il empoche les deux sans autre problème de conscience. Gigolo au quart ...'; 'En rafale, le dégrisement. Le voir comme un play-boy – ou gorby-boy! – brutal (pas trop cependant) et jouisseur (pourquoi non). Me dire que j'ai perdu un an et demi pour un homme qui, en partant, me demande s'il peut prendre le paquet de Marlboro ouvert, sur la table', *Se perdre*, pp. 151, 163, 207, 223.

56 '[U]ne vérité brute, instantanée, contradictoire, qui s'exprime plus librement parce qu'elle n'entre pas dans la cohérence d'une oeuvre', Annie Ernaux and Fabrice Thumerel, 'Ambivalences et ambiguïtés du journal intime: entretien avec Annie Ernaux', in Fabrice Thumerel (ed.), *Annie Ernaux*, pp. 245–51 (p. 247).

57 '[C]omme si ce dernier *m'autorisait* à le faire, comme s'il fallait que la vie soit devenue "forme", forme littéraire concertée, avec un coefficient de généralité, pour que je la livre ensuite dans son immédiateté, son caractère informe', Annie Ernaux and Philippe Lejeune, 'Un singulier journal au féminin', in Fabrice Thumerel (ed.), *Annie Ernaux*, pp. 253–8 (p. 258).

58 *Une femme*, pp. 99, 102.

59 'En quelques semaines, le désir de se tenir l'a abandonnée. Elle s'est affaissée, avançant à demi courbée, la tête penchée. Elle a perdu ses lunettes ...', ibid., p. 97.

60 Ibid., pp. 96, 102–3.

61 'Souvent, j'écrivais sur une feuille la date, l'heure, et "il va venir" avec d'autres phrases, des craintes, qu'il ne vienne pas, qu'il ait moins de désir. Le soir, je reprenais cette feuille, "il est venu", notant en désordre des détails de cette rencontre', *Passion simple*, p. 18.

62 '[F]ournir toutes les pièces,' *L'Écriture comme un couteau*, p. 39.

63 Alain Girard, *Le Journal intime* (Paris: Presses Universitaires de France, 1963), p. 568; 'dans le quotidien et dans la perspective que le quotidien délimite', Maurice Blanchot, *Le Livre à venir* (Paris: Gallimard, 1959), p. 252.

64 '[L]a forme livre n'est pas faite pour le journal. Publier un journal, c'est vouloir faire entrer une éponge dans une boîte d'allumettes', Philippe Lejeune, *Signes de vie: le pacte autobiographique 2* (Paris: Seuil, 2005), pp. 94–5.

65 '[B]ien sûr, chaque séquence raconte, etc., mais ce n'est pas construit comme un récit avec un début, un milieu et une fin – aucun phénomène de séquence comme l'analysent Barthes, Brémond ou d'autres: *il est écrit dans l'ignorance de sa fin*', ibid., pp. 66–7 (Lejeune's emphasis).

66 '[L]e temps impose la structure, et la vie immédiate est la matière. C'est donc plus limité, moins libre, je n'ai pas le sentiment de

"construire" une réalité, seulement de laisser une trace d'existence, de *déposer* quelque chose, sans finalité particulière, sans délai aucun de publication, du pur *être-là*', *L'Écriture comme un couteau*, p. 23.

67 *Se perdre*, pp. 26, 41, 172.

68 Paul Ricoeur, *Temps et Récit II: la configuration dans le récit de fiction* (Paris: Seuil, 1984), pp. 159–60.

69 Ibid., pp. 164–5. Müller's term is discussed by Ricoeur.

70 The reader only partly shares the narrator's perspective in the diary texts, since Ernaux's prefaces provide us with a foreknowledge of the ending about which the diary-narrator is ignorant.

71 Annie Ernaux and Marc Marie, *L'Usage de la photo* (Paris: Gallimard, 2005), pp. 60, 64; pp. 85, 89.

72 Ibid., pp. 134–5, 162–3.

73 Ibid., pp. 47, 51.

74 '[R]endre les mots et les phrases inébranlables, les paragraphes impossibles à bouger', *L'Usage de la photo*, p. 62; 'J'ai peur de découvrir ce qu'il écrit. J'ai peur de découvrir son altérité, cette dissemblance des points de vue que le désir et le quotidien partagé recouvrent, que l'écriture dévoilera d'un seul coup', p. 196.

75 '[L]'écriture sous les photos, en multiples fragments – qui seront eux-mêmes brisés par ceux, encore inconnus en ce moment, de M. –, m'offre, entre autres choses, l'opportunité d'une *mise en récit minimale* de cette réalité', *L'Usage de la photo*, pp. 76–7.

76 Ibid., pp. 30, 32.

77 Ibid., p. 196.

78 '[U]n dispositif de "triangulation" pour évoquer quelque chose de finalement indicible', Ernaux and Lejeune, 'Un singulier journal au féminin', in Thumerel (ed.), *Annie Ernaux*, pp. 253–8 (p. 255).

79 Even here, perhaps, choice of discourse cannot be separated from time of narrating. Arguably, the underlying contrast between *Ce qu'ils disent ou rien* and subsequent representation is that between a teenage narrator recounting her recent past and a mature narrator reflecting on her more distant youth. For an exploration of issues other than the time of narrating involved in Ernaux's revisitings, see Alison Fell's article, cited above.

80 Tiphaine Samoyault, 'Agenda, addenda: le temps de vivre, le temps d'écrire', in Thumerel (ed), pp. 71–8 (p. 74).

81 'Je ne pensais pas à la fin de mon livre. Maintenant, je sais qu'elle approche … Bientôt je n'aurai plus rien à écrire', *La Place*, p. 101.

82 'Je passe de l'imparfait, ce qui était – mais jusqu'à quand? –, au présent – mais depuis quand? – faute d'une meilleure solution. Car je ne peux rendre compte de l'exacte transformation de ma passion pour A., jour après jour, seulement m'arrêter sur images, isoler des signes d'une réalité dont la date d'apparition – comme en histoire générale – n'est pas définissable avec certitude', *Passion simple*, p. 66n.

83 '[P]ar un effort de la conscience critique', *Les Années*, p. 238.

84 '[L]es signes de ce qui m'attendait réellement, je les ai tous négligés', *La Femme gelée* (Paris: Gallimard, 1981), p. 123.

85   '[À] dix ans, les choses sont énormes, on patauge, on ne voit rien, le manque d'expérience', *Les Armoires vides*, p. 90.

86   *La Honte*, pp. 51, 134.

87   'La femme que je suis en 95 est incapable de se replacer dans la fille de 52 qui ne connaissait que sa petite ville, sa famille, et son école privée, n'avait à sa disposition qu'un lexique réduit. Et devant elle, l'immensité du temps à vivre. Il n'y a pas de vraie mémoire de soi', *La Honte*, p. 39.

88   *L'Usage de la photo*, p. 193.

89   'Écrire a été une façon de sauver ce qui n'est plus déjà ma réalité, c'est-à-dire une sensation me saisissant de la tête aux pieds dans la rue, mais est devenu "l'occupation", un temps circonscrit et achevé', *L'Occupation* (Paris: Gallimard, 2002), pp. 73–4.

90   'Alors que je peux me rappeler exactement tout ce qui est associé à ma relation avec A., les émeutes d'octobre en Algérie, la chaleur et le ciel voilé du 14 juillet 89, même les détails les plus futiles, comme l'achat d'un mixer en juin, la veille d'un rendez-vous, il m'est impossible de relier la rédaction d'une page précise à une pluie battante ou à l'un des événements qui se sont produits dans le monde depuis cinq mois, la chute du mur à Berlin et l'exécution de Ceauçescu. Le temps de l'écriture n'a rien à voir avec celui de la passion', *Passion simple*, pp. 60–1.

91   An early exception to this rule is *Ce qu'ils disent ou rien*, rather unexpectedly, since neither its teenage protagonist nor the teenage narrator are writers in any real sense. Its two references to Anne's abortive attempts to write her life story (pp. 64, 106), each time as a third-person autofiction and each time abandoned as inauthentic, recount an aspect of the protagonist's life that Ernaux's adult narrators are reluctant to acknowledge.

92   *Se perdre*, p. 211.

93   *Je ne suis pas sortie de ma nuit'*, pp. 11–12.

94   These anxieties are recounted in *Se perdre*, pp. 184, 211.

95   '[I]ls ont ce qu'ils méritent, ils m'ont fait trop chier à être comme ils étaient', *Les Armoires vides*, p. 177.

96   Ibid., pp. 89, 99; *Ce qu'ils disent ou rien*, pp. 51–2.

97   '[*Les Armoires vides*] sera lu par la critique comme un roman, par les lecteurs comme un roman autobiographique. Pas comme un roman par mes proches, évidemment. En première lieu ma mère, qui vivait alors chez moi. Avec beaucoup d'intelligence mais aussi de soumission devant la violence que je lui infligeais – elle a dû souffrir énormément à cause de ce livre – elle a joué le jeu, fait comme si tout était inventé … Elle avait souhaité que j'écrive, elle n'avait pas imaginé que ce serait ça, un livre qui n'avait rien à voir avec ce qu'elle aimait, l'amour – "la romance" comme elle disait –, et tout avec le réel, avec notre vie, le commerce, avec elle', *L'Écriture comme un couteau*, p. 27.

98   In *Passion simple*, Ernaux recounts S. telling her, 'tu n'écriras pas un livre sur moi', p. 76. The avoidance is thus not absolute, but even this example denies any importance of her writing self to her relationship: the following line claims she has borne out his words.

99 See *L'Écriture comme un couteau*, p. 137.
100 '[U]ne crainte que je ne m'en prenne à elle de façon violente ou retorse, que je fasse un esclandre', *L'Occupation*, p. 29.
101 The incident is described in Thomas, *Annie Ernaux*, p. 158.
102 Merleau, 'The Confessions of Annie Ernaux', p. 83.
103 'En dehors de ses obligations de travail, cours et copies, son temps est consacré à la gestion de ses goûts personnels et de ses désirs, lecture, films, téléphone, correspondance et aventures amoureuses', *Les Années*, p. 175.
104 Ibid., p. 179.
105 'Je me demande si, comme je le fais, ne pas séparer sa vie de l'écriture ne consiste pas à transformer spontanément l'expérience en description', *L'Usage de la photo*, p. 112.
106 'Je ne *suis* pas écrivain, j'écris, puis je vis', *Se perdre*, p. 299; 'Je ne me pense jamais écrivain, juste comme quelqu'un qui écrit, qui *doit* écrire', *L'Écriture comme un couteau*, p. 19.
107 'Là, je pouvais prendre le temps d'apprivoiser cet espace, de faire surgir du vide ce que je pense, cherche, éprouve quand j'écris – ou tente d'écrire – mais qui est absent quand je n'écris pas', *L'Écriture comme un couteau*, p. 12.
108 'Nous continuons les prises de vue ... Mais il me semble que nous ne regardons plus de la même façon le spectacle que nous découvrons, qu'il n'y a plus cette douleur qui nous poussait à fixer la scène. Photographier n'est plus le *dernier* geste. Il appartient à notre entreprise d'écriture. Une forme d'innocence est perdue', *L'Usage de la photo*, p. 171.
109 Ibid., p. 76.
110 'Je ne fais pas l'amour comme un écrivain, c'est-à-dire en me disant que "ça servira" ou avec distance. Je fais l'amour comme si c'était toujours – et pourquoi ne le serait-ce pas – la dernière fois, en simple vivante', ibid., p. 32.
111 '[L]e piège de l'individuel', *La Place*, p. 45; 'une sorte d'autobiographie impersonelle', *Les Années*, p. 240; 'J'ai évité le plus possible de me mettre en scène et d'exprimer l'émotion qui est à l'origine de chaque texte', *Journal du dehors*, p. 9.
112 '[C]e n'est plus *mon* désir, *ma* jalousie, qui sont dans ces pages, c'est *du* désir, *de la* jalousie', *L'Occupation*, p. 48.
113 '[U]n livre sur lui, ni même sur moi'; 'Je me demande si je n'écris pas pour savoir si les autres n'ont pas fait ou ressenti des choses identiques, sinon, pour qu'ils trouvent normal de les ressentir', *Passion simple*, pp. 76, 65.
114 *L'Écriture comme un couteau*, p. 151.
115 'Dans tous ces textes, il y a la même *objectivation*, la même mise à distance, qu'il s'agisse de faits psychiques dont je suis, j'ai été, le siège, ou de faits socio-historiques. Et, dès *Les Armoires vides*, mon premier livre, je ne dissocie pas intime et social ... Quand j'écris, tout est chose, matière devant moi, extériorité, que ce soit mes sentiments, mon corps, mes pensées ou le comportement des gens dans

le RER. Dans *L'Événement*, le sexe traversé par la sonde, les eaux et le sang, tout ce qu'on range dans l'intime, est là, de façon nue, mais qui renvoie à la loi d'alors, aux discours, au monde social en général', *L'Écriture comme un couteau*, pp. 152–3.

116 These shifts even affect grammatical agreements, as when Ernaux writes of herself as a parent in the 1960s: 'on ne se résolvait pas à … se montrer nus devant ses enfants', and then, six lines later (in a new paragraph): 'Le suicide de Gabrielle Russier nous avit bouleversées' (p. 110). The 'nus' in the first sentence is masculine, used to refer to both men and women; 'bouleversées' in the second refers to women only.

117 'J'ai mis de moi-meme beaucoup plus que prévu dans ces textes', *Journal du dehors*, p. 9.

118 'les signes d'une condition partagée avec d'autres', *La Place*, p. 45.

119 'à la jointure du familial et du social, du mythe et de l'histoire'; 'des images purement affectives', *Une femme*, pp. 23, 52.

120 Ernaux, Magill and Stephenson, 'Entretien', p. 75.

121 '[D]es *organisations inconnues* d'écriture'; 'des texts dont la forme meme est donnée par la réalité de ma vie', *L'Usage de la photo*, p. 76.

122 *Se perdre*, pp. 222, 240, 277; *Passion simple*, p. 76; *L'Usage de la photo*, p. 196.

2   Pascal Quignard and the Fringes of Narrarive

1 The eleven books were *Albucius*, *La Raison*, *Sur le doigt qui montre cela*, and the eight volumes of the *Petits Traités*.

2 '[V]oix de basse de la grande littérature française', Sjef Houppermans, Christine Bosman Delzons and Danièle de Ruyter-Tognati (eds), *Territoires et terres d'histoire: perspectives, horizons, jardins secrets dans la littérature française d'aujourd'hui* (Amsterdam: Rodopi, 2005), Introduction, p. 11.

3 Quignard's translation, *Alexandra de Lycophron* (Paris: Mercure de France, 1971, 2nd edn 2001) is the text which sold sixty-eight copies in ten years, as he mentions in an interview, 'Pascal Quignard: Écrire n'est pas un choix, mais un symptôme', *La Quinzaine Littéraire*, 1–15 November 1990, 17–19 (p. 17); Quignard details the *Traités'* publication difficulties on the back cover of the Folio edition; critical reception of *Les Ombres errantes* is discussed in an interview with Jean-Louis Ezine, 'Quignard: L'Aveu', *Le Nouvel Observateur*, 6–12 January 2005, 54–6 (p. 54).

4 '[L]a représentation d'un événement ou d'une suite d'événements, réels ou fictifs, par le moyen du langage, et plus particulièrement du langage écrit', Gérard Genette, 'Frontières du récit', in *Communications*, 8 (1966), 158–69 (p. 158).

5 See, for instance, Gerald Prince, *Narratology: The Form and Functioning of Narrative* (Berlin: Mouton, 1982), p. 4, or Mieke Bal, *Narratology: Introduction to the Theory of Narrative*, 2nd edn (Toronto: University of Toronto Press, 1997), p. 4.

6 Bal, *Narratology*, p. 8.
7 'Eugène commençait à se sentir très mal à l'aise'; 'une de ces maisons légères, à colonnes minces, à portiques mesquins, qui constituent le *joli* à Paris, une véritable maison de banquier', Honoré de Balzac, *Le Père Goriot* (1834, published 1835) (Paris: Gallimard, coll. Folio, 1971), pp. 104, 192.
8 Mikhail Bakhtin, 'The Problem of Speech Genres', in Mikhail Bakhtin, *Speech Genres and Other Late Essays*, trans. by Vern W. McGee, ed. by Caryl Emerson and Michael Holquist (Austin, TX: University of Texas Press, 1986), pp. 60–102 (p. 99).
9 'Jésus baissé pour écrire', Tome IV, XXIe traité; *Petits Traités*, 2 vols (Paris: Gallimard, 1997), I, pp. 513–27; first published in 8 vols (Paris: Maeght, 1990).
10 'La langue devient semblable aux statues des dieux'; 'cette anormale, douteuse, brutale, contentieuse – au point d'être soit interprétée comme maléfique, soit interprétée comme divine – "fission de l'oral" qu'est toute pratique de l'écriture'; 'c'est le corps de dieu lui-même qui, tour à tour se dressant, se baissant, mime ou danse de façon énigmatique une sorte de partage, ou d'admonition, ou d'hésitation entre ces deux mondes', *Petits Traités*, I, pp. 518, 523, 519.
11 'Cneius Naevius prit part à la première guerre punique. On rapporte qu'il fut blessé au-dessus du genou et à la hanche. Son bras ne tremblait pas. Il avait encore la vertu des origines, non celle d'un guerrier, qui n'est qu'humain, mais celle d'un chasseur, qui est tout animal qui poursuit et dévore', ibid., p. 526.
12 'Monstrueuse simultanéité. Incroyable et mystérieuse intrusion pour ceux dont la meute fut celle des loups, voyant, sidérés, la première lettre au bout du doigt d'une prostituée', ibid., p. 526.
13 *Rhétorique spéculative* (Paris: Gallimard, 1995), p. 149.
14 'Hermit' references come in *Rhétorique spéculative*, p. 197 and the book-length interview, Pascal Quignard and Chantal Lapeyre-Desmaison, *Pascal Quignard le solitaire: rencontre avec Chantal Lapeyre Desmaison* (Paris: Galilée, 2006), p. 32; 'Deserter' reference is in Pascal Quignard and Jean-Louis Pautrot, 'Dix questions à Pascal Quignard', *Études françaises*, 40.2 (2004), 87–92 (p. 88); the autobiographical sketch is 'Pascal Quignard par lui-même', in Adriano Marchetti (ed.), *Pascal Quignard: la mise au silence* (Seyssel: Champ Vallon, 2000), pp. 191–2 (p. 192).
15 A literal hermit appears in the *conte*, 'L'Image et le jadis', in *Revue des sciences humaines*, 260 (2000) 9–18; more figuratively, Chenogne, the protagonist of *Le Salon du Wurtemberg*, withdraws to a life of reclusive writing at the end of the novel. La Bruyère (*Un gêne technique à l'égard des fragments*) and Porcius Latron (*La Raison*) are among Quignard's more reclusive biographical subjects.
16 The story of Cäcilia Müller can be pieced together from various references in Quignard's work and interviews, including *Le Nom sur le bout de la langue* (Paris: Gallimard, 1995), first published by POL, 1993, p. 59, *Vie secrète* (Paris: Gallimard, 1998), pp. 16 and 331, *Sur le*

jadis (Paris: Grasset, 2002), p. 134; Laypeyre-Desmaison, *Pascal Quignard le solitaire*, pp. 59, 169, and Quignard and Ezine, p. 56. In the Ezine interview, Quignard asserts this episode to be the source of all his books, but expressed in none of them.

17 See, for instance, Quignard's discussion of 'fascination' in *Vie secrète*, pp. 145–67, or 'jadis' in *Sur le jadis*, pp. 139–44.

18 '[C]elui qui n'a pas de secret n'a pas d'âme', Lapeyre-Desmaison, *Pascal Quignard le solitaire*, p. 61.

19 In interview, Quignard stresses the importance to him of the novel's multiple viewpoints, including female ones, which are denied him in the *traités*. He describes the novel as 'the only heterosexual genre', 'Dix questions à Pascal Quignard', p. 91.

20 Examples of this structure can be found in 'La Voix perdue', in Marchetti (ed.), pp. 5–34, and 'L'Image et le jadis'.

21 'A chaque fois que l'argumentation me paraît perdre pied dans quelque chose de mou j'invente une histoire ... Au moins dans les histoires on abandonne l'idée de savoir exactement ce qu'on exprime dans ce qu'on communique', *Pascal Quignard le solitaire*, p. 62.

22 'Réfute-t-on un poème?', Michel Deguy, 'L'Écriture sidérante', in Marchetti (ed.), pp. 43–64 (p. 49).

23 '[L]a vérité ne m'éclaire pas, et que l'appétit de dire ou celui de penser ne lui sont peut-être jamais tout-à-fait soumis', *La Leçon de musique* (Paris: Gallimard, 2002), first published by Hachette, 1987, p. 15; 'qu'on n'oublie pas que je ne dis rien qui soit sûr', *Abîmes* (Paris: Grasset, 2002), p. 108.

24 'Le récit s'égare entre la fiction qui ne prend pas et la méditation qui se méprend. Aucune révélation n'accompagne en effet cette dernière. Le narrateur expérimente conjointement la vacuité de la conscience et celle de l'écriture', Bruno Blanckeman, *Les Récits indécidables: Jean Echenoz, Hervé Guibert, Pascal Quignard* (Villeneuve d'Ascq: Presses Universitaires du Septentrion, 2000), pp. 161–2.

25 Given the immense range of Quignard's references, it is perhaps understandable that he should produce occasional slips in the further reaches of his knowledge, and it is not difficult for the cultivated reader to catch him out from time to time. On English literature, for instance, Quignard refers to the Brontë's home as Hathord (for Haworth; *Les Ombres errantes*, Paris: Grasset, 2002, p. 155), and that of Du Maurier's Rebecca as Wanderley (Manderley; *Sur le jadis*, p. 154). Other errors include the assertion that Vladimir Propp's folk-tale morphology was intended to apply to all narrative (*Rhétorique spéculative*, p. 142), or a discussion of the Korean writing system which misspells its inventor's name and wrongly labels it non-alphabetic (*Petits Traités*, I, p. 320). More serious charges are brought by the Classicist Rémy Poignault, who examines Quignard's representation of Fronto in *Rhétorique spéculative*, and accuses him of asserting guesswork (such as Fronto's birthdate) as fact, of misrepresenting and misquoting him, and, in the case of the most important quota-

tion, which opens the *traité* and underpins the whole volume of essays, of inventing it entirely (p. 13). Rémy Poignault, 'Fronton revu par Pascal Quignard', in Rémy Poignault (ed.), *Présence de l'antiquité grecque et romaine au XXe siècle: actes du colloque à Tours (30 novembre – 2 décembre 2000)* (Tours: Centre de recherches A. Piganiol, 2002), pp. 145–74.

26 *La Raison* (Paris: Le Promeneur, 1990), p. 52; *Petits Traités*, I, p. 191.

27 *Terrasse à Rome* (Paris: Gallimard, 2000), p. 9.

28 Ibid., p. 12.

29 'Marie-José portait une robe à rayures jaunes et blanches boutonnée jusqu'au cou'; 'Elle avait relevé ses cheveux noirs en un petit chignon sur la nuque ... et que retenait un ruban de velours jaune. Sa robe était rayée de jaune', *L'Occupation américaine* (Paris: Seuil, 1994), pp. 135, 138.

30 'En 397, Aurelius Ambrosius mourut à Milan. On dit que la mort l'interrompit alors qu'il écrivait le mot *mortem*'; 'Aurelius Prudentius Clemens mourut en écrivant le mot *dolorosus*', *Les Tablettes de buis d'Apronenia Avitia* (Paris: Gallimard, 1984), pp. 22, 31.

31 '[L]a *pietas* romaine n'a nullement le sens de la "piété" qui en dérive'; 'la *castitas* romaine n'a nullement le sens de la "chasteté" qui en dérive', *Le Sexe et l'effroi* (Paris: Gallimard, 1994), pp. 24, 26.

32 Repetition is a symptom of obsessive compulsive disorder, and there may be an autobiographical link in the naming of food to Quignard's own compulsion to know the name of anything he ingests. 'Always under the threat of anorexia', he will summon restaurant chefs from their kitchen to name unknown items on his plate, and refuse to eat what cannot be named (Lapeyre-Desmaison, *Pascal Quignard le solitaire*, p. 145). There are also hints that there may be a system behind these recurring foods, flowers, people and places. Quignard claims to have had a rivalry with Georges Perec over writing under the constraint of concealed systems: 'We made the following rule: you could not claim victory unless any innovation was invisible.' (Pascal Quignard, Marcel Gauchet and Pierre Nora, 'La Déprogrammation de la littérature', in *Écrits de l'éphémère* (Paris: Galilée, 2005), pp. 233–49 (p. 241). First published in *Le Débat*, 54 (April 1989)). Quignard has kept his silence better than Perec: he gives no indication of which text(s) are implicated out of those published before Perec's death in 1982, but *Carus* seems a possible candidate.

33 '[C]ette manière d'agenda, d'éphéméride, de pense-bête, de notes journalières', *Les Tablettes de buis*, pp. 14–15.

34 'Je ne suis pas intéressé à "faire revivre les grands morts", je me moque de faire revenir les Romains, de ressusciter Hadrien et de lui faire tenir un discours idiot du dix-neuvième siècle', 'Pascal Quignard: "Écrire n'est pas un choix, mais un symptôme"', *La Quinzaine littéraire*, 1–15 November 1990, 17–19 (p. 18). The text in question is Marguerite Yourcenar's 1951 novel, *Mémoires d'Hadrien*.

35 'Curieuse façon que j'ai de noter ces souvenirs. L'ordre qui les relie ne cesse de me faire défaut et pourtant il s'impose à moi comme l'évidence', *Le Salon du Wurtemberg* (Paris: Gallimard, 1986), p. 105.

36 *Les Escaliers de Chambord* (Paris: Gallimard, 1989), p. 59.
37 *Le Salon du Wurtemberg*, p. 205.
38 Quignard comments on the novel's construction: 'It's a difficult book. Each chapter comes under a particular literary genre: witness statement, letter, folk tale, portrait, dialogue ... It wasn't easy to do and nobody even notices! It's a book I particularly enjoyed writing because it demonstrates my own way of working.' ('C'est un livre difficile. Chaque chapitre relève d'un genre littéraire particulier: déposition, lettre, conte, tableau, dialogue ... Ce n'était pas facile à faire et personne d'ailleurs ne s'en est rendu compte! C'est un livre que j'ai beaucoup aimé écrire car il met sous les yeux une manière de procéder qui est la mienne.') Pascal Quignard and Catherine Argand, 'Pascal Quignard' (interview), *Lire*, September 2002, consulted online at *http://www.lire.fr/entretien.asp/idC=43001/idTC=4/idR=201/idG=3* (last accessed 30 October 2008).
39 'Le graveur sent une odeur poignante. Il lève les yeux sur le visage du jeune homme qui l'égorge. Il le regarde: il est bouleversé par ses traits. Il le contemple. Il ne crie pas. Curieusement il pense à une gravure sur bois de Jan Heemkers, qui était son maître à Bruges', *Terrasse à Rome*, p. 98.
40 'Il se trouve que l'an 1667 Meaume mourut à Utrecht dans la demeure de Gérard Van Honthorst et un burin, lui-même signé à gauche et daté décembre 1666, en apporterait la preuve si besoin était. Le graveur dut quitter Rome à la fin de l'an 1664. Soit à l'automne 1666. Ce point est incertain', ibid., p. 82.
41 Chapters 35 and 36; pp. 100–5.
42 'C'est en –58 que l'amphithéâtre accueillit cinq crocodiles et un hippopotame. C'est là qu'Albucius les découvrit. Il avait onze ans et c'est sans doute pourquoi il en parla toujours. Et c'est trois ans plus tard qu'il vit le premier rhinocéros: ramené par César lui-même. En janvier –58, César fait préparer les livres qu'il compte emporter en Gaule. Cicéron en habit de deuil est poursuivi dans les rues de Rome par les bandes de matraqueurs payés par Clodius. Ils hurlent et frappent. Ils entendent venger les hommes qui servaient Catilina et que Cicéron a mis à mort. Cicéron est blessé par des pierres et couvert de seaux d'excréments humains qu'on déverse sur lui. Le peuple se joint aux bandes de Clodius et crie qu'il a lésé les droits à la liberté. Cicéron quitte Rome. Les Helvètes quittent en masse la Suisse dans le dessein de s'établir le long du golfe de Biscaye. Cicéron se lave dans une grande vasque de pierre grise. Il espère qu'il va se séparer d'une odeur putride, César détruit le pont qui enjambe le Rhône', *Albucius* (Paris: Gallimard, 2004), first published by POL in 1990, pp. 48–9.
43 '[Les] mots les plus vils, [les] choses les plus basses et [les] thèmes les plus inégaux', ibid., p. 42.
44 'Le père de Sénèque le philosophe lui demanda un jour des exemples de "sordidissima". Albucius répondit: "Et rhinocerotem et latrinas et spongias" (Les rhinocéros, les latrines et les éponges.) Plus

tard il ajouta aux choses sordidissimes les animaux familiers, les adultères, la nourriture, la mort des proches, les jardins', ibid., p. 43.

45 '[O]ù la plupart des genres littéraires existants étaient coupillés et mêlés', ibid., p. 21.

46 '"Démantibuler" cela veut dire démandibuler. Dé-mandibuler, cela revient à rendre inopérante la mastication. Cela laisse crue la chair, et cela laisse les morceaux entiers ... J'adore les parataxes déroutantes, l'ordre qui ne marche pas, les mondes déchirés, les listes chinoises, les poubelles, les greniers. J'ai un respect infini pour les enfers, schéol, brocantes et autres dépôts', *Pascal Quignard le solitaire*, p. 161.

47 Michel Foucault, *Les Mots et les choses* (Paris: Gallimard, 1966), p. 7; the story in question is 'The Analytical Language of John Wilkins', from Borges's 1952 collection, *Otras Inquisiciones (Other Inquisitions)*.

48 'De même que l'amour humain a ses figures, le langage humain a ses *imagines*, ses *prosôpa*, ses saillies qui font brèche, qui déchirent le langage lui-même. Loggin recommande les asyndètes, les anaphores, toutes les ruptures de liaison dont peut disposer le rhéteur. Le désordre nu du langage désordonne la pensée qui cherche, tandis que les conjonctions entravent l'élan ou désamorcent le jet pneumatique', *Rhétorique spéculative*, p. 67.

49 *Ethelrude et Wolframm* (Paris: Galilée, 2006), p. 14.

50 'Elle pose les mains sur ses poignets. Puis elle posa sa tête sur ses mains. Elle songe. Elle songea', *Villa Amalia* (Paris: Gallimard, 2006), p. 242.

51 'Quand il arriva pour son deuxième cours, ce fut Madeleine, très mince, les joues roses, qui ouvrit la grande porte cochère. "Parce que je vais me baigner," dit-elle, "je vais relever mes cheveux." Sa nuque était rose, avec des petits poils noirs ébouriffés dans la clarté. Comme elle levait ses bras, ses seins se serraient et gonflaient. Ils se dirigèrent vers la cabane de Monsieur de Sainte Colombe. C'était une belle journée de printemps. Il y avait des primevères et il y avait des papillons. Marin Marais portait sa viole à l'épaule', *Tous les matins du monde* (Paris: Gallimard, 1991), p. 52.

52 *Albucius*, p. 199; *Rhétorique spéculative*, p. 146.

53 'Qu'on pardonne ces fragments, ces spasmes que je soude. La vague qui se brise emprunte au soleil une part précipitée de sa clarté. Cette brusquerie est comme un rêve de voleur. La mort aussi enlève vite et ne restitue rien', *Petits Traités*, I, p. 25.

54 'Son existence sature l'attention, sa multiplication édulcore l'effet que sa brièveté prépare. Il faut peut-être présenter sous forme de problème l'incapacité de fabriquer un objet dont la lecture soit continue. Il faut aussi mettre en avant le peu de satisfaction, tout à la fois au regard de la pensée et au regard de la beauté, où ces rognures ou ces lambeaux abandonnent', *Une gêne technique à l'égard des fragments* (Montpellier: Fata Morgana, 1986), p. 21.

55 'En fait le fragment trahit plus de circularité, d'autonomie et d'unité que le discours suivi qui masque vainement ses ruptures à force de

roueries plus ou moins manifestes, de transitions sinueuses, de maladroites cimentations, et expose finalement sans cesse à la vue ses coutures, ses ourlets, ses *rentraitures*', ibid., p. 43.

56 '[L]es historiens ont peur et font semblant de croire que ce qui arrive dans le monde des hommes est cohérent', *Albucius*, p. 110; 'les plus beaux livres ... désigne avec le doigt des trous, des fragilités, des esseulements et des peurs – quelque chose qui a été fui plutôt qu'assouvi', *Petits Traités*, I, p. 282.

57 *Une gêne technique*, p. 36.

58 '[C]e qui affaiblit certains auteurs de roman à thèse, c'est que, renonçant à la pensée interrogative, ils ont déjà trouvé', Jean-Yves Tadié, *Le Roman au xxe siècle* (Paris: Belfond, 1990), p. 180.

59 '[L]e fragment permet de renouveler sans cesse 1) la posture du narrateur, 2) l'éclat bouleversant de l'attaque', *Une gêne technique*, p. 54.

60 Sylviane Coyault, 'Sous prétexte de biographie: *Tous les matins du monde* de Pascal Quignard', in Sylviane Coyault (ed.), *Des Récits poétiques contemporains* (Clermont-Ferrand: CRLMC Université Blaise Pascal, 1996), pp. 183–96 (p. 188).

61 'Dix questions à Pascal Quignard', p. 90.

62 '"Une intrigue!", tel est le cri dès que le cri devient langage. Et voilà une raison pour laquelle je ne crois pas aux romans sans intrigues. Chacune de nos vies est un continent que seul un récit aborde. Et non seulement il faut un récit pour accoster et s'associer sa propre expérience, mais un héros pour assurer la narration, un moi pour dire je', 'La Déprogrammation de la littérature', p. 236.

63 'La temporalité ne peut pas devenir humaine si elle n'est pas articulée sur un mode narratif. C'est-à-dire l'action, le réel, une intrigue, une scène de chasse – c'est déjà un récit verbal', *La Leçon de musique*, p. 63.

64 Bruno Blanckeman, '"J'obéis les yeux fermés à ma propre nuit"', in Philippe Bonnefis and Dolorès Lyotard (eds), *Pascal Quignard: figures d'un lettré* (Paris: Galilée, 2005), pp. 87–97 (p. 93).

65 Chantal Lapeyre-Desmaison, *Mémoires d'origine: un essai sur Pascal Quignard* (Paris: Les Flohic, 2001), p. 198.

66 *Une gêne technique*, pp. 20, 24; 'Pascal Quignard & Marie-Laure Picot: un entretien', *CCCP* 10.2 (2004), 5–13 (p. 9).

67 *Une gêne technique*, p. 32; Alain Robbe-Grillet, *Le Miroir qui revient* (Paris: Minuit, 1984), p. 27.

68 'Je vous ai dit que vous n'auriez rien de moi, ni de l'ordre de la vie privée, ni de l'ordre de la création, par incapacité. Je ne suis pas le tiers de ce qui se passe à ce moment là', *Pascal Quignard le solitaire*, pp. 86–7.

69 'Sartre écrit en fait – à quelques pauvres stéréotypes américains près – le même roman que Mauriac, comme le Nouveau Roman s'inscrit en réalité dans la même lignée formelle. C'est le règne du même sous couvert de rupture théorique et non pas rhétorique. Il aboutit aujourd'hui, avec le resserrement supplémentaire des possibilités

morphologiques introduit par le Nouveau Roman, à un académisme complet. On en connaît par cœur les prescriptions plus ou moins affamantes et presque religieuses: le roman à l'intérieur du roman, la désintégration de l'action, la moribonderie, le silence, la blancheur, les dialogues langue de bois dont la pauvreté hèle la profondeur, les quelques calembours, la désidentification des personnages, la dérision de l'intrigue ... Je ne sais pourquoi, quand je m'approche de la rue Bernard-Palissy, un ennui doux et vieillot m'envahit', 'La Déprogrammation de la littérature', p. 243. Rue Bernard-Palissy is the home of Les Éditions de Minuit, publishers of the *nouveau roman* and of 'minimalist' writers like Jean Echenoz and Jean-Philippe Toussaint.

70 In 2000, eleven years after the original interview, Quignard returns to the subject: '[Deprogramming literature] is an illusion I nourished. It's always a vain dream. Things always reprogramme themselves somehow. Synthesis always wins out over analysis. The lava always solidifies. Order always returns.' ('C'est une illusion que je nourrissais. C'est un rêve toujours perdu. Cela se reprogramme toujours on ne sait comment. La *synthesis* gagne toujours sur *l'analysis*. La lave sèche toujours. L'ordre revient toujours.') *Pascal Quignard le solitaire*, p. 165.

71 'Ne songez plus qu'à l'énergie, au détail sans raison, au jeu', 'La Déprogrammation de la littérature', p. 249.

72 *Petits Traités*, I, p. 58; *Rhétorique spéculative*, p. 184; *La Leçon de musique*, p. 62; Gilles Dupuis, 'Une Leçon d'écriture: le style et l'harmonie chez Pascal Quignard', in Marchetti (ed.), pp. 119–30.

73 *Albucius*, p. 74; *Rhétorique spéculative*, p. 140; *Abîmes*, p. 141.

74 Dominique Viart, 'Les "Fictions critiques" de Pascal Quignard', in *Études françaises* 40.2 (2004), 25–37 (p. 32).

75 *Vie secrète*, p. 17.

76 '[À] la frange de la fiction ... à la frange de la noèse. Extraordinairement agénérique', *Pascal Quignard le solitaire*, p. 214.

77 *Rhétorique spéculative*, p. 143.

78 'Je cherche à écrire un livre où je songe en lisant. J'ai admiré de façon absolue ce que Montaigne, Rousseau, Stendhal, Bataille ont tenté. Ils mêlaient la pensée, la vie, la fiction, le savoir comme s'il s'agissait d'un seul corps', *Vie secrète*, p. 298.

79 'Ce ne sont plus exactement des traités. Je m'approche peu à peu de Tchouang-tseu que j'ai tant cité en m'entretenant avec vous. J'espère qu'on ne saura plus démêler fiction ou pensée', *Pascal Quignard le solitaire*, p. 211.

80 For example, by Pautrot, p. 175.

3 Marie Darrieussecq and the Voice of the Mind

1   The novel reached a print run of 400,000 copies in its first year, and has since been published in forty countries. Marie Darrieussecq and John Lambeth, 'Entretien avec Marie Darrieussecq', *The French Review*, 79 (2006), 806–18 (813).

2   All published by POL in Paris. Darrieussecq's other works include the novella *Claire dans la forêt* (Paris: Éditions des femmes, 1996), a collection of short stories, *Zoo* (Paris: POL, 2006), and the non-fiction *Précisions sur les vagues* (Paris: POL, 1999) and *Le Bébé* (Paris: POL, 2002).

3   'Discours du récit', pp. 225–67.

4   *Nouveau Discours du récit*, pp. 30–3.

5   'Discours du récit', p. 203.

6   In interview, Darrieussecq discusses how her choice of first- or third-person narrative can be motivated by the theme of the novel. Asked about the change from first- to third-person between *Naissance des fantômes* and *Le Mal de mer*, she replies: 'It isn't really a choice. It's more instinctive, I mean, in that novel I wanted to talk about a character in the grip of depression. Anxiety is first-person because it's a kind of mental panic, while depression is being outside of oneself or alongside oneself', Marie Darrieussecq and Jeannette Gaudet, '"Des livres sur la liberté": conversation avec Marie Darrieussecq', *Dalhousie French Studies*, 59 (2002), 108–18 (p. 108).

7   'Elle coupe une jolie rose, deux pétales seulement se sont cambrés hors du bouton, ce n'est pas encore une fleur, deux pétales à demi ouverts. Elle remercie elle ne sait qui ou quoi, elle rend grâce, pour le sursis du matin, le flot de respiration, le bonheur qui est une chose énorme et liquide', *Bref séjour chez les vivants*, pp. 7–8.

8   In the jargon of narrative theory, generally avoided here but occasionally useful for its precision, *heterodiegetic* narration is recounted from outside the world of the text (diegesis), as with classic third-person narratives, and *homodiegetic* narration is told by a narrator who exists within the world of the story. *Autodiegetic* is sometimes used for homodiegetic narrators who tell the story of their own experience.

9   In the interview with John Lambeth, Darrieussecq describes in detail her relationship with Sarraute, whom she describes as her 'grand-mère spirituelle', and its influence on her work. Darrieussecq and Lambeth, 'Entretien avec Marie Darrieussecq', p. 809.

10 '[M]ouvements indéfinissables, qui glissent très rapidement aux limites de notre conscience.' Sarraute's definition of tropisms is to be found in *L'Ère du soupçon: essais sur le roman* (Paris: Gallimard, 1956), p. 8.

11 'Elle achètera un test demain, non, il faut attendre d'avoir du retard. On devrait le sentir tout de suite. D'ailleurs elle ne sent rien il faut bien voir les choses en face: elle ne sent rien. Assise à la terrasse de la *Biela* attendant Jimena. Ici avant c'était quoi, un magasin de cycles. Les premiers vélos de Buenos Aires', *Bref séjour chez les vivants*, p. 231.

12 'Je me rappelle cette attraction de fête foraine, à Blackpool. Elle, maman, claustrophobe restée à l'extérieur. Tous les trois, Pierre John et moi, pourquoi je pense à ça, où était Anne? assis sur un banc, la brochette Johnson, avec trois autres visiteurs nous attendions; au centre d'une pièce, comment dire, normale, un buffet, une table, des tableaux, une théière sur le buffet. Je me souviens', *Bref séjour chez les vivants*, p. 93.

13 Dorrit Cohn, *Transparent Minds: Narrative Modes for Presenting Consciousness in Fiction* (Princeton, NJ: Princeton University Press, 1978), p. 14.

14 'Si vous faites attention non à ce que vous pensez mais à la forme de votre pensée, vous vous apercevez – ce sont des évidences mais qu'on oublie toujours – que vous faites rarement des phrases complètes sujet–verbe–complément. Il y a des morceaux de rêves, un fantasme, un souvenir, des chansons', Marie Darrieussecq and Alain Nicolas, 'Marie et les cerveaux' (interview), *L'Humanité*, 13 September 2001, 8.

15 '*Bref séjour chez les vivants* ... est un livre qui essaie de mettre sur la page le fonctionnement du cerveau. Je me suis amusée aussi du côté de la neurobiologie, mais ce n'est pas du tout un livre scientifique. Ça part de cette idée très simple que quand on pense, on ne pense pas en phrases, ou très rarement. C'est très rare qu'on a une phrase construite dans la tête. On a des images, des souvenirs, un bout de musique qui passe, une idée mais vague. C'est rare qu'on les formule. Comment mettre ça sur le papier? Ce n'est pas le "stream-of-consciousness" qui est déjà très écrit. C'est vraiment très peu narratif et plus proche de la poésie', Darrieussecq and Gaudet, p. 117.

16 Francis Crick, *The Astonishing Hypothesis: The Scientific Search for the Soul* (London: Simon and Schuster, 1994), p. 3.

17 Jacques Mehler and others, 'A Precursor to Language Acquisition in Young Infants', *Cognition*, 29 (1988), 143–78; Wilder Penfield, *The Excitable Cortex in Conscious Man* (Liverpool: Liverpool University Press, 1958); *Bref séjour chez les vivants*, pp. 167–9, p. 183. A list of scientific works consulted by Darrieussecq can be found in Shirley Jordan's enlightening article, '"Un grand coup de pied dans le château de cubes": Formal Experimentation in Marie Darrieussecq's *Bref séjour chez les vivants*', *MLR*, 100 (2005), 51–67 (p. 62).

18 'Il y a sans doute un travail neuronal du deuil, des dérivations, des impasses et des court-circuits, toute une éléctricité à revoir, des synapses à reviser', *Tom est mort*, pp. 68–9; 'une zone en rouge sur une carte du cerveau'; 'comme si la schizophrénie bouchait des zones du cerveau, transformait des artères en impasses et des centres nerveux en terrains vagues', *Le Pays*, pp. 38, 162.

19 'Ça m'a comme qui dirait réveillée. Mes neurones se sont remis en place', *Truismes*, p. 92.

20 *Fictions contemporaines au féminin: Marie Darrieussecq, Marie NDiaye, Marie Nimier, Marie Redonnet* (Paris: L'Harmattan, 2002), p. 56.

21 'ce choc au coeur, l'adrénaline lâchée d'un coup, une vague élec-
    trique qui vient buter au bout des doigts et paralyse la gorge'; 'les
    doigts à travers lesquels je détaillais, comme au microscope à l'in-
    frarouge, les influx nerveux jaillis du cerveau', *Naissance des fantômes*,
    pp. 21, 136.

22 'J/e ne pensais à rien ... Dans le cerveau des masses roulaient, s'artic-
    ulaient ou s'annulaient, se formaient et se déformaient. Les rouages
    des hanches, genoux, chevilles, fonctionnaient à plein, le piston des
    bras s'activaient, l'air tapissaient à grands jets le fond des poumons.
    Les fluides circulaient, décrassaient, défatiguaient. L'oxygène irra-
    diait, le cerveau respirait', *Le Pays*, p. 13.

23 Sigmund Freud, *From the History of an Infantile Neurosis* [*Aus der
    Geschichte einer infantilen Neurose*] (1918), in *The Standard Edition of the
    Complete Works of Sigmund Freud*, ed. by James Strachey (London:
    Hogarth Press, 1953–74), vol. 17, pp. 7–122.

24 Peter Brooks, *Reading for the Plot: Design and Intention in Narrative*
    (Cambridge, MA: Harvard University Press, 1992); first published,
    New York: Knopf, 1984, p. 269.

25 Ibid., p. 276.

26 Barthes's theory of the hermeneutic code is expounded in *S/Z* (Paris:
    Seuil, 1970). A more detailed discussion follows in the chapter on
    Jean Echenoz.

27 The relationship between cognitive science and psychoanalysis is
    explored further in my article, 'Darrieussecq's Mind', *French Studies*,
    62 (2008), 429–41.

28 'Chaque photon décollant de l'enveloppe d'Edmée se jetant en ligne
    droite sur les rétines de Peter pour refaire, avec la mémoire propre à
    la lumière, son image à elle, Edmée. Et avec autant infaillibilité, ses
    nerfs optiques à elle inversant l'image, gauche-droite, et les lobes de
    son cerveau le remettant dans le bon sens, *zig zag*, voilà Peter', *White*,
    pp. 79–80.

29 '[Darrieussecq] refuse toute explication psychologique, mais docu-
    mente avec minutie les sensations physiques ressenties', Catherine
    Rodgers, '"Entrevoir l'absence des bords du monde" dans les romans
    de Marie Darrieussecq', in *Nouvelles écrivaines: nouvelles voix?*, ed. by
    Nathalie Morello and Catherine Rodgers (Amsterdam: Rodopi,
    2002), pp. 83–103 (p. 87); 'une lutte pour arriver à dire le réel en
    contournant les lieux communs et en particulier les lieux communs
    de la psychologie', Darrieussecq and Lambeth, 'Entretien avec Marie
    Darrieussecq', p. 808.

30 'Ma grossesse la plus longue', *Naissance des fantômes*, p. 51.

31 '[C]e mariage, et pas d'enfants'; 'une entité qui, sans jamais me
    donner un enfant, avait cependant vécu avec moi un certain temps',
    Naissance des fantômes, pp. 72, 117.

32 '[C]es trois syllabes, ton-ma-ri, qui sonnaient de plus en plus phoné-
    tiquement à mes oreilles (une occlusive dentale, une occlusive
    labiale, une liquide vibrante)', *Naissance des fantômes*, p. 75.

33 'Je lui demanderais de me décrire les maisons, les rues, les fontaines, le ciel, et ce qu'il avait rêvé que seraient nos enfants', ibid., pp. 141–2.

34 'Nous verrions les mêmes couleurs, les mêmes formes, et je cesserais de me demander si mon mari (si les chats, les oiseaux, les poissons et les mouches aux yeux à facettes) sentait et voyait tout de même ce que moi je sentais et voyais', ibid., p. 142, and repeated as the closing lines of the novel.

35 'Il y a longtemps que je cherche auprès de la science des métaphores qui fonctionnent. Je côtoie beaucoup de scientifiques, et je pense qu'on fait le même métier. On cherche le meilleur outil possible pour décrire le monde. Pour moi cet outil est fait de mots', Darrieussecq and Nicolas, 'Marie et les cerveaux', p. 8.

36 '[La science] est un réservoir de métaphores, tout simplement ... Le discours de la science m'apporte, entre autres, tout le vocabulaire de l'atomisation. Quand quelqu'un se désintègre, le monde se désintègre autour de lui et là, la science nucléaire m'apporte des mots, molécule, particule, atome, neutron', Darrieussecq and Gaudet, '"Des livres sur la liberté"', 115. *Naissance des fantômes* offers a clear illustration of Darrieussecq's comments here. The narrator of the novel discusses the double-slit experiment, quantum physics's famous demonstration of wave-particle duality at the sub-atomic level, in the context of her sense of unreality among the familiar 'solid' objects of her apartment once her husband has gone (p. 93); later, in the effect of fog, a solid wall appears to dissolve into 'millions of particles of wall' (p. 102), again drawing on the language of particle physics as a metaphor for the narrator's loss of her grounding in the world.

37 'enveloppe encéphalique tendue comme un tambour', *White*, p. 100; 'sous l'abrasion de mes neurones', *Naissance des fantômes*, p. 32; *Le Mal de mer*, pp. 104–5.

38 'On se dirige vers le marchand de glaces. Son coeur cogne devant les bacs colorés, elle peine à lire, ses talons chauffent. La pression se fait plus forte autour de sa main, ... elle ne sait plus quoi faire de ce grand creux dans sa poitrine, des fourmis qui dévorent ses talons, de la tension rapace qui monte au long de ses mollets pour prendre toute la place', *Le Mal de mer*, pp. 44–5.

39 'au lieu d'écrire "je me sentais très angoissée" ... j'essaie de trouver d'autres façons, j'essaie d'ouvrir de nouvelles fenêtres de qu'est-ce que c'est l'angoisse, qu'est-ce que c'est être seule, qu'est-ce que c'est avoir un corps', Darrieussecq and Lambeth, 'Entretien avec Marie Darrieussecq', p. 808.

40 Ibid., pp. 811–12.

41 Darrieussecq, 'Être libéré de soi', *Le Magazine littéraire*, March 2008, 58.

42 The examples are Cohn's, *Transparent Minds*, p. 105.

43 Édouard Dujardin, 'Le Monologue intérieur: son apparition, ses origines, sa place dans l'oeuvre de James Joyce' (1931), in Édouard

Dujardin, *Les Lauriers sont coupés, suivi de Le Monologue intérieur*, ed. by Carmen Licari (Rome: Bulzoni, 1977), pp. 189–273 (p. 230). Cohn disputes Dujardin's claim to have invented the form *ex nihilo*, citing several antecedents in passages of longer works.

44   '[Des] phrases directes réduites au minimum syntaxial'; 'la pensée la plus intime, la plus proche de l'inconscient, antérieurement à toute organisation logique, c'est-à-dire en son état naissant', Dujardin, *Les lauriers sont coupés*, p. 230.

45   Robert Humphrey, *Stream of Consciousness in the Modern Novel* (Berkeley, CA: University of California Press, 1954), p. 24.

46   Cohn, *Transparent Minds*, p. 56.

47   Ibid., p. 223.

48   'Quelle chaleur déjà, huit heures et demi et ce type qui s'est garé à notre place, c'est pourtant écrit, *privado*, je vais encore devoir appeler les flics, et ces pensées que j'avais achetées pour être bleues les voilà mauves, et ces roses, vingt boutons qui pointent, sur ces plants-là au moins je ne me suis pas fait avoir, gonflés à craquer sève qui monte', *Bref séjour chez les vivants*, p. 167.

49   'Le parvis. Est-ce qu'on appelle ça un parvis? Depuis le temps que j'attends. Quelqu'un d'autre pourrait venir, quelqu'un d'autre que lui. À moins qu'il ne se déguise. Un recruteur. Quelqu'un qui me donnerait quelque chose. Une mission. De l'argent, immédiatement. Qu'est-ce que ça fait? On ferme les yeux. Vulgaire en pensée. Vulgaire tout court. À la maternité, *et comment l'appellerez-vous, cette petite?* Anne. *Anne comment?* Anne tout court. Le nombre de fois où John et maman, en anglais ou en français, m'ont raconté', ibid., p. 8.

50   'Retirons nos gants; il faut les jeter négligemment sur la table, à côté de l'assiette; plutôt dans la poche du pardessus; non, sur la table; ces petites choses sont de la tenue générale. Mon pardessus au porte-manteau; je m'assieds; ouf! j'étais las. Je mettrai dans la poche de mon pardessus mes gants. Illuminé, doré, rouge, avec les glaces cet étincellement; quoi? le café; le café où je suis', Dujardin, *Les Lauriers sont coupés*, p. 103.

51   James Joyce, *Ulysses* (1922) (Harmondsworth: Penguin, 1992), p. 872.

52   This is an issue common to all stand-alone stream-of-consciousness narratives. In Simone de Beauvoir's 'Monologue', for instance, the narrator informs us at the opening, 'I've drawn the curtains', setting the scene for herself as she does for the reader. *La Femme rompue* (Paris: Gallimard, 1967), pp. 85–188 (p. 87).

53   Darrieussecq cites Joyce's influence in Darrieussecq and Nicolas, 'Marie et les cerveaux', p. 8.

54   '"Fin", "début", "continu", "discontinu", "séparé", "ensemble": est-il donc possible qu'il n'ait aucune idée de ces concepts ? J'ai du mal à croire à une telle virginité du cerveau. Qu'il faille parler pour penser, que les notions ne viennent qu'avec les mots, la théorie me paraît pauvre', *Le Bébé*, p. 112.

55   *White*, p. 55.

56 'Elle a ce sentiment maintenant, d'avoir pensé à tout. La lampe fonctionne, dénichant au bas des arbres la bruyère, et des cratères de sable. Les dix mille francs sont dans sa poche; il faut cesser d'avoir peur, qu'ils tombent, que le vent les déloge, que la petite joue avec. La liasse est déjà un peu entamée, on lui a rendu des pièces sur le pain au lait et le jus d'orange. Elle remonte lentement, elle a les oeufs, le plaid, voilà, c'est ce qu'elles vont faire, manger et dormir ici', *Le Mal de mer*, pp. 12–13.

57 '*je ne peux plus penser* est la dernière pensée formulée par E avant qu'elle n'oublie sa personne, phrases réflexes et syllogismes, et la façon dont l'espace et le temps la clôturent. Le plaisir se polarise et les images affluent, le lac s'agrandit, s'étale, son sexe est un point du lac, une île autour de laquelle ondulent les ponts suspendus, c'est la dernière image dans le cerveau d'Edmée quand la jouissance la rapte – annule jusqu'aux images – elle crie', *White*, pp. 210–11.

58 William James, *The Principles of Psychology*, 3 vols (1890) (Cambridge, MA: Harvard University Press, 1981), I, p. 233.

59 'si [nos] idées trouvent des mots préexistants pour les exprimer, cela fait pour chacune l'effet d'une bonne fortune inespérée; et, à vrai dire, il a souvent fallu aider la chance, et forcer le sens du mot pour qu'il se modelât sur la pensée. L'effort est cette fois douloureux, et le résultat aléatoire. Mais c'est alors seulement que l'esprit se sent ou se croit créateur. Il ne part plus d'une multiplicité d'éléments tout faits pour aboutir à une unité composite où il y aura un nouvel arrangement de l'ancien. Il s'est transporté tout d'un coup a quelque chose qui paraît à la fois un et unique, qui cherchera ensuite à s'étaler tant bien que mal en concepts multiples et communs, donnés d'avance dans des mots', Henri Bergson, *Les Deux Sources de la morale et de la religion* (Paris: Alcan, 1932), p. 43.

60 For a critique of the Sapir–Whorf hypothesis of linguistic determinism, see Steven Pinker, *The Language Instinct* (London: Allen Lane, 1994), pp. 55–82.

4 Jean Echenoz and the Uses of Digression

1 '"Vous aimez Robbe-Grillet, bien sûr" ... sur le ton de l'évidence, comme si mon livre découlait naturellement de cette influence', Jean Echenoz, *Jérôme Lindon* (Paris: Minuit, 2001), p. 13.

2 Jean Echenoz, 'Un Musée imaginaire', *La Quinzaine littéraire*, 16–31 May 1989, 13.

3 '[D]eux écrivains auxquels certains d'entre nous doivent, sinon tout, du moins presque tout', Jean Echenoz, 'Neuf notes sur *Fatale*', postface to Jean-Patrick Manchette, *Fatale* (1977) (Paris: Gallimard, 1996), pp. 147–54 (p. 153).

4 Jean-Claude Lebrun, *Jean Echenoz* (Paris: Rocher, 1992), p. 78.

5 Randa Sabry, *Stratégies discursives: digression, transition, suspens* (Paris: Éditions de l'École des Hautes Études en Sciences Sociales, 1992), p. 7. Christine Montalbetti is one of the few other theorists to have

taken up digression in recent years, both in her critical work and creatively in her fiction.

6 Pierre Bayard, 'Proust et la digression', *Revue des lettres modernes: histoire des idées et des littératures*, 1533–40 (2001), 235–51.

7 'Balzac écrit mal, son incapacité à maîtriser différents discours, dont certains n'ont rien à faire dans une écriture narrative romanesque, en est une des preuves les plus manifestes', Éric Bordas, 'Pratiques balzaciennes de la digression', *L'Année balzacienne*, 20.1 (July 1999), 293–316 (p. 295).

8 'Il y a digression lorsque la narration *se désolidarise* de l'histoire (de l'action, du sujet), s'en détourne pour parler d'autre chose ou d'elle-même, et, du coup, saper sa propre orientation vers une fin déterminée (qui est non seulement de mener mais de mener à bien l'histoire)', Sabry, p. 138.

9 '[L]'ensemble des unités qui ont pour fonction d'articuler, de diverses manières, une question, sa réponse, et les accidents variés qui peuvent ou préparer la question ou retarder la réponse', Roland Barthes, *S/Z* (1970), in *Oeuvres complètes*, III, pp. 119–345 (pp. 131–2).

10 Brooks, *Reading for the Plot*, p. 18.

11 Genette, 'Frontières du récit', in *Communications*, 8 (1966) (*L'Analyse structurale du récit*), 158–69 (168).

12 Genette, revisiting his discussion on narrative duration from *Discours du récit*, suggests that, in addition to the four 'speeds' of narrative highlighted in that study (*pause, scene, summary, ellipsis*), he ought to have included *reflexive digression* as a fifth, since its interruption of narrative discourse is qualitatively different from the pause created by, say, a descriptive passage. *Nouveau discours du récit* (Paris: Seuil, 1983), p. 25.

13 '[C]ausons ensemble jusqu'à ce qu'ils se soient rejoints', Denis Diderot, *Oeuvres*, ed. by André Billy (Paris: Gallimard, coll. Pléiade, 1951), p. 525.

14 'Mes deux premiers livres, *Le Méridien de Greenwich* et *Cherokee*, reposaient sur mes souvenirs du roman noir. *L'Équipée malaise* tient du roman d'aventures, un genre que j'aime beaucoup et qui offre plus de souplesse. En mêlant des ingrédients qui sont des terrains d'aventures plutôt propices à la littérature et au cinéma, comme la Malaisie, un cargo battant complaisamment pavillon cypriote, une mutinerie, un trafic d'armes, la culture du caoutchouc, on peut jouer ... Un système se met en place à partir duquel on peut tricher', Yann Plougastel, 'Jean Echenoz ne connaît pas la Malaisie, et alors?', *L'Événement du jeudi*, 5–11 February 1987, 80–1.

15 'Il était habillé comme Ferrer aurait toujours souhaité, à la galerie, qu'il le fût. Seul accroc dans le tableau quand Delahaye se laissa tomber dans un fauteuil et que les revers de son pantalon se haussèrent: les élastiques de ses chaussettes semblaient hypotendus. Vous êtes très bien, comme ça, dit Ferrer. Vous les trouvez où, vos vêtements? Je n'avais plus rien à me mettre, répondit Delahaye, j'ai dû m'acheter quelques petites choses ici. On trouve des trucs pas mal

du tout dans le quartier du centre, vous n'imaginez pas comme c'est moins cher qu'en France. Puis il se redressa dans son fauteuil, rajusta sa cravate légèrement décentrée par l'émotion, sans doute, et remonta ses mi-bas affaissés en vrille sur ses chevilles. C'est ma femme qui m'a offert ces chaussettes, ajouta-t-il distraitement, mais elles tombent, voyez-vous. Elles ont tendance à tomber. Ah, dit Ferrer, ça c'est normal. Ça tombe toujours, les chaussettes qu'on vous offre. C'est juste, sourit Delahaye crispé, c'est très bien observé, je peux vous offrir un verre?', *Je m'en vais* (Paris: Minuit, 1999), p. 230.

16 'Tout cela ne nous avançait pas terriblement, donc on se tut une minute ou deux faute d'arguments', ibid., p. 233.

17 'Nous n'avons pas pris le temps, depuis presque un an pourtant que nous le fréquentons, de décrire Ferrer physiquement. Comme cette scène un peu vive ne se prête pas à une longue digression, ne nous y éternisons pas: disons rapidement qu'il est un assez grand quinquagénaire brun aux yeux verts, ou gris selon le temps ...', ibid., p. 234.

18 'Les jours s'écoulèrent ensuite, faute d'alternative, dans l'ordre habituel', *Je m'en vais*, p. 236. The allusion is to the opening line of Beckett's *Murphy* (Paris: Bordas, 1947): 'Le soleil brillait, n'ayant pas d'alternative, sur le rien de neuf.'

19 Bessard-Banquy, *Le Roman ludique*, p. 103.

20 Schoots, p. 102.

21 *Les Grandes Blondes* (Paris: Minuit 1995), p. 124. These monologues are to a degree recuperated into the subplot of Personnettaz's romantic education, demonstrating his fear of women and sexuality in his listening discomfort.

22 'Mais nous savons qu'elle a quitté Sydney, nous connaissons déjà ce trajet, réglons donc tout cela très vite et résumons', ibid.

23 'À moins qu'une âme sensible leur eût porté main forte, leurs efforts conjugués durent aboutir puisque deux heures plus tard ils roulaient à nouveau, pleins phares à fond sur la voie de gauche', ibid., p. 102.

24 Blanckeman, *Les Récits indécidables*, p. 39.

25 'Il se passe en effet quelque chose avec le jazz. Le travail que j'ai pu effectuer à un certain moment sur les genres a peut-être quelque chose à voir avec le standard, soit un thème devenu classique indéfiniment repris par toutes sortes de musiciens qui ont trouvé là une unité mélodique, harmonique, séduisante, intéressante, fertile, et chacun va le traiter à sa façon en le magnifiant et le sabotant à la fois. J'ai en particulier une grande admiration pour Thelonius Monk qui n'a eu de cesse de reprendre, outre ses propres compositions, des standards majeurs tels que *Just a gigolo* et de les pervertir pour les détruire et les magnifier à la fois, pour les dilater. Saboter pour dilater, c'est une formule dont je ferais bien mon programme. Ou détruire pour embellir. Créer un maximum d'obstacles par rapport à une forme fixe pour la déstabiliser, la casser, l'affaiblir, la torturer, mais non dans un but pervers, plutôt pour lui faire faire un quart de

tour. On trouve par ailleurs dans le jazz des éléments de syncope, de coupure, de faux pas, de piège, de rupture, de dissonance qui sont pour moi très précieux sur le plan de l'écriture', Jean Echenoz, 'Il se passe quelque chose avec le jazz', *Europe*, 820–1 (August–September 1997), 200.

26 Jean-Louis Ezine and Jean-François Josselin, 'Pour ou contre Echenoz?', *Le Nouvel Observateur*, 16 September 1999, consulted online at *http://hebdo.nouvelobs.com/hebdo/parution/p1819/articles/ a23541-.html?xtmc=echenozcontre&xtcr=1* (last accessed 30 October 2008).

27 Pierre Lepape, 'Pour raconter cette époque', *Le Monde*, 24 March 1990; quoted in Christine Jérusalem, *Jean Echenoz: géographies du vide* (Saint-Étienne: Publications de l'Université de Saint-Étienne, 2005), p. 7.

28 'À peine ébauché, chaque livre de Jean Echenoz se met à tanguer et à rouler et ne paraît plus vouloir tenir le cap prévu, mais il se met à croiser en cours de route tout ce bric-à-brac d'objets flottants qui tendent à en devenir progressivement le véritable centre d'intérêt ... Au bout de la lecture, ce n'est cependant pas une impression de dissémination ni d'incohérence qui perdure et prédomine, mais bien plutôt celle d'un système extrêmement rigoureux, voire d'une constellation dont toutes les parties, grandes ou petites, jusqu'à la moindre poussière d'étoile, seraient soumises à une même impérieuse loi de gravitation', Jean-Claude Lebrun, *Jean Echenoz*, p. 38.

29 Blanckeman, *Les Récits indécidables*, p. 46.

30 Emer O'Beirne, 'Televisual Narratives: Echenoz and Toussaint', *Contemporary French and Francophone Studies*, 10 (2006), 239–48 (p. 245).

31 Aspects of *Nous Trois* which connect it to *bande dessinée* in the French tradition include its sensationalist visual imagery, in both the earthquake and the space-flight halves of the narrative, its cast of beautiful yet superficially drawn characters, its foregrounding of the comic and its refusal of pathos (most notably in its flippancy towards the deaths in the Marseille disaster). Suspicious parallels to *Objectif lune* occur in Meyer's casual invitation into space, and the subsequent journey to the astronautics base, pp. 116–26.

32 '[E]n travelling', *Au piano* (Paris: Minuit, 2003), p. 49; 'plans généraux'; 'plan moyen', *Nous Trois* (Paris: Minuit, 1992), p. 71; *Cherokee* (Paris: Minuit, 1983), pp. 21, 55.

33 *Ravel* (Paris: Minuit, 2006), pp. 52–61.

34 *Je m'en vais*, pp. 46–7.

35 'Elle continuait de choisir au hasard sur sa carte ... Cela produirait une errance en dents de scie, pas très contrôlée: s'il se pourrait qu'on fît quelque détour pour l'avancer, il arriverait aussi qu'elle dût s'adapter à une destination, ceci équilibrant cela. Son itinéraire ne présenterait ainsi guère de cohérence, s'apparentant plutôt au trajet

brisé d'une mouche enclose dans une chambre', *Un an* (Paris: Minuit, 1997), p. 63.

36   *L'Équipée malaise* (Paris: Minuit, 1986), pp. 189–91; *Je m'en vais*, chapter 17 (pp. 115–23).

37   *L'Équipée malaise*, pp. 228–9.

38   *Je m'en vais*, p. 190.

39   *Un an*, pp. 50, 80.

40   Ibid., pp. 24, 37, 41, 109.

41   '[S]ans lien ni suite entre eux'; 'une somme parfaite, un catalogue de nature et de culture organisé avec soin en ordre', *Le Méridien de Greenwich* (Paris: Minuit, 1979), pp. 238, 246.

42   'The Figure in the Carpet' (1896), the title of which becomes a metaphor for the hidden theme of a writer's oeuvre; in Henry James, *Selected Tales*, ed. by John Lyon (Harmondsworth: Penguin, 2001), pp. 284–313.

43   '[T]out ira par deux, toujours plus ou moins par deux', *L'Équipée malaise*, p. 49. See, for instance, Fieke Schoots's discussion in *Passer en douce à la douane: l'écriture minimaliste de Minuit* (Amsterdam: Rodopi, 1997), pp. 118–19.

44   'Vous ferez une rencontre, souffla-t-elle doucement dans son oreille. Et vous partirez en voyage, un petit voyage. Et puis vous allez gagner beaucoup d'argent', *Cherokee*, p. 12.

45   Ferrer's apparent death was a singular kind of heart attack, from which he recovered without ill effect; Delahaye's death was faked as part of his scheme to rob Ferrer; Ferrer perpetuates the lie as part of the deal he has reached with Delahaye.

46   *Je m'en vais*, pp. 192–5, 125; *Un an*, p. 48.

47   *Les Grandes Blondes*, pp. 200, 141; *Au piano*, pp. 15–16, 167.

48   '[I]ls vous imposent d'être petit, moche et méchant', *Au piano*, p. 214.

49   *Je m'en vais*, p. 194; *Un an*, p. 70.

50   Tzvetan Todorov, *Introduction à la littérature fantastique* (Paris: Seuil, 1970).

51   'Au mieux, Béliard est une illusion. Au mieux il est une hallucination forgée par l'esprit déréglé de la jeune femme. Au pire il est une espèce d'ange gardien, du moins peut-il s'apparenter à cette congrégation. Envisageons le pire', *Les Grandes Blondes*, p. 36.

52   *Jérusalem*, p. 171.

53   Echenoz and Jean-Baptiste Harang, 'Jean Echenoz, Arctique de Paris' (Interview), *Libération*, 'Livres', 16 September 1999, 1–2 (1).

54   'Max préféra vite regarder son ticket. Comme il ne se passe pas grand-chose dans cette scène, on pourrait l'occuper en parlant de ce ticket. C'est qu'il y aurait pas mal de choses à dire sur ces tickets, sur leurs usages annexes – cure-dents, cure-ongles ou coupe-papier, plectre ou médiator, marque-page et ramasse-miettes, cale ou cylindre pour produits stupéfiants, paravent de maison de poupée, microcarnet de notes, souvenir, support de numéro de téléphone que vous gribouillez pour une fille en cas d'urgence – et leurs divers

destins – pliés en deux ou en quatre dans le sens de la longueur et susceptibles alors d'être glissés sous une alliance, une chevalière, un bracelet-montre, pliés en six et jusqu'en huit en accordéon, déchirés en confettis, épluchés en spirale comme une pomme, puis jetés dans les corbeilles du réseau, sur le sol du réseau, puis jetés hors du réseau, dans le caniveau, dans la rue, chez soi pour jouer à pile ou face: face magnétisée, pile section urbaine –, mais ce n'est peut-être pas le moment de développer tout cela', *Au piano*, pp. 71–2.

55　　Georges Perec, *L'Infra-ordinaire* (Paris: Seuil, 1989); Alain Robbe-Grillet, *Les Gommes* (Paris: Minuit, 1953), p. 161.

56　　'[Q]u'est-ce que c'est que ce nom idiot récupéré sur les anciens tickets de métro'; 'il y a toujours une petite part d'arbitraire dans les décisions', *Au piano*, pp. 148–9.

57　　*Ravel*, pp. 46–7, 108.

58　　*Nous Trois*, pp. 13–14, 60.

59　　*L'Équipée malaise*, pp. 205, 123.

60　　'Cette route est loin des plages, on ne voit pas la mer, on le regrette. On aimerait bien regarder naître et grossir les vagues et se renverser, voir indéfiniment chacune d'elles décliner sa version, son interprétation de la vague idéale, on pourrait comparer leur allure, leur conception, leur succession, leur son, mais non, Victoire descendit du car vers quinze heures à Mimizan', *Un an*, pp. 48–9.

61　　'Je suis obligé de tout reprendre au conditionnel, d'exprimer la frustration de ne pas pouvoir décrire les vagues, d'imaginer la description qu'on pourrait en faire ... C'est comme si une section rythmique imposait un autre tempo. On est alors bien obligé d'être dans la contradiction et de profiter de cette contradiction-là. Cela fait qu'on travaille avec un intérêt différent et plus grand que si on suivait la pente des intentions premières. On se fait violence à soi, on fait violence au récit, aux autres ... Ça bouscule les choses, ce qui est un intérêt majeur de la littérature', Jean Echenoz and Hervé Delouche, 'Pour ce livre, cette histoire-là, je n'ai jamais pensé à quelqu'un d'autre qu'une femme ...', *Regards*, 1997, consulted online at *www.regards.fr/archives/1997/199707/199707inv01.html*.

62　　*Je m'en vais*, p. 240; *L'Équipée malaise*, p. 122.

63　　*Ravel*, p. 76; *Je m'en vais*, p. 189.

64　　*Les Grandes Blondes*, p. 250; *Ravel*, p. 70; 'Continuons d'avancer, maintenant, accélérons'; 'accompagnons-les jusqu'à leur véhicule ... laissons-les s'en aller. Revenons chez Paul'; 'Mais ça marchera beaucoup mieux, Maurice, ça marchera cent mille fois mieux que *La Madelon*'; 'Personellement, je commence à en avoir un peu assez, de Baumgartner'; 'vous prévoyez le pire, on vous comprend' ; 'pas mal de gens que vous ne devez pas connaître ... d'autres dont vous avez peut-être entendu parler'; 'vous, je vous connais, par contre, je vous vois d'ici. Vous imaginiez que Max était encore un de ces hommes à femmes, un de ces bons vieux séducteurs ... Eh bien pas du tout', *Au piano*, p. 60.

65 'Les partis pris systématiques de la seconde personne, tels qu'on les trouve chez le Butor de *La Modification* ou le Perec d'*Un homme qui dort*, ne m'intéressent pas en tant que systèmes. Mais j'aime bien sûr ces ouvertures-là, recourir à la première, deuxième ou troisième personne du singulier ou du pluriel comme on filmerait une scène avec trois caméras. Puisque par ailleurs le livre rencontre tôt ou tard un lecteur, je trouve normal de s'adresser à lui, de lui dire "tu" ou "vous" – plutôt "vous", d'ailleurs – quitte à l'abandonner aussitôt à un regard d'ensemble. Pour fuir tout projet formaliste précis', 'Il se passe quelque chose avec le jazz', p. 201.

66 'Le lendemain, vers midi et demie, Béliard vint chercher Max histoire de vous socialiser un peu, expliqua-t-il. Ce ne serait pas bon pour vous de rester isolé dans votre coin, il ne faut pas rester coupé du monde, il est toujours bon d'échanger. Ce serait donc le premier repas que Max prendrait hors de sa chambre, au sortir de laquelle on croisa Doris dans le couloir. Elle était là, paraissant traîner dans le secteur sans avoir grand-chose à faire, comme si elle n'attendait que de rencontrer Max. Et, bien que celui-ci, nous l'avons dit, n'eût jamais été ce qu'on appelle un séducteur, jamais été sensible aux appels plus ou moins subliminaux qu'on pouvait lui adresser car jamais assez sûr de lui pour les considérer comme tels, il lui sembla que Doris le regardait plus précisément, lui souriait avec plus d'acuité. Même son maquillage et sa démarche, plus souple et dansante qu'à l'ordinaire, n'étaient pas les mêmes que les autres fois, comme si quelque chose, enfin je ne sais pas. Mais qu'est-ce que tu te racontes. Qu'est-ce que tu vas imaginer', *Au piano*, pp. 130–1.

67 'Parce que j'aimerais aussi que la lecture se fasse dans le même sens que l'écriture, je veux dire littéralement dans tous les sens.' 'Il se passe quelque chose avec le jazz', p. 201.

68 'Meyer feuilleta celui-ci, croyant reconnaître une devanture sur le trajet d'un des convois, devanture entrevue dans la poussière opaque comme il venait de quitter le centre commercial en compagnie de Mercedes. Il referma le magazine quand je parus au fond du couloir, réglant un des poignets de ma combinaison', *Nous Trois*, pp. 176–7.

69 'Que ce personnage nommé DeMilo s'exprime par le "je", ce n'est qu'un de ses attributs, parmi d'autres, mais cela ne lui confère aucun droit de priorité sur la narration. Le seul droit qu'il a, c'est celui de parler ainsi, à la première personne', Interview with Claude Murcia, 'Décalage et hors-champ', *Artpress*, 175 (December 1992), 56–9; reprinted in Schoots, p. 169 n.

70 Echenoz compares his use of verb tenses to a gearbox in Echenoz and 'J.-C. L.', 'Jean Echenoz: l'image du roman comme un moteur de fiction me séduit en ce moment' (Interview), *L'Humanité*, 'Culture', 11 October 1996, consulted online at *http://www. humanite.fr/journal/archives.html*.

71 Michel Volkovitch, 'Les Temps verbaux chez Jean Echenoz', in Christine Jérusalem and Jean-Bernard Vray (eds), *Jean Echenoz: 'une tentative modeste de description du monde'* (Sainte-Étienne: Publications de l'Université de Sainte-Étienne, 2006), pp. 267–76 (p. 268).

72   Colin Nettelbeck, 'The "Post-Literary" Novel: Echenoz, Pennac and Company', *French Cultural Studies*, 14 (June 1994), 113–38 (p. 127). Nettelbeck gives an example from *Le Méridien de Greenwich*: 'temps suffisant pour qu'ils sympathisassent, mieux se connussent, et de se revoir convinssent' (p. 171).

73   'Vers six heures il entendit Alice rentrer, sans pour autant suspendre son travail: il passerait la fin de l'après-midi à préciser quelques nuances des deux mouvements, *Pressentiment* suivi de *Mort*, de la Sonate 1.X.1905 de Janácek, après quoi il monterait retrouver Alice affairée dans la cuisine. Tiens, dirait-il, du poisson. Oui, répondrait Alice, pourquoi? Non, rien, dirait Max en mettant la table, j'aime bien le poisson, où as-tu rangé les couverts à poisson?', *Au piano*, p. 35.

74   Marc Augé, *Non-lieux: introduction à une anthropologie de la surmodernité* (Paris: Seuil, 1992).

75   'Il enfila quelques affaires sans prendre garde à leur assortiment, se proposant vaguement d'acheter des chaussures un de ces jours – celles-ci devaient facilement faire soixante mille au compteur. Mais, outre cette perspective, rien d'autre à faire aujourd'hui; ni plus ni moins qu'hier. Et rien ne mine comme l'oisiveté derrière la République, dans un deux-pièces opaque de la rue Yves-Toudic', *Les Grandes Blondes*, p. 198.

76   The noise of corduroy trousers appears in *Un an*, pp. 33–4; beer bubbles are described in *Le Méridien de Greenwich*, pp. 172–3; the cashiers' conversation in *Nous Trois*, p. 212. Viart's comment is taken from his essay, 'Jean Echenoz et l'ésthétique du dégagement', in Jérusalem and Vray (eds), pp. 243–54 (p. 248).

77   'j'ai fait quelques années de sociologie à l'université, j'ai toujours envie de marquer les situations par des objets, par des systèmes de discours, par des types d'échanges', Echenoz and 'J.-C. L.'

78   Echenoz and Jean-Baptiste Harang, 'Jean Echenoz, Arctique de Paris', 2.

79   *Ravel*, pp. 19–20; *L'Équipée malaise*, p. 69.

80   Davis and Fallaize, pp. 89–91.

81   For example, *Nous Trois*, pp. 83–4, *Lac*, p. 63.

82   *Au piano*, p. 181; *Nous Trois*, pp. 144–7; *L'Équipée malaise*, p. 79.

83   See, in particular, Jean Baudrillard, *L'Échange symbolique et la mort* (Paris: Gallimard, 1976). Critical discussions of Baudrillard's ideas in relation to Echenoz's fiction include Davis and Fallaize, pp. 94–7, Schoots, pp. 97–9, and Jérusalem, pp. 124–5.

84   Gianfranco Rubino, 'L'Évidence du narrateur', in Jérusalem and Vray (eds), pp. 221–9 (p. 221).

85   'Le roman – la forme romanesque – n'avait pas très bonne presse à l'époque, on baignait plutôt dans la théorie. On ne parlait pas trop d'écrire des romans, des fictions, on parlait de produire des *textes*. Ponctuation dynamitée, narration déconstruite, etc., c'était extrêmement intéressant. Je produisais moi-même, seul dans mon coin, pas mal de textes. Et puis, à un moment donné, j'ai dû en avoir assez, je me suis dit: 'je ne vais plus produire un texte, je vais tâcher d'écrire

un roman', Interview with Cathérine Argand and Jean-Maurice de Montrémy, *Lire*, September, 1992, pp. 36–41.

86 'Pourquoi j'ai pas fait poète', in *Revue de littérature générale*, 95.1 ('La mécanique lyrique') (Paris: POL, 1995).

87 Schoots, p. 183.

88 Viart, 'Jean Echenoz et l'ésthétique du dégagement', p. 252.

5 Patrick Modiano and the Problem of Endings

1 Modiano's major texts to date are *La Place de l'étoile* (Paris: Gallimard, 1968); *La Ronde de nuit* (Paris: Gallimard, 1970); *Les Boulevards de ceinture* (Paris: Gallimard, 1972); *Villa Triste* (Paris: Gallimard, 1975); *Livret de famille* (Paris: Gallimard, 1977); *Rue des Boutiques Obscures* (Paris: Gallimard, 1978); *Une jeunesse* (Paris: Gallimard, 1981); *De si braves garçons* (Paris: Gallimard, 1982); *Quartier perdu* (Paris: Gallimard, 1984); *Dimanches d'août* (Paris: Gallimard, 1986); *Remise de peine* (Paris: Seuil, 1987); *Vestiaire de l'enfance* (Paris: Gallimard, 1989); *Voyage de noces* (Paris: Gallimard, 1990); *Fleurs de ruine* (Paris: Seuil, 1991); *Un cirque passe* (Paris: Gallimard, 1992); *Chien de printemps* (Paris: Seuil, 1993); *Du plus loin de l'oubli* (Paris: Gallimard, 1996); *Dora Bruder* (Paris: Gallimard, 1997); *Des inconnues* (Paris: Gallimard, 1999); *La Petite Bijou* (Paris: Gallimard, 2001); *Accident nocturne* (Paris: Gallimard, 2003); *Un pedigree* (Paris: Gallimard, 2005); *Dans le café de la jeunesse perdue* (2007).

2 Jérôme Garcin, 'Sans famille: rencontre avec Patrick Modiano', *Le Nouvel Observateur*, 2 October 2003, 56–9 (p. 58).

3 Modiano's filmography includes screenwriting credits for three films (each credit shared with the director): Louis Malle's *Lacombe Lucien* (1974, screenplay published by Gallimard, 1974), Pascal Aubier's *Le Fils de Gascogne* (1995) and Jean-Paul Rappeneau's *Bon Voyage* (2003). In addition, three of his novels have been adapted by others for the screen: *Une jeunesse*, filmed by Moshé Mizrahi in 1983, *Villa triste*, filmed by Patrice Leconte as *Le Parfum d'Yvonne* in 1994, and *Dimanches d'août*, filmed by Manuel Poirier as *Te quiero* in 2001. Modiano's relationship with the cinema is explored by Colin Nettelbeck in his article, 'Modiano's Stylo: A Novelist in the Age of Cinema', *French Cultural Studies* 17 (2006), 35–54. The collaborations with Le Tan are *Memory lane* (Paris: POL, 1981) and *Poupée blonde* (Paris: POL, 1983).

4 'J'ai l'impression depuis plus de trente ans d'écrire le même livre – c'est-à-dire l'impression que les vingt livres publiés séparément ne forment, en fait, qu'un seul livre', 'Rencontre avec Patrick Modiano à l'occasion de la publication de *La Petite Bijou*' (2001), interview posted on the Gallimard website, *http://www.gallimard.fr/catalog/html/ event/index/index_modia.html.*

5 The terms 'demi-monde' and 'haut pègre' ('high-class mobsters') are Modiano's own to describe his father's associations, in *Un pedigree*, p. 18.

6   Akane Kawakami, *A Self-Conscious Art: Patrick Modiano's Postmodern Fictions* (Liverpool: Liverpool University Press, 2000), p. 110.

7   John Flower, 'Introduction', in John Flower (ed.), *Patrick Modiano* (Amsterdam: Rodopi, 2007), pp. 7–18 (p. 7).

8   *Villa Triste*, p. 21.

9   *Accident nocturne*, p. 117; *Un pedigree*, p. 11.

10   '[T]oute cette soirée passée avec eux dans la demi-pénombre de la terrasse était empreinte de la douceur d'un rêve. Et de nouveau, le long des rues vides de Neuilly, je croyais entendre le claquement des sabots et le bruissement des feuillages d'il y a vingt ans', *De si braves garçons*, p. 160.

11   'la transparence du temps', *Vestiaire de l'enfance*, p. 151.

12   'Moi aussi, à partir d'aujourd'hui, je ne veux plus me souvenir de rien', *Quartier perdu*, p. 184.

13   See Thierry Laurent, *L'Oeuvre de Patrick Modiano: une autofiction* (Lyon: Presses Universitaires de Lyon, 1997) and Dervila Cooke, *Present Pasts: Patrick Modiano's (Auto)Biographical Fictions* (Amsterdam: Rodopi, 2005).

14   Aristotle, *Poetics*, in D. A. Russell and Michael Winterbottom (eds), *Classical Literary Criticism* (Oxford: Oxford University Press, 1989), pp. 51–90 (pp. 60–1).

15   Vladimir Propp, *Morphology of the Folktale* (1928), trans. by Laurence Scott, revised and ed. by Louis A. Wagner (Austin: University of Texas Press, 1971).

16   Umberto Eco applies a Proppian analysis to Ian Fleming's spy thrillers in 'James Bond: une combinatoire narrative', *Communications*, 8 (1966), 83–99.

17   Armine Kotin Mortimer, *La Clôture narrative* (Paris: José Corti, 1985).

18   See J. Hillis Miller, *Ariadne's Thread: Story Lines* (New Haven: Yale University Press, 1992).

19   J. Hillis Miller, 'The Problematic of Ending in Narrative', *Nineteenth-Century Fiction*, 33 (1978), 3–7 (p. 4).

20   Kotin Mortimer, *La Clôture narrative*, p. 221.

21   Frank Kermode, *The Sense of an Ending: Studies in the Theory of Fiction* (Oxford: Oxford University Press, 1967).

22   Ibid., p. 46.

23   Brooks, *Reading for the Plot*, p. 23.

24   Jonathan Culler, *The Pursuit of Signs* (London: Routledge, 1988), pp. 188–208.

25   D. A. Miller, *Narrative and its Discontents: Problems of Closure in the Traditional Novel* (Princeton, NJ: Princeton University Press, 1981), p. 274.

26   Ibid., p. ix. Miller's example of *Great Expectations* also helps to illustrate the deterministic limits in his theory: Dickens's novel reaches equal stability in both of its alternative endings: whether Pip loses Estella definitively or gains her definitively, the narrative has reached a state of quiescence.

27 Marianna Torgovnik, *Closure in the Novel* (Princeton, NJ: Princeton University Press, 1981), p. 206. Torgovnik's examples are Erica Jong's *Fear of Flying* (1973) and Bernard Malamud's *The Tenants* (1971).

28 Torgovnik, *Closure in the Novel*, pp. 13–18.

29 'Je ne sais pas combien de temps je suis resté au bord de ce lagon. Je pensais à Freddie. Non, il n'avait certainement pas disparu en mer. Il avait décidé, sans doute, de couper les dernières amarres et devait se cacher dans un atoll. Je finirais bien par le trouver. Et puis, il me fallait tenter une dernière démarche: me rendre à mon ancienne adresse à Rome, rue des Boutiques Obscures, 2. Le soir est tombé. Le lagon s'éteignait peu à peu à mesure que sa couleur verte se résorbait. Sur l'eau couraient encore des ombres gris mauve, en une vague phosphorescence. J'avais sorti de ma poche, machinalement, les photos de nous que je voulais montrer à Freddie, et parmi celles-ci, la photo de Gay Orlow, petite fille. Je n'avais pas remarqué jusque-là qu'elle pleurait. On le devinait à un froncement de ses sourcils. Un instant, mes pensées m'ont emporté loin de ce lagon, à l'autre bout du monde, dans une station balnéaire de la Russie du Sud où la photo avait été prise, il y a longtemps. Une petite fille rentre de la plage, au crépuscule, avec sa mère. Elle pleure pour rien, parce qu'elle aurait voulu continuer de jouer. Elle s'éloigne. Elle a déjà tourné le coin de la rue, et nos vies ne sont-elles pas aussi rapides à se dissiper dans le soir que ce chagrin d'enfant?', *Rue des Boutiques Obscures*, pp. 250–1.

30 Despite its fairy-tale name, the Via delle Botteghe Oscure is in fact a real street in Rome.

31 Viktor Shklovsky, *O teorii prozy* (1929), reprinted as 'La Construction de la nouvelle et du roman', trans. by Tzvetan Todorov, in *Théorie de la littérature*, ed. by Tzvetan Todorov (Paris: Seuil, 1966), pp. 170–96. Discussing Shklovsky's idea, Frank Kermode remarks: 'Such endings have nothing to do with ravelling or unravelling. They simply say the cold got colder, or the plain stretched out interminably. Everybody recognizes the gesture', 'Sensing Endings', *Nineteenth-Century Fiction*, 33.1 (June 1978), 144–58 (p. 146).

32 Philippe Hamon, 'Clausules', *Poetique: Revue de Theorie et d'Analyse Litteraires* 24 (1975), 495–526.

33 The symbolism of turning away from the search captures in miniature what the later parts of the story have already been recounting. Roland has already approached the heart of the mystery as he approaches the place where he was near-fatally betrayed as he tried to flee the Occupation into Switzerland. When, at that point, he tells the taxi driver to return him to the station (p. 235), and immediately afterwards arranges his flight to Polynesia, he has already begun to flee the past trauma which he earlier wished to confront.

34 Modiano's autobiography, *Un pedigree*, follows this rule, although his other non-fiction text, *Dora Bruder*, does not.

35 *De si braves garçons*, p. 186; *Vestiaire de l'enfance*, p. 151; *Du plus loin de l'oubli*, p. 181.

36   'Une douzaine d'années avait passé depuis que l'on ne m'appelait
     plus "la Petite Bijou" et je me trouvais à la station de métro Châtelet à
     l'heure de pointe. J'étais dans la foule qui suivait le couloir sans fin,
     sur le tapis roulant. Une femme portait un manteau jaune. La
     couleur du manteau avait attiré mon attention et je la voyais de dos,
     sur le tapis roulant. Puis elle marchait le long du couloir où il était
     indiqué "Direction Château-de-Vincennes". Nous étions maintenant
     immobiles, serrés les uns contre les autres au milieu de l'escalier, en
     attendant que le portillon s'ouvre. Elle se tenait à côté de moi. Alors
     j'ai vu son visage. La ressemblance de ce visage avec celui de ma mère
     était si frappante que j'ai pensé que c'était elle', *La Petite Bijou*, p. 9.
37   Ibid., pp. 10, 12.
38   'La voix de Véra Valadier avait changé … Peut-être pensait-elle à ce
     temps proche – les années passent si vite – où sa fille serait grande et
     où elle, Véra, hanterait les couloirs du métro pour l'éternité avec un
     manteau jaune', ibid., p. 119.
39   'Je restais devant la porte, sans sonner. Souvent, quand je revenais
     seule dans le grand appartement près du Bois de Boulogne et que je
     sonnais, personne ne m'ouvrait. Alors je descendais l'escalier et j'al-
     lais téléphoner dans un café, un peu plus loin, sur l'avenue. Le
     patron me regardait avec gentillesse, les clients aussi. Ils avaient l'air
     de savoir qui j'étais. Ils avaient dû se renseigner. Un jour, l'un d'eux
     avait dit: "C'est la petite du 129." Je n'avais pas d'argent et on ne me
     faisait pas payer la communication. J'entrais dans la cabine télé-
     phonique. L'appareil fixé au mur était trop haut pour moi et il fallait
     que je me dresse sur la pointe des pieds pour composer le numéro:
     PASSY 15 28. Mais personne ne répondait …', ibid., pp, 77–8,
40   '"J'ai l'impression que vos souvenirs d'enfance vous préoccupent
     beaucoup", m'a-t-il dit. C'était depuis le soir où j'avais vu la femme
     en manteau jaune dans le métro. Avant, j'y pensais à peine', ibid.,
     p. 143.
41   'Les lettres qui m'étaient destinées et qui venaient du Maroc avaient
     dû rester fermées … Elles portaient sur leurs enveloppes une
     mauvaise adresse, ou un simple faute d'orthographe, et cela avait
     suffi pour qu'elles s'égarent, les unes après les autres, dans un
     bureau de poste inconnu. A moins qu'on ne les ait renvoyées au
     Maroc, mais il n'y avait déjà plus personne là-bas. Elles s'étaient
     perdues, comme le chien', ibid., p. 167.
42   'Ils ont détruit l'hôtel de Verdun', *Villa Triste*, p. 13.
43   'Ainsi cette enveloppe. Avait-elle existé dans la réalité? Où n'était-ce
     qu'un objet qui faisait partie de mon rêve?', *Voyage de noces*, p. 108.
44   'Il n'avait plus beaucoup de réalité. Le sang même qui avait giclé de
     ses lèvres et lui avait inondé le menton ne paraissait pas être du sang
     véritable mais un artifice de cinéma', *Dimanches d'août*, p. 75.
45   These structures gain a philosophical justification in Modiano's most
     recent novels, where Nietzsche's idea of the eternal return becomes a
     preoccupation of the narrators. See *Accident nocturne*, p. 60; *Dans le
     café de la jeunesse perdue*, p. 133.

46 'Il me semblait que je ne parviendrais jamais à retrouver la moindre
    trace de Dora Bruder. Alors le manque que j'éprouvais m'a poussé à
    l'écriture d'un roman, *Voyage de noces*, un moyen comme un autre
    pour continuer à concentrer mon attention sur Dora Bruder, et peut-
    être, me disais-je, pour élucider ou deviner quelque chose d'elle, un
    lieu où elle était passée, un détail de sa vie', *Dora Bruder*, p. 53.

47 Georges Perec, *W ou le souvenir de l'enfance* (Paris: Denoël, 1975).
    Perec's memoir alternates the story of his childhood under the
    Occupation with chapters of a fantasy narrative, the setting of which
    gradually comes to resemble the kind of concentration camp in
    which his mother died.

48 *Dora Bruder*, p. 54.

49 Stioppa, who appears on p. 48 of *Un pedigree*, was previously seen in
    Rue des Boutiques Obscures and *Remise de peine*; Gay Orloff (*Un pedigree*,
    p. 18) is very reminiscent of the character Gay Orlow in *Rue des
    Boutiques Obscures*; Freddie McEvoy, an Australian bobsleigh cham-
    pion in *Un pedigree* (p. 17), recalls Pedro McEvoy, a possible alias of
    the narrator in *Rue des Boutiques Obscures*, and the fourth story of *De si
    braves garçons*, involving a character named Pedro and another
    named McFowles, the latter of whom is to die in a bobsleigh acci-
    dent.

50 *Un pedigree*, pp. 37, 69.

51 Ibid., pp. 116, 65.

52 *Accident nocturne*, pp. 10, 86; *Un pedigree*, pp. 112, 33.

53 Morawski appears in *Un pedigree*, p. 65 and *Accident nocturne*, p. 147;
    Sologne in *Un pedigree*, p. 93 and *Accident nocturne*, p. 25; the café
    rendezvous in *Un pedigree*, p. 90 and *Accident nocturne*, p. 140; and the
    young woman in *Un pedigree*, p. 96 and *Accident nocturne*, p. 86.

54 'Nous sommes restés seuls dans le salon, quelques minutes, et je fais
    un effort de mémoire pour rassembler le plus de détails possible. Les
    portes-fenêtres qui donnaient sur le boulevard étaient entrouvertes à
    cause de la chaleur. C'était au 19 du boulevard Raspail. En 1965. Un
    piano à queue tout au fond de la pièce. Le canapé et les deux
    fauteuils étaient du même cuir noir. La table basse, en métal argenté.
    Un nom comme Devez ou Duvelz. La cicatrice sur la joue. Le
    chemisier dégrafé. Une lumière très vive de projecteur, ou plutôt de
    torche électrique. Elle n'éclaire qu'une parcelle du décor, un instant
    isolé, laissant le reste dans l'ombre, car nous ne saurions jamais la
    suite des événements et qui étaient, au juste, ces deux personnes',
    Fleurs de ruine, pp. 23–4.

55 'cette sorte de pan lumineux, découpé au milieux d'indistinctes
    ténèbres', Marcel Proust, *Du côté de chez Swann* (1913) (Paris:
    Flammarion, 1987), p. 140.

56 'Plus je considérais la façade blanche, plus j'avais la sensation de
    l'avoir déjà vue – une sensation fugitive comme les bribes d'un rêve
    qui vous échappent au réveil, ou bien un reflet de lune', *Accident
    nocturne*, p. 114. Such failures are also prefigured in Proust in the
    Hudimesnil episode of *A l'ombre des jeune filles en fleurs*.

57 Kawakami, *A Self-conscious Art*, p. 23.

58   'La sensation de vide m'a envahi, encore plus violente que d'habi-
     tude. Elle m'était familière. Elle me prenait, comme à d'autres des
     crises de paludisme ... De tout ce que j'ai pu éprouver au cours des
     années où j'écrivais mes livres à Paris, cette impression d'absence et
     de vide est la plus forte. Elle est comme un halo de lumière blanche
     qui m'empêche de distinguer les autres détails de ma vie de cette
     époque-là et qui brouille mes souvenirs. Aujourd'hui, je sais la
     manière de surmonter ce vertige. Il faut que je me répète doucement
     à moi-même mon nouveau nom: Jimmy Sarano, ma date et mon lieu
     de naissance, mon emploi du temps, le nom des collègues de Radio-
     Mundial que je rencontrerai le jour même, le résumé du chapitre
     des *Aventures de Louis XVII* que j'écrirai, mon adresse, 33, Mercedes
     Terrace, bref, que je m'agrippe à tous ces points de repère pour ne
     pas me laisser aspirer par ce que je ne peux nommer autrement que:
     le vide', *Vestiaire de l'enfance*, p. 101. As we learn in a further section of
     this same passage, Sarano shares Modiano's birthplace, and is only a
     digit away from sharing his birthdate.

59   Josane Duranteau, 'L'Obsession de l'anti-héros', *Le Monde*,
     11 November 1972, 13; Jean Montalbetti, 'La Haine des professeurs:
     instantané Patrick Modiano', *Les Nouvelles littéraires*, 13 June 1968,
     2; Jean-Louis Ezine, 'Sur la sellette: Patrick Modiano ou le passé
     antérieur', *Les Nouvelles littéraires*, 6–12 October 1975, 5. All of these
     comments on literature are collected in Alan Morris, *Patrick Modiano*
     (Oxford: Berg, 1996), p. 7.

60   'J'ai souvent le sentiment que des gens de ma génération ont une
     infirmité par rapport à ceux de la génération précédente: notre
     pouvoir de concentration s'est affaibli. La génération précédente est
     parvenue à faire une oeuvre globale, une sorte de cathédrale. Je
     pense à Proust ou à Lawrence Durrell et à son *Quatuor d'Alexandrie*.
     Ces gens vivaient dans un monde où l'on pouvait se concentrer
     davantage tandis que pour les gens de ma génération, c'est fragmen-
     taire. On arrive peut-être à faire un truc global, mais avec des
     fragments, si vous voulez ...', Patrick Modiano and Laurence Liban,
     'Entretien', *Lire*, October 2003; consulted online at *http://www.lire.fr/
     entretien.asp/idC=45605/idTC=4/idR=201/idG=3*.

61   Colin Nettelbeck, 'Jardinage dans les ruines: Modiano et l'espace
     littéraire français contemporain', in John E. Flower (ed.), *Patrick
     Modiano* (Amsterdam: Rodopi, 2007), pp. 19–32 (p. 23).

62   Kawakami, *A Self-conscious Art*, p. 132.

63   Ibid., p. 46.

64   André Gide, *Les Faux-monnayeurs* (Paris: Gallimard, 1925), p. 322.

65   Kotin Mortimer, *La Clôture narrative*, p. 183.

66   As another character in *Les Faux-monnayeurs* opines: 'Trying to
     resolve things is the business of you novelists. In life nothing is
     resolved, everything continues', p. 308. Balzac, who has been a
     primary point of reference for this study, expresses a similar opinion
     in a postface to *La Fille aux yeux d'or*, in which he describes his novel
     as true in its details but unrealistic in its narrative form, as 'nothing

in nature has a poetic denouement', Postface, *La Fille aux yeux d'or* (1834–5) (Paris: Flammarion, 1988), p. 302.

The Return of the Story

1 'Il faut croire que je m'inscris dans la tradition des écrivains français qui posent des questions au monde d'aujourd'hui et ne renient pas la narration balzacienne', Michel Houellebecq and Jérôme Garcin, '"Je suis un prophète amateur": un entretien avec Michel Houellebecq', *Le Nouvel Observateur*, 25–31 August 2005, 8–10 (pp. 9–10).

2 '— Pourquoi venir à New York pour écrire dessus? me demande le grand écrivain en caressant sa barbe blanche. Moi, quand j'écris un roman qui se passe à Berlin, je ne vais pas à Berlin pour l'écrire. — C'est que je fais de l'Ancien Roman. Je laisse la nouveauté aux jeunes comme vous', Frédéric Beigbeder, *Windows on the World* (Paris: Gallimard, coll. Folio, 2004), first published by Grasset, 2003, p. 271.

3 'Cet effacement progressif des relations humaines n'est pas sans poser certains problèmes au roman. Comment en effet entreprendrait-on la narration de ces passions fougueuses, s'étalant sur plusieurs années, faisant parfois sentir leurs effets sur plusieurs générations? Nous sommes loin des *Hauts de Hurlevent*, c'est le moins qu'on puisse dire. La forme romanesque n'est pas conçue pour peindre l'indifférence, ni le néant; il faudrait inventer une articulation plus plate, plus concise et plus morne', Michel Houellebecq, *Extension du domaine de la lutte* (Paris: Nadeau, 1994), p. 42.

4 Le Clézio's first novel, *Le Procès-verbal* (1963), slips between the confused and hallucinatory account of its schizophrenic first-person narrator and that of an impersonal narrator who may be the protagonist in disguise, while the text itself includes crossings-out legible and illegible, extracts from books and newspapers the narrator reads, and page-long gaps mid-sentence. Le Clézio's subsequent career has seen a gradual development towards more subtle and conventional narrative structures: his more recent novels may alternate narratives from different times and places, or adopt the fairy-tale logic of magic realism in their plot development, but ostentatious narrative invention is put behind him.

Select Bibliography

Annie Ernaux

Les Armoires vides (Paris: Gallimard, 1974)
Ce qu'ils disent ou rien (Paris: Gallimard, 1977)
La Femme gelée (Paris: Gallimard, 1981)
La Place (Paris: Gallimard, 1984) (Prix Renaudot, 1984)
Une femme (Paris: Gallimard, 1988)
Passion simple (Paris: Gallimard, 1992)
Journal du dehors (Paris: Gallimard, 1993)
'Je ne suis pas sortie de ma nuit' (Paris: Gallimard, 1997)
La Honte (Paris: Gallimard, 1997)
La Vie extérieure, 1993–1999 (Paris: Gallimard, 2000)
L'Événement (Paris: Gallimard, 2000)
Se perdre (Paris: Gallimard, 2001)
L'Occupation (Paris: Gallimard, 2002)
'Préface', in Fabrice Thumerel (ed.), *Annie Ernaux: une oeuvre de l'entre-deux* (Arras: Artois Presses Université, 2004), pp. 7–10
Les Années (Paris: Gallimard, 2008)
(with Claire-Lise Tondeur) 'Entretien avec Annie Ernaux', *The French Review*, 69 (1995), 37–44
(with Pierre-Louis Fort) 'Entretien avec Annie Ernaux', *The French Review*, 76 (2003), 984–94
(with Frédéric-Yves Jeannet) *L'Écriture comme un couteau: entretien avec Frédéric-Yves Jeannet* (Paris: Stock, 2003)
(with Michèle M. Magill and Katherine S. Stephenson) 'Entretien', in Michèle M. Magill and Katherine S. Stephenson, *Dit de femmes: entretiens d'écrivaines françaises* (Birmingham, AL: Summa, 2003), pp. 73–88
(with Philippe Lejeune) 'Un singulier journal au féminin', in Thumerel (ed.), pp. 253–8
(with Marie-Madeleine Million-Lajoinie) 'A propos des journaux extérieurs' (interview), in Thumerel (ed.), pp. 259–65
(with Fabrice Thumerel) 'Ambivalences et ambiguïtés du journal intime' (interview), in Thumerel (ed.), pp. 245–52
(with Loraine Day) '"Entraîner les lecteurs dans l'effarement du réel": Interview with Annie Ernaux', *Romance Studies*, 23 (2005), 223–36
(with Marc Marie) *L'Usage de la photo* (Paris: Gallimard, 2005)
Davis, Colin and Elizabeth Fallaize, *French Fiction in the Mitterrand Years: Memory, Narrative, Desire* (Oxford: Oxford University Press, 2000)

Fell, Alison S., 'Recycling the Past: Annie Ernaux's Evolving *Écriture de Soi*', *Nottingham French Studies*, 41 (2002), 60–9

Fernandez-Recatala, Denis, *Annie Ernaux* (Monaco: Rocher, 1994)

McIlvanney, Siobhán, 'Recuperating Romance: Literary Paradigms in the Works of Annie Ernaux', *Forum for Modern Language Studies*, 32 (1996), 240–50

—— *Annie Ernaux: The Return to Origins* (Liverpool: Liverpool University Press, 2001)

Merleau, Chloë Taylor, 'The Confessions of Annie Ernaux: Autobiography, Truth and Repetition', *Journal of Modern Literature*, 28 (2004), 65–88

Motte, Warren, 'Annie Ernaux's Understatement', *The French Review*, 69 (1995), 55–67

Thomas, Lynn, *Annie Ernaux: An Introduction to the Writer and her Audience* (Oxford and New York: Berg, 1999)

Thumerel, Fabrice (ed.), *Annie Ernaux: une oeuvre de l'entre-deux* (Arras: Artois Presses Université, 2004)

Tondeur, Claire-Lise, *Annie Ernaux ou l'exil intérieur* (Amsterdam: Rodopi, 1996)

Pascal Quignard

Lycophron, Alexandra (translation) (Paris: Mercure de France, 1971, 2nd edn 2001)

Le Lecteur (Paris: Gallimard, 1976)

Carus (Paris: Gallimard, 1979); folio edition 'revue et corrigée par l'auteur', 1990

Les Tablettes de buis d'Apronenia Avitia (Paris: Gallimard, 1984)

Le Salon du Wurtemberg (Paris: Gallimard, 1986)

Une gêne technique à l'égard des fragments (Montpellier: Fata Morgana, 1986); reprinted by Galilée, 2005

La Leçon de musique (Paris: Hachette, 1987); reprinted by Gallimard (Folio), 2002

Les Escaliers de Chambord (Paris: Gallimard, 1989)

Albucius (Paris: POL, 1990); reprinted by Gallimard (Folio), 2004

Kong Souen-Long, Sur le doigt qui montre cela (translation) (Paris: Chandeigne, 1990)

Petits Traités, 8 vols (Paris: Maeght, 1990); reprinted in 2 vols by Gallimard (Folio), 1997

La Raison (Paris: Le Promeneur, 1990)

Tous les matins du monde (Paris: Gallimard, 1991)

La Frontière (Lisbon: Quetzal, 1992); reprinted by Gallimard (Folio), 1994

Le Nom sur le bout de la langue (Paris: POL, 1993); reprinted by Gallimard (Folio), 1995

L'Occupation américaine (Paris: Seuil, 1994)

Le Sexe et l'effroi (Paris: Gallimard, 1994)

Rhétorique spéculative (Paris: Calmann-Lévy, 1995); reprinted by Gallimard (Folio), 1997

La Haine de la musique (Paris: Calmann-Lévy, 1996); reprinted by Gallimard (Folio), 1997

Vie secrète (Paris: Gallimard, 1998)

Terrasse à Rome (Paris: Gallimard, 2000)

'L'Image et le jadis', in *Revue des sciences humaines*, 260 (2000) 9–18

'Pascal Quignard par lui-même', in Adriano Marchetti (ed.), *Pascal Quignard: la mise au silence* (Seyssel: Champ Vallon, 2000), pp. 191–2

'La Voix perdue', in Marchetti (ed.), pp. 5–34.

Les Ombres errantes: Dernière Royaume I (Paris: Grasset, 2002)

Sur le jadis: Dernière Royaume II (Paris: Grasset, 2002)

Abîmes: Dernière Royaume III (Paris: Grasset, 2002)

Écrits de l'éphémère (Paris: Galilée, 2005)

Les Paradisiaques: Dernière Royaume IV (Paris: Grasset, 2005)

Sordidissimes: Dernière Royaume V (Paris: Grasset, 2005)

'Le Roi au pied mouillé', in Philippe Bonnefis and Dolorès Lyotard (eds), *Pascal Quignard: figures d'un lettré* (Paris: Galilée, 2005), pp. 11–14

Ethelrude et Wolframm (Paris: Galilée, 2006)

Villa Amalia (Paris: Gallimard, 2006)

(with Catherine Argand), 'Pascal Quignard', *Lire*, September 2002, consulted online at *http://www.lire.fr/entretien.asp/idC=43001/idTC=4/idR=201/idG=3* (last accessed 30 October 2008)

(with Jean-Louis Ezine) 'Quignard: L'Aveu', *Le Nouvel Observateur*, 6–12 January 2005, pp. 54–6

(with Chantal Lapeyre-Desmaison) *Pascal Quignard le solitaire: rencontre avec Chantal Lapeyre-Desmaison* (Paris: Les Flohic Éditions, 2001)

(with Jean-Louis Pautrot) 'Dix questions à Pascal Quignard', *Études françaises*, 40.2 (2004), 87–92

(with Marie-Laure Picot) 'Pascal Quignard un entretien', *CCCP* 10.2 (2004), 5–13

(with *Quinzaine littéraire* interviewer) 'Pascal Quignard: Écrire n'est pas un choix, mais un symptôme', *La Quinzaine littéraire*, 1–15 November 1990, 17–19

Blanckeman, Bruno, *Les Récits indécidables: Jean Echenoz, Hervé Guibert, Pascal Quignard* (Villeneuve d'Ascq: Presses Universitaires du Septentrion, 2000)

Bonnefis, Philippe, *Pascal Quignard: son nom seul* (Paris: Galilée, 2001)

—— and Dolorès Lyotard (eds), *Pascal Quignard: figures d'un lettré* (Paris: Galilée, 2005)

Coyault, Sylviane, 'Sous prétexte de biographie: *Tous les matins du monde* de Pascal Quignard', in Sylviane Coyault (ed.), *Des Récits poétiques contemporains* (Clermont-Ferrand: CRLMC Université Blaise Pascal, 1996), pp. 183–96

Lapeyre-Desmaison, Chantal, *Mémoires d'origine: un essai sur Pascal Quignard* (Paris: Les Flohic, 2001)

Marchetti, Adriano (ed.), *Pascal Quignard: la mise au silence* (Seyssel: Champ Vallon, 2000)

Pautrot, Jean-Louis, 'La Voix narrative chez Pascal Quignard: de l'oracle à la fraternité', in Michael Bishop and Christopher Elson (eds), *French Prose in 2000* (Paris: Rodopi, 2002), pp. 173–82

Poignault, Rémy, 'Fronton revu par Pascal Quignard', in Rémy Poignault (ed.), *Présence de l'antiquité grecque et romaine au XXe siècle: actes du colloque à Tours (30 novembre – 2 décembre 2000)* (Tours: Centre de recherches A. Piganiol, 2002), pp. 145–74.

Viart, Dominique, 'Les "Fictions critiques" de Pascal Quignard', in *Études françaises* 40.2 (2004), 25–37

Marie Darrieussecq

Truismes (Paris: POL, 1996)

Naissance des fantômes (Paris: POL, 1998)

Le Mal de mer (Paris: POL, 1999)

Précisions sur les vagues (Paris: POL, 1999)

Bref séjour chez les vivants (Paris: POL, 2001)

Le Bébé (Paris: POL, 2002)

White (Paris: POL, 2003)

Claire dans la forêt, suivi de *Penthésilée, premier combat* (Paris: Editions des femmes, 2004)

Le Pays (Paris: POL, 2005)

Zoo (Paris: POL, 2006)

Tom est mort (Paris: POL, 2007)

'Être libéré de soi', *Le Magazine littéraire* (March 2008), p. 58

(with Jeannette Gaudet) '"Des livres sur la liberté": conversation avec Marie Darrieussecq', *Dalhousie French Studies*, 59 (2002), 108–18

(with John Lambeth) 'Entretien avec Marie Darrieussecq', *The French Review*, 79 (2006), 806–18

(with Alain Nicolas) 'Marie et les cerveaux', *L'Humanité*, 13 September 2001, 8

Jordan, Shirley, '"Un grand coup de pied dans le château de cubes": Formal Experimentation in Marie Darrieussecq's *Bref séjour chez les vivants*', *MLR*, 100 (2005), 51–67

Kemp, Simon, 'Homeland: Voyageurs et patrie dans les romans de Marie Darrieussecq', in Audrey Lasserre and Anne Simon (eds), *Nomadismes des romancières contemporaines de langue française* (Paris: Presses Sorbonne Nouvelle, 2008), pp. 159–66

Robson, Kathryn, 'Virtual reality: the subject of loss in Marie Darrieussecq's *Naissance de fantômes* and Regine Detambel's *La Chambre d'echo*', *Australian Journal of French Studies*, 61 (2004), 3–15

Rodgers, Catherine, '"Entrevoir l'absence des bords du monde" dans les romans de Marie Darrieussecq', in *Nouvelles écrivaines: nouvelles voix?*, ed. by Nathalie Morello and Catherine Rodgers (Amsterdam: Rodopi, 2002)

Sarrey-Strack, Colette, *Fictions contemporaines au féminin: Marie Darrieussecq, Marie NDiaye, Marie Nimier, Marie Redonnet* (Paris: L'Harmattan, 2002)

Jean Echenoz

Le Méridien de Greenwich (Paris: Minuit, 1979)

Cherokee (Paris: Minuit, 1983)

L'Équipée malaise (Paris: Minuit, 1986)

Lac (Paris: Minuit, 1989)

'Un Musée imaginaire', *La Quinzaine littéraire*, 16–31 May 1989, 13

Nous Trois (Paris: Minuit, 1992)

Les Grandes Blondes (Paris: Minuit, 1995)

'Pourquoi j'ai pas fait poète', in *Revue de littérature générale*, 95.1 ('La mécanique lyrique') (Paris: POL, 1995)

'Neuf notes sur *Fatale*', postface to Jean-Patrick Manchette, *Fatale* (1977) (Paris: Gallimard, 1996), pp. 147–54

'Il se passe quelque chose avec le jazz', *Europe*, 820–1 (August–September 1997)

Un an (Paris: Minuit, 1997)

Je m'en vais (Paris: Minuit, 1999)

Jérôme Lindon (Paris: Minuit, 2001)

Au piano (Paris: Minuit, 2003)

Ravel (Paris: Minuit, 2006)

(with Cathérine Argand and Jean-Maurice de Montrémy) 'Jean Echenoz', *Lire*, September 1992, 36–41

(with Hervé Delouche) 'Pour ce livre, cette histoire-là, je n'ai jamais pensé à quelqu'un d'autre qu'une femme ...', *Regards*, 1997, consulted online at *www. regards.fr/archives/1997/199707/199707inv01.html* (last accessed 30 October 2008)

(with Jean-Baptiste Harang) 'Jean Echenoz, Arctique de Paris', *Libération*, 'Livres', 16 September 1999, 1–2

(with 'J.-C. L.' [Jean-Claude Lebrun?]) 'Jean Echenoz: l'image du roman comme un moteur de fiction me séduit en ce moment', *L'Humanité*, 'Culture', 11 October 1996, consulted online at *http://www.humanite.fr/journal/archives.html* (last accessed 30 October 2008)

(with Claude Murcia) 'Décalage et hors-champ', *Artpress*, 175 (December 1992), 56–9

Bessard-Banquy, Olivier, *Le Roman ludique: Jean Echenoz, Jean-Philippe Toussaint, Éric Chévillard* (Lille: Presses Universitaires du Septentrion, 2003)

Blanckeman, Bruno, *Les Récits indécidables: Jean Echenoz, Hervé Guibert, Pascal Quignard* (Villeneuve d'Ascq: Presses Universitaires du Septentrion, 2000)

Davis, Colin and Elizabeth Fallaize, *French Fiction in the Mitterrand Years: Memory, Narrative, Desire* (Oxford: Oxford University Press, 2000)

Ezine, Jean-Louis and Jean-François Josselin 'Pour ou contre Echenoz?', *Le Nouvel Observateur*, 16 September 1999, consulted online at *http://hebdo.nouvelobs.com/hebdo/parution/p1819/articles/a23541-.html?xtmc =echenozcontre&xtcr=1* (last accessed 30 October 2008)

Jérusalem, Christine, *Jean Echenoz: géographies du vide* (Saint-Étienne: Publications de l'Université de Saint-Étienne, 2005)

—— and Jean-Bernard Vray (eds), *Jean Echenoz: 'une tentative modeste de description du monde'* (Sainte-Étienne: Publications de l'Université de Sainte-Étienne, 2006)

Kemp, Simon, *Defective Inspectors: Crime Fiction Pastiche in Late-Twentieth-Century French Literature* (Oxford: Legenda, 2006)

—— 'Urban Hell: Infernal Cities in Butor and Echenoz', in Christian Emden, Catherine Keen and David Midgley (eds), *Imagining the City*, I (London & Berne: Peter Lang, 2006), pp. 95–108
Lebrun, Jean-Claude, *Jean Echenoz* (Paris: Rocher, 1992)
Lepape, Pierre, 'Pour raconter cette époque', *Le Monde*, 24 March 1990
Nettelbeck, Colin, 'The "Post-Literary" Novel: Echenoz, Pennac and Company', *French Cultural Studies*, 14 (June 1994), 113–38
O'Beirne, Emer, 'Televisual Narratives: Echenoz and Toussaint', *Contemporary French and Francophone Studies*, 10 (2006), 239–48
Plougastel, Yann, 'Jean Echenoz ne connaît pas la Malaisie, et alors?', *L'Événement du jeudi*, 5–11 February 1987, pp. 80–1
Schoots, Fieke, *'Passer en douce à la douane': l'écriture minimaliste de Minuit* (Amsterdam: Rodopi, 1997)

Patrick Modiano

La Place de l'étoile (Paris: Gallimard, 1968)
La Ronde de nuit (Paris: Gallimard, 1970)
Les Boulevards de ceinture (Paris: Gallimard, 1972)
Villa Triste (Paris: Gallimard, 1975)
Livret de famille (Paris: Gallimard, 1977)
Rue des Boutiques Obscures (Paris: Gallimard, 1978)
Une jeunesse (Paris: Gallimard, 1981)
Memory lane (Paris: Hachette, 1981)
De si braves garçons (Paris: Gallimard, 1982)
Poupée blonde (Paris: POL, 1983)
Quartier perdu (Paris: Gallimard, 1984)
Dimanches d'août (Paris: Gallimard, 1986)
Remise de peine (Paris: Seuil, 1987)
Vestiaire de l'enfance (Paris: Gallimard, 1989)
Voyage de noces (Paris: Gallimard, 1990)
Fleurs de ruine (Paris: Seuil, 1991)
Un cirque passe (Paris: Gallimard, 1992)
Chien de printemps (Paris: Seuil, 1993)
Du plus loin de l'oubli (Paris: Gallimard, 1996)
Dora Bruder (Paris: Gallimard, 1997)
Des inconnues (Paris: Gallimard, 1999)
La Petite Bijou (Paris: Gallimard, 2001)
Éphéméride (Paris: Mercure de France, 2002)
Accident nocturne (Paris: Gallimard, 2003)
Un pedigree (Paris: Gallimard, 2005)
Dans le café de la jeunesse perdue (Paris: Gallimard, 2007)
(with Gallimard interviewer) 'Rencontre avec Patrick Modiano à l'occasion de la publication de *La Petite Bijou*' (2001), Gallimard website, http://www.gallimard.fr/catalog/html/event/index/index_modia.html (last accessed 30 October 2008)
(with Jérôme Garcin) 'Sans famille: rencontre avec Patrick Modiano', *Le Nouvel Observateur*, 2 October 2003, 56–9

(with Laurence Liban) 'Entretien', *Lire*, October 2003. Consulted online at *http://www.lire.fr/entretien.asp/idC=45605/idTC=4/idR=201/idG=3* (last accessed 30 October 2008)

(with Louis Malle) *Scénario de Lacombe Lucien* (Paris: Gallimard, 1974)

Cooke, Dervila, *Present Pasts: Patrick Modiano's (Auto)Biographical Fictions* (Amsterdam: Rodopi, 2005)

Flower, John E. (ed.), *Patrick Modiano* (Amsterdam: Rodopi, 2007)

Kawakami, Akane, *A Self-Conscious Art: Patrick Modiano's Postmodern Fictions* (Liverpool: Liverpool University Press, 2000)

Laurent, Thierry, *L'Oeuvre de Patrick Modiano: une autofiction* (Lyon: Presses Universitaires de Lyon, 1997)

Morris, Alan, *Patrick Modiano* (Oxford: Berg, 1996)

Nettelbeck, Colin, 'Modiano's Stylo: A Novelist in the Age of Cinema', *French Cultural Studies* 17 (2006), 35–54

Other Literature, Criticism and Theory

Aristotle, *Poetics*, in D. A. Russell and Michael Winterbottom (eds), *Classical Literary Criticism* (Oxford: Oxford University Press, 1989), pp. 51–90 (pp. 60–1)

Augé, Marc, *Non-lieux: introduction à une anthropologie de la surmodernité* (Paris: Seuil, 1992)

Baert, Frank and Dominique Viart (eds), *La Littérature française contemporaine: questions et perspectives* (Leuven/Louvain: Presses Universitaires de Louvain, 1993)

Bakhtin, Mikhail, *Speech Genres and Other Late Essays*, trans. by Vern W. McGee, ed. by Caryl Emerson and Michael Holquist (Austin, TX: University of Texas Press, 1986).

Bal, Mieke, *Narratology: Introduction to the Theory of Narrative*, 2nd edn (Toronto: University of Toronto Press, 1997)

Balzac, Honoré de, *Le Père Goriot* (1834, published 1835) (Paris: Gallimard, coll. Folio, 1971)

—— *La Fille aux yeux d'or* (1834–5) (Paris: Flammarion, 1988)

Bancquart, Marie-Claire and Pierre Cahné, *Littérature française du XXe siècle* (Paris: Presses Universitaires de France, 1992)

Barkow, Jerome H., Leda Cosmides and John Tooby, *The Adapted Mind: Evolutionary Psychology and the Generation of Culture* (Oxford: Oxford University Press, 1992)

Barthes, Roland, *Oeuvres complètes*, ed. by Éric Marty, 5 vols (Paris: Seuil, 2002)

Baudrillard, Jean, *L'Échange symbolique et la mort* (Paris: Gallimard, 1976)

Bayard, Pierre, 'Proust et la digression', *Revue des lettres modernes: histoire des idées et des littératures*, 1533–40 (2001), 235–51

Beauvoir, Simone de, *La Femme rompue* (Paris: Gallimard, 1967)

Beckett, Samuel, *Murphy* (Paris: Bordas, 1947)

Beigbeder, Frédéric, *Windows on the World* (Paris: Grasset, 2003), reprinted by Gallimard (Folio), 2004

Bergson, Henri, *Essai sur les données immédiates de la conscience* (1927) (Paris: Presses Universitaires de France, 2003)

—— *Les Deux Sources de la morale et de la religion* (Paris: Alcan, 1932)
Bishop, Michael and Christopher Elston (eds), *French Prose in 2000*
(Amsterdam: Rodopi, 2002)
Blanchot, Maurice, *Le Livre à venir* (Paris: Gallimard, 1959)
Blanckeman, Bruno, *Les fictions singulières: étude sur le roman français contemporain* (Paris: Prétexte, 2002)
—— and Jean-Christophe Millois (eds), *Le Roman français aujourd'hui: transformations, perceptions, mythologies* (Paris: Prétexte, 2004)
——, Aline Mura-Brunel and Marc Dambre (eds), *Le Roman français au tournant du XXIe siècle* (Paris: Presses de la Sorbonne Nouvelle, 2004)
Bon, François, *Daewoo* (Paris: Fayard, 2004)
Bordas, Éric, 'Pratiques balzaciennes de la digression', *L'Année balzacienne*,
20.1 (July 1999), 293–316
Bourdieu, Pierre, *La Distinction: critique sociale du jugement* (Paris: Minuit,
1979)
Brooks, Peter, *Reading for the Plot: Design and Intention in Narrative*
(Cambridge, MA: Harvard University Press, 1992); first published, New
York: Knopf, 1984
Brunel, Pierre, *Glissements du roman français au XXe siècle* (Paris: Klincksieck,
2001)
—— *Où va la littérature française aujourd'hui?* (Paris: Vuibert, 2002)
Butor, Michel, 'Réponses à *Tel Quel*', in *Essais sur le roman* (Paris: Gallimard,
1992)
Cixous, Hélène, 'Le Rire de la Méduse', *L'Arc*, 61 (1975), 39–54
Cohn, Dorrit, *Transparent Minds: Narrative Modes for Presenting Consciousness
in Fiction* (Princeton, NJ: Princeton University Press, 1978)
Combe, Dominique, 'Retour du récit, retour au récit (et à Poésie et récit)',
Degrés: Revue de Synthèse à Orientation Sémiologique 111 (Autumn 2002),
b1–b16
Cousseau, Anne, 'Postmodernité: du retour au récit à la tentation
romanesque', *Études sur le roman du second demi-siècle*, cahier no. 1 (2002),
5–17
Crick, Francis, *The Astonishing Hypothesis: The Scientific Search for the Soul*
(London: Simon and Schuster, 1994)
Culler, Jonathan, *The Pursuit of Signs* (London: Routledge, 1981)
Davis, Colin and Elizabeth Fallaize, *French Fiction in the Mitterrand Years:
Memory, Narrative, Desire* (Oxford: Oxford University Press, 2000)
Dennett, Daniel C., *Consciousness Explained* (1991) (Harmondsworth:
Penguin, 1993)
Diderot, Denis, *Oeuvres*, ed. by André Billy (Paris: Gallimard, coll. Pléiade,
1951)
Didier, Béatrice, *L'Écriture-femme* (Paris: Presses Universitaires de France,
1981)
Djebar, Assia, *Femmes d'Alger dans leur appartement* (Paris: Albin Michel,
2002)
Djian, Philippe, *37,2° le matin* (Paris: Barrault, 1985)
Doubrovsky, Serge, *Autobiographiques: de Corneille à Sartre* (Paris: Presses
Universitaires de France, 1988)

Dujardin, Édouard, *Les Lauriers sont coupés, suivi de Le Monologue intérieur*, ed. by Carmen Licari (Rome: Bulzoni, 1977)

Eco, Umberto, 'James Bond: une combinatoire narrative', *Communications*, 8 (1966), 83–99

Flory, Eli, 'La Rentrée littéraire au banc d'essai', *Le Magazine des livres*, September-October 2007, 4–11

Foucault, Michel, *Les Mots et les choses* (Paris: Gallimard, 1966)

Freud, Sigmund, *The Standard Edition of the Complete Works of Sigmund Freud*, ed. James Strachey (London: Hogarth Press, 1953–74), 22 vols

Genette, Gérard, 'Frontières du récit', in *Communications*, 8 (1966) (*L'Analyse structurale du récit*), 158–69

—— 'Discours du récit: essai de méthode', in *Figures III* (Paris: Seuil, 1972), pp. 65—282

—— 'Récit fictionnel, récit factuel', in *Fiction et Diction* (1979) (Paris: Seuil, coll. 'Points', 2004), pp. 91–118

—— *Nouveau discours du récit* (Paris: Seuil, 1983)

Gide, André, *Les Faux-monnayeurs* (Paris: Gallimard, 1925)

Girard, René, *Le Journal intime* (Paris: Presses Universitaires de France, 1963)

Godard, Henri, *Le Roman modes d'emploi* (Paris: Gallimard, 2006)

Goodman, Nelson, 'Twisted Tales; or, Story, Study and Symphony', in W. J. T. Mitchell (ed.), *On Narrative* (Chicago: University of Chicago Press, 1980), pp. 99–115

Gracq, Julien, *Préférences* (Paris: José Corti, 1961)

Guichard, Thierry, et al., *Le Roman français contemporain* (Paris: Culturesfrance, 2007)

Hamon, Philippe, 'Clausules', *Poetique: Revue de Theorie et d'Analyse Litteraires* 24, (1975), 495–526

Hobson, Allan, *Dreaming: An Introduction to the Science of Sleep* (Oxford: Oxford University Press, 2002)

Holmes, Diana, *Romance and Readership in Twentieth-Century France: Love Stories* (Oxford: Oxford University Press, 2006)

Houellebecq, Michel, *La Possibilité d'une île* (Paris: Fayard, 2005)

—— and Jérôme Garcin, '"Je suis un prophète amateur": un entretien avec Michel Houellebecq', *Le Nouvel Observateur*, 25–31 August 2005, 8–10

Houppermans, Sjef, Christine Bosman Delzons and Danièle de Ruyter-Tognati (eds), *Territoires et terres d'histoire: perspectives, horizons, jardins secrets dans la littérature française d'aujourd'hui* (Amsterdam: Rodopi, 2005)

Humphrey, Robert, *Stream of Consciousness in the Modern Novel* (Berkeley, CA: University of California Press, 1954)

James, Henry, *Selected Tales*, ed. by John Lyon (Harmondsworth: Penguin, 2001)

James, William, *The Principles of Psychology*, 3 vols (1890) (Cambridge, MA: Harvard University Press, 1981)

Jameson, Fredric, *Postmodernism, or, The Cultural Logic of Late Capitalism* (London: Verso, 1991)

Jourde, Pierre, *La Littérature sans estomac* (Paris: L'Esprit des péninsules, 2002)

Joyce, James, *Ulysses* (1922) (Harmondsworth: Penguin, 1992)

Kermode, Frank, *The Sense of an Ending: Studies in the Theory of Fiction* (Oxford: Oxford University Press, 1967)

—— 'Sensing Endings', *Nineteenth-Century Fiction*, 33.1 (June 1978), 144–58

Kernel, Brigitte, *Mes étés d'écrivains: grands entretiens* (Paris: Belfond, 2003)

Kibédi-Varga, Aron, 'Le Récit postmoderne', *Littérature*, 77 (February 1990), 3–22 (p. 16)

Kotin Mortimer, Armine, *La Clôture narrative* (Paris: José Corti, 1985)

Lebrun, Jean-Claude and Claude Prévost, *Nouveaux Territoires romanesques* (Paris: Messidor, 1990)

Lejeune, Philippe, *Le Pacte autobiographique* (Paris: Seuil, 1975)

—— *Signes de vie: le pacte autobiographique 2* (Paris: Seuil, 2005)

Lindon, Jérôme and Jean-Pierre Salgas, 'Jérôme Lindon: "On ne se baigne pas deux fois dans le même fleuve" ', *La Quinzaine littéraire*, 16 May 1989, 34

Maulpoix, Jean-Michel, *Histoire de la littérature française – XXe siècle, 1950/1990* (Paris: Hatier, 1991)

Mehler, Jacques, and others, 'A Precursor to language acquisition in young infants', *Cognition*, 29 (1988), 143–78

Meyer, Catherine (ed.), *Le Livre noir de la psychanalyse: vivre, penser et aller mieux sans Freud* (Paris: Les Arènes, 2005)

Miller, D. A., *Narrative and its Discontents: Problems of Closure in the Traditional Novel* (Princeton, NJ: Princeton University Press, 1981)

Miller, J. Hillis, 'The Problematic of Ending in Narrative', *Nineteenth-Century Fiction*, 33 (1978), 3–7

—— *Ariadne's Thread: Story Lines* (New Haven: Yale University Press, 1992)

Millet, Richard, *Désenchantement de la littérature* (Paris: Gaillmard, 2007)

Motte, Warren, *Small Worlds: Minimalism in Contemporary French Literature* (Lincoln, NE: University of Nebraska Press, 1999)

—— *Fables of the Novel* (Chicago, IL: Dalkey Archive Press, 2003)

Nadeau, Maurice, 'L'État des lieux', *La Quinzaine littéraire*, 16 May 1989, n° spécial, 'Où va la littérature française', 3–4

Oulipo, *La Littérature potentielle* (Paris: Gallimard, 1973)

Penfield, Wilder, *The Excitable Cortex in Conscious Man* (Liverpool: Liverpool University Press, 1958)

Perec, Georges, *W ou le souvenir d'enfance* (Paris: Denoël, 1975)

—— *L'Infra-ordinaire* (Paris: Seuil, 1989)

Pinker, Steven, *The Language Instinct* (London: Allen Lane, 1994)

—— *How the Mind Works* (New York: Norton, 1997)

Prince, Gerald, *Narratology: The Form and Functioning of Narrative* (Berlin: Mouton, 1982)

Propp, Vladimir, *Morphology of the Folktale* (1928), trans. by Laurence Scott, revised and ed. by Louis A. Wagner (Austin: University of Texas Press, 1971)

Ricardou, Jean, *Pour une théorie du nouveau roman* (Paris: Seuil, 1971)

Ricoeur, Paul, *Temps et récit*, 3 vols (Paris: Seuil, 1983–5)

Robbe-Grillet, Alain, *Les Gommes* (Paris: Minuit, 1953)

—— *Pour un nouveau roman* (Paris: Minuit, 1961)

—— 'Sur le choix des générateurs', in *Nouveau Roman: hier, aujourd'hui II: Pratiques*, ed. by Jean Ricardou and Françoise van Rossum-Guyon (Paris: UGE, collection '10/18', 1971), pp. 157–62

—— *Le Miroir qui revient* (Paris: Minuit, 1984)

Sabry, Randa, *Stratégies discursives: digression, transition, suspens* (Paris: Éditions de l'École des Hautes Études en Sciences Sociales, 1992)

Salgas, Jean-Pierre, '1960–1990: Romans mode d'emploi', in Yves Mabin (ed.), *Le Roman français contemporain* (Paris: Publications de la Ministère des Affaires Étrangères, 1993), pp. 5–37

Sarraute, Nathalie, *L'Ère du soupçon* (Paris: Gallimard, 1956)

—— *Enfance* (Paris: Gallimard, 1983)

Sartre, Jean-Paul, *La Nausée* (Paris: Gallimard, 1938)

Shklovsky, Viktor, *O teorii prozy* (1929), reprinted as 'La Construction de la nouvelle et du roman', trans. by Tzvetan Todorov, in *Théorie de la littérature*, ed. Tzvetan Todorov (Paris: Seuil, 1966), pp. 170–96

Sollers, Philippe, *L'Écriture et l'expérience des limites* (Paris: Seuil, 1968)

—— *Paradis* (Paris: Seuil, 1981)

Tadié, Jean-Yves, *Le Roman au XXe siècle* (Paris: Belfond, 1990)

Todorov, Tzvetan, *Introduction à la littérature fantastique* (Paris: Seuil, 1970)

—— *La Littérature en péril* (Paris: Flammarion, 2007)

Torgovnik, Marianna, *Closure in the Novel* (Princeton, NJ: Princeton University Press, 1981)

Vercier, Bruno, and Dominique Viart, *La Littérature française au présent: héritage, modernité, mutations* (Paris: Bordas, 2005)

Viart, Dominique, *Le Roman français au XXe siècle* (Paris: Hachette, 1999)

Index